COMMENTARY

ON THE

EPISTLES TO THE SEVEN CHURCHES IN ASIA.

COMMENTARY

ON THE

EPISTLES TO THE SEVEN CHURCHES IN ASIA.

REVELATION II. III.

BY

RICHARD CHENEVIX TRENCH, D.D.

DEAN OF WESTMINSTER.

NEW YORK:
CHARLES SCRIBNER, 124 GRAND STREET.
PUBLISHED BY ARRANGEMENT WITH THE AUTHOR.
1863.

PREFACE.

In this publication I at length accomplish, however imperfectly, a wish which I have cherished for a large number of years. During the time that I fulfilled my pleasant labours at King's College, I lectured three times to the theological students there on these seven Epistles; and the lectures to them delivered constitute the groundwork of the present volume, though much has been added, and some little changed, in the final revision which I have given to my work before venturing to challenge a larger audience for it. I confess that each time I have gone over these Epistles I have become more conscious of the manifold difficulties which they present; and more than once have been half disposed not to offer to others, in the way of interpretation of them, what has so little satisfied myself. I have not, however, held my hand. There has ever seemed to me a very useful warning contained in that German proverb which says, "The best is oftentimes the enemy of the good;" and without claiming for an instant that title of *good* for my book, I do not doubt that many a good book has remained unwritten, or, perhaps, being written, has remained unpublished, because there floated before the mind's eye of the author, or possible author, the ideal of a better or a best, which has put him out of all conceit with his good; meanwhile some other, having no ideal at all before him, either to stimulate or to repress, steps in and poorly fills the place which the other would have filled, if not excellently, yet reasonably, well. I repeat that thus saying, I am as far as possible from implicitly claiming for my book this quality of good; but still it may contain, I trust it does contain, enough of profit in it to justify me in giving it into the hands of men.

And indeed, if there is much in the difficulties with which these Epistles abound to repel and deter, there is much also in these same difficulties to allure and attract. And not in these only. The number of aspects in which they present themselves to us as full of interest is extraordinary.

For example, the points of peculiar attraction which they offer to the student of ecclesiastical history are many. Who are these Angels of the Churches? What do we learn from their evident preëminence in their several Churches, about the government and constitution of the Church in the later apostolic times? or is it lawful to draw any conclusions? Again, was there a body of heretics actually bearing the name of Nicolaitans in the times of St. John? And those that had the doctrine of Balaam, and the followers of the woman Jezebel, with what heretics mentioned elsewhere shall we identify these? Or, once more, what is the worth of that historico-prophetical scheme of interpretation adopted by our own Joseph Mede and Henry More, and many others down even to the present day; who see in these seven Epistles the mystery of the whole evolution of the Church from the days of the Apostles to the close of the present dispensation? Was this so intended by the Spirit? or is it only a dream and fancy of men?

Nor less is there a strong attraction in these Epistles for those who occupy themselves with questions of pure exegesis, from the fact of so many unsolved, or imperfectly solved, problems of interpretation being found in them. It is seldom within so small a compass that so many questions to which no answer with perfect confidence can be given, occur. What, for instance, is the exact meaning, and what the etymology, of χαλκολίβανος (i. 15; ii. 18)? what the interpretation of the white stone with the new name written upon it (ii. 17)? why is Pergamum called "Satan's seat" (ii. 13)? with many other questions of the same kind.

Nor can any one, I think, attentively studying, fail to be struck with what one might venture to call the entire originality of these seven Epistles, with their entire unlikeness, in some points at least, to any thing else in Scripture. Contemplate, for instance, the titles of Christ here, "the Amen," "the Faithful and True Witness," "the Beginning of the Creation of God," "He that hath the seven Spirits of God," and others which I might name. While the analogy of faith is perfectly preserved, while there is no difficulty in harmonizing what is here said of Christ's person and offices with what is taught elsewhere, yet how wholly new a series of titles are these. It is the same with the promises; some, it is true, as "the tree of life," "the crown of life," "the new name," have been anticipated in other parts of Scripture, yet how many appear here for the first time; and set forth what Augustine so grandly calls "beatæ vitæ magna secreta," under aspects as novel as they are animating and alluring;

such are "the hidden manna," the "white stone," the "white raiment," the "pillar in the temple of God," and "the morning star." And very striking, as combined with this originality, with this free movement of the Spirit here, is the strict and rigid symmetrical arrangement of these Epistles, the way in which they are all laid out upon the same plan, distributed according to exactly the same ever-recurring laws. The surprise which we feel on tracing this for the first time, is similar to that which overtakes one who, attempting any thing like a critical study of the Psalms, discovers the rigid laws to which, so far as concerns the form, they are for the most part submitted, or rather, which they have imposed on themselves, and to which they delight to conform.

Then, once more, the purely theological interest of these Epistles is great. I have already referred to the titles of Christ, the entirely novel aspects under which the glory of the Son of God is here set forth. But they have another and profounder interest. Assuredly there is enough in these two chapters alone to render Arianism entirely untenable by any one who, admitting their authority, should consent to be bound in their interpretation by the ordinary rules of fairness and truth. On this matter I have several times dwelt in the course of my interpretation.

And, finally, the practical interest of these Epistles in their bearing on the whole pastoral and ministerial work is extreme. It is recorded of the admirable Bengel that it was his wont above all things to recommend the study of these Epistles to youthful ministers of Christ's word and sacraments. And indeed to them they are full of teaching, of the most solemn warning, of the strongest encouragement. We learn from these Epistles the extent to which the spiritual condition of a Church is dependent upon that of its pastors; the guilt, not merely of teaching, but of allowing, error; how there may be united much and real zeal for the form of sound words with a lamentable decay of the spirit of love; or, on the other hand, many works and active ministries of love, with only too languid a zeal for the truth once delivered; with innumerable lessons more. For one who has undertaken the awful ministry of souls, I know almost nothing in Scripture so searching, no threatenings so alarming, no promises so comfortable, as are some which these Epistles contain.

Surely, if all this be so, it is very much to be regretted that while every chapter of every other book of the New Testament is set forth to be read in the Church, and, wherever there is daily service, is read in the Church, three times in the year, and some, or portions of some, are read oftener there, while even of the Apocalypse itself two chapters and portions of others have been admitted into the service, under no circumstances whatever can the second and third chapter ever be heard in the congregation. Any one who knows, or at all guesses, how small the amount of the private reading of the Scriptures among our people, and the extent, therefore, to which the stated public reading in the congregation is the source of whatever knowledge of it the great mass of our people possess, the means by which they are at all leavened by it, must deeply regret that chapters so rich in doctrine, in exhortation, in reproof, in promises, should thus be withheld from them. Certainly, if at any time a reconsideration of the portions of Scripture appointed to be read in the Church should find place, the slight cast on these chapters, and in them on the Apocalypse itself, with the injury inflicted on the people by their total omission, ought not to be allowed to continue.

But to bring these prefatory remarks to a close. Whether the attempt here made to draw out some of the riches contained in this portion of God's Word may have any interest for others, I know not: but for myself this volume must ever retain a very solemn interest. Besides the serious solemnity of giving any work that professes to be a work for God into the hands of men, I can never disconnect this book from two great sorrows which fell on me, while it was preparing for, and passing through, the press; sorrows which have left me far poorer than before; and yet, I would humbly hope, richer too, if better able to speak to others of truths whose price and value has been brought home with new power to myself; if theology has been thus more closely connected for me with life, and with life's toil and burden, from which it is ever in danger of being dissociated and divorced. It is my earnest hope that so it may prove; and in this hope I humbly commend my book, with all its shortcomings, to Him who can alone make it profitable to any.

Deanery, Westminster,
July 31, 1861.

COMMENTARY

ON THE

EPISTLES TO THE SEVEN CHURCHES IN ASIA.

REVELATION II. III.

INTRODUCTION, REV. i. 4—20.

Ver. 4. "*John to the seven Churches*[1] *in Asia.*" —So far as the Apocalypse is allowed to witness for its own authorship, it is difficult to refuse to find in these words a strong internal argument that we have here an authentic work of St. John. The writer avouches himself as "*John;*" but, though there may have been Johns many in the Church at this time, John the Presbyter and others, still it is well-nigh impossible to conceive any other but John *the Apostle* who would have named himself

[1] Lest any should charge me with a slovenly omission at the very outset of my work, let me observe that the words "*which are,*" finding here a place in most modern editions of our Bible, have no place in the exemplar edition of 1611.

by this name alone, with no further style or addition. We instinctively feel that for any one else there would have been an affectation of simplicity, concealing a most real arrogance, in the very plainness of this title, in the assumption that thus to mention himself was sufficient to ensure his recognition, or that he had a right to appropriate this name in so absolute a manner to himself. The unique position in the Church of St. John, the beloved Apostle, and now the sole surviving Apostle, the one remaining link between the faithful of this time and the earthly life of their Lord, abundantly justified in him that which would have ill become any other; just as a king or queen, as representative persons in a nation, will sign by their Christian names only, but not any other besides. Despite all which has been urged to avoid this conclusion, it is assuredly either John the Apostle and Evangelist who writes the Apocalypse; or one who, assuming his style and title, desires to pass himself off as John—in other words a *falsarius*. Are the opposers of St. John's authorship of this Book prepared for the alternative?

Of the seven Churches which St. John addresses here I reserve to speak in particular when we reach the nominal enumeration of them (ver. 11); but as this is the only place where they are described as Churches "*in Asia*," it may be needful to say a few words concerning the "Asia" which is intended. We may trace two opposite movements going on in the names of countries, analogous to like movements which are continually finding place in other words. Sometimes they grow more and more inclusive, are applied in their later use to far wider tracts of the earth than they were in their earlier. It is thus with the name "Italy." Designating at one time only the extreme southern point of the central peninsula of Europe, the name crept up and up, till in the time of Augustus it obtained the meaning which it has ever since retained, including all within the Alps. "Holland" is another example in the same kind. Some names, on the other hand, of the widest reach at the beginning, gradually contract their meaning, till in the end they designate no more than a minute fraction of that which they designated at the beginning. "Asia" furnishes a good example of this. In the New Testament, as generally in the language of men when the New Testament was written, Asia meant not what it now means for us, and had once meant for the Greeks, one namely of the three great continents of the old world (Æschylus, *Prom.* 412; Pindar, *Olymp.* 7. 18; Herodotus, iv. 38), nor yet even that region which geographers about the fourth century of our era began to call "Asia Minor;" but a strip of the western seaboard containing hardly a third portion of this: cf. 1 Pet. i. 1; Acts ii. 9; vi. 9. "Asia vestra," says Cicero (*Pro Flacc.* 27), addressing some Asiatics, "constat ex Phrygiâ, Mysiâ, Cariâ, Lydiâ;" its limits being nearly identical with those of the kingdom which Attalus III. bequeathed to the Roman people. Take "Asia" in this sense, and there will be little or no exaggeration in the words of the Ephesian silversmith, that "almost throughout all Asia" Paul had turned away much people from the service of idols (Acts xix. 26); words which must seem to exceed even the limits of an angry hyperbole to those not acquainted with this restricted use of the term.

"*Grace be unto you and peace.*"—This opening salutation may fitly remind us (for in reading the Apocalypse we are often in danger of forgetting it), that the Book is an Epistle, that, besides containing within its bosom those seven briefer Epistles addressed severally to the seven Churches in particular, it is itself an Epistle addressed to them as a whole, and as representing in their mystic unity all the Churches, or the Church (ii. 7, 11, 23, &c.). Of this larger Epistle, namely the Apocalypse itself, these seven Churches are the original receivers; not as having a nearer or greater interest in it than any other portion of the Universal Church; though as members of that Church they have an interest in it as near and great as can be conceived (i. 3; xxii. 18, 19); but on account of this their representative character, of which there will be occasion presently to speak. And being such an Epistle, it opens with the most frequently recurring apostolic salutation: "*Grace and peace.*" This is the constant salutation of St. Paul (Rom. i. 7; 1 Cor. i. 3, &c.), with only the exception of the two Epistles to Timothy, where "mercy" finds place between "grace and peace;" cf. 2 John 3; the salutation also of St. Peter in both his Epistles; while St. James employs the less distinctively Christian "greeting" (*χαίρειν*, i. 1; cf. Acts xxiii. 26).

"*From Him which is and which was, and which is to come.*"—On the departure from the ordinary rules of grammar, and apparent violation of them in these words, *ἀπὸ ὁ ὢν, καὶ ὁ ἦν, καὶ ὁ ἐρχόμενος*, there will be something more to say when we reach the first clause of the next verse. Doubtless the immutability of God, "the same yesterday, and to-day, and for ever" (Heb. xiii. 8), is intended to be expressed in this immutability of the name of God, in this absolute resistance to change or even modification which that name here presents. "I am the Lord; I change not" (Mal. iii. 6), this is what is here declared; and there could be no stronger consolation for the faithful than thus to be reminded that He who is from everlasting to everlasting, "with whom is no variableness, neither shadow of turning" (Jam. i. 17), was on their side; how then should they "be afraid of a man that shall die, and the son of man which shall be made as grass" (Isai. li. 12, 13)?

And yet we must not understand the words, "*and which is to come*," as though they declared the "æternitas a parte *post*" in the same way as "*which was*" expresses the "æternitas a parte *ante*." It is difficult to understand how so many should assume without further question that ὁ ἐρχόμενος here is = ὁ ἐσόμενος, and that thus we have the eternity of God expressed here, so far as it can be expressed, in forms of time: "He who was, and is, *and shall be*." But how ὁ ἐρχόμενος should ever have this significance it is hard to perceive. There is a certain ambiguity about our translation; it cannot be accused of incorrectness; yet, on the other hand, one does not feel sure that when our Translators rendered, "*which is to come*," they did not mean "*which is to be*." The Rheims, which is here kept right by the Vulgate ("et qui *venturus est*"), so renders the words as to exclude ambiguity, "*and which shall come*." If any urge that "*which is, and which was*," present and past, require to be completed with a future, "*and which shall be*," to this it may be replied, that plainly they do not require to be so completed, seeing that at xi. 17, no such complement finds place; for the words καὶ ὁ ἐρχόμενος have no right to a place there in the text. And then, on the other hand, there is every thing to recommend the grammatical interpretation. What is the key-note to this whole Book? Surely it is, "I come quickly. The world seems to have all things its own way, to kill my servants; but I come quickly." With this announcement the Book begins, i. 7; with this it ends, xxii. 7, 12, 20; and this is a constantly recurring note through it all, ii. 5, 16; iii. 11; vi. 17; xi. 18; xiv. 7; xvi. 15; xviii. 20. It is Christ's word of comfort, or, where they need it, of warning, to his friends; of terror to his foes. Origen further notes the evidence which this language, rightly interpreted, yields for the equal divinity of the Son with the Father (*De Princ.* § 10): "Ut autem unam et eandem omnipotentiam Patris ac Filii esse cognoscas, audi hoc modo Joannem in Apocalypsi dicentem, Hæc dicit Dominus Deus, qui est, et qui erat, et qui venturus est, omnipotens. Qui enim venturus est, quis est alius nisi Christus?"—There should be no comma dividing "*which is*" from the clause following, "*and which was.*" These rather form one sentence, which is to be balanced with the other, "*and which is to come.*"

"*And from the seven Spirits which are before*

his throne."—Some have understood by "*the seven Spirits*," the seven principal Angels, the heavenly realities of which "the seven princes of Persia and Media, which saw the king's face, and which sat the first in the kingdom" (Esth. i. 14), the "seven counsellors" (Ezra vii. 14), were a kind of earthly copy; room for whom had been found in the later Jewish angelology (Tob. xii. 15), and the seal of allowance set on the number seven in this very Book (Rev. viii. 2). And these have not been merely Roman Catholic expositors, such as Bossuet and Ribera, tempted to this interpretation by their zeal for the worshipping of Angels; but others with no such temptations, as Beza, Hammond, Mede (in a sermon on Zech. iv. 10, *Works*, 1672, p. 40; cf. pp. 833, 908). They claim some of the Fathers for predecessors in the same line of interpretation; Hilary, for example, *Tract. in Ps.* 118, *Lit.* 21, § 5. Clement of Alexandria is also claimed by Hammond; but neither in the passage cited nor in the context (*Strom.* vi. 16) can I find that he affirms anything of the kind. But this interpretation, which after all is that only of a small minority either of ancients or moderns, must be rejected without hesitation. Angels, often as they are mentioned in this Book, are never called "Spirits." So too, in testimony of their ministering condition, their creaturely state, they always *stand* (Rev. viii.

2; Luke i. 19; 1 Kings xxii. 19, 21), but these Spirits "*are*" (ἐστιν) before the throne. Again, how is it possible to conceive the Apostle desiring grace and peace to the Church from the Angels, let them be the chiefest Angels which are, and not from God alone? or how can we imagine Angels, created beings, interposed here between the Father and the Son, and thus set as upon an equal level with Them; the Holy Ghost meanwhile being omitted, as according to this interpretation He must be, in this solemn salutation of the Churches? Where again would be the singular glory claimed for Himself by the Son in those words, "He that hath the seven Spirits of God" (iii. 1)? what transcendant prerogative in the fact that these Angels, no less than all created things, were within his dominion?

There is no doubt that by "*the seven Spirits*" we are to understand, not indeed the sevenfold operations of the Holy Ghost, but the Holy Ghost sevenfold in his operations. Neither need there be any difficulty in reconciling this interpretation, as Mede urges, with the doctrine of his personality. It is only that He is regarded here not so much in his personal unity, as in his manifold energies; for "there are diversities of gifts, but the same Spirit" (1 Cor. xii. 4). The matter could not be put better than it is by Richard of St. Victor: "Et a septem

Spiritibus, id est, a septiformi Spiritu, qui simplex quidem est per naturam, septiformis per gratiam;" and compare Delitzsch, *Bibl. Psychologie*, pp. 34, 147. The manifold gifts, operations, energies of the Holy Ghost are here represented under the number seven, being, as it is, the number of completeness in the Church. We have anticipations of this in the Old Testament. When the prophet Isaiah would describe how the Spirit should be given not by measure to Him whose name is The Branch, the enumeration of the gifts is sevenfold (xi. 2); and the seven eyes which rest upon the stone which the Lord has laid can mean nothing else but this (Zech. iii. 9; cf. iv. 10; Rev. v. 6). On the number "seven," and its significance in Scripture and elsewhere, but above all in this Book, there will be something presently to be said.

Ver. 5. "*And from Jesus Christ, who is the faithful witness.*"—In the last of these seven Epistles He calls Himself "the faithful and true witness" (iii. 14); as, therefore, we shall meet these words again, and they will be there more conveniently dealt with, I will not now do more than quote Richard of St. Victor's noble comment upon them: "Testis fidelis, quia de omnibus quæ per Eum testificanda erant in mundo testimonium fidele perhibuit. Testis fidelis, quia quæcunque audivit a Patre fideliter discipulis suis nota fecit.

Testis fidelis, quia viam Dei in veritate docuit, nec Ei cura de aliquo fuit, nec personas hominum respexit. Testis fidelis, quia reprobis damnationem, et electis salvationem nunciavit. Testis fidelis, quia veritatem quam verbis docuit, miraculis confirmavit. Testis fidelis, quia testimonium Sibi a Patre nec in morte negavit. Testis fidelis, quia de operibus malorum et bonorum in die judicii testimonium verum dabit."—A reference to the original, where the nominative *ὁ μάρτυς ὁ πιστός* is in apposition to the genitive *Ἰησοῦ Χριστοῦ*, will show that we have here one of the many departures from the ordinary grammatical construction, with which this Book abounds. The officious emendations of transcribers have caused a large number of these, though not this one, to disappear from our received text; but in any critical edition of the Greek original we are struck by their immense multitude. To regard these, which some have done, as evidences of St. John's helplessness in the management of Greek, is to regard them altogether from a wrong point of view. Rather, we should say, to take the case immediately before us, the doctrinal interest here overbears the grammatical. Düsterdieck very well: "Das Gewicht der Vorstellungen selbst durchbricht die Schranken der regelrechten Form; die abrupte Redeweise hebt die gewaltige Selbständigkeit aller drei Prädicate."

At all costs that all-important ὁ μάρτυς ὁ πιστός, with the other two titles of the Lord which follow, shall be maintained in the dignity and emphasis of the casus rectus. Cf. xx. 2, where ὁ ὄφις ὁ ἀρχαῖος (changed in the received text into τὸν ὄφιν τὸν ἀρχαῖον) is in like manner in apposition to τὸν δράκοντα, and compare further xiv. 12; but above all, and as making quite clear that St. John adopted these constructions with his eyes open, and for a distinct purpose, the remarkable ἀπὸ ὁ ὢν κ. τ. λ. of the verse preceding that now under consideration.[1]

"*The first begotten of the dead.*"—Cf. Col. i. 18, where very nearly the same language occurs, and the same title is given to the Lord: ὁ πρωτότοκος τῶν νεκρῶν here, πρωτ. ἐκ τ. νεκρῶν there. The phrases are not precisely identical in meaning; and even were they so, the suggestion of Hengstenberg, that St. John here builds upon St. Paul, setting his seal to the prior Apostle's word, seems to me highly unnatural. Glorious as this language is, who does not feel how easily two Apostles, quite independent of one another, might have arrived at it to express the same blessed truth? Christ is indeed "*the first begotten of the dead,*" notwithstanding that such raisings from the grave as that of the widow's son

[1] There is a good discussion on these grammatical anomalies in the Apocalypse in Lücke's *Einleitung*, pp. 458–464.

and Lazarus went before. There was for them no repeal of the sentence of death, but a respite only; not to say that even during their period of respite they carried about with them a body of death. Christ first so rose from the dead, that He did not, and could not, die any more (Rom. vi. 9); in this respect was "the first-fruits of them that slept" (1 Cor. xv. 20, 23), the Prince of life (Acts iii. 15). Alcuin: "Primogenitus ideo dicitur quia nullus ante Ipsum non moriturus surrexit." In this "*first begotten*" (or "first born from the dead," as it is Col. i. 18), I do not see the image of the grave as the womb that bare him (λύσας τὰς ὠδῖνας τοῦ θανάτου, Acts ii. 24); but remembering how often τίκτειν = γεννᾶν, I should rather put this passage in connection with Ps. ii. 7, "Thou art my Son; this day have I begotten Thee." It will doubtless be remembered that St. Paul (Acts xiii. 33; cf. Heb. i. 5) claims the fulfilment of these words not in the eternal generation before all time of the Son; still less in his human conception in the Blessed Virgin's womb; but rather in his resurrection from the dead; "declared to be the Son of God with power by the resurrection from the dead" (Rom. i. 4). On that verse in Ps. ii., and with reference to Acts xiii. 32, Hilary, the depth and distinctly theological value of whose exposition seems to me at this day very imperfectly recognised, has these words: "Filius meus es Tu, Ego hodie genui Te; non ad Virginis partum, neque ad eam quæ ante tempora est generationem, sed ad primogenitum ex mortuis pertinere apostolica auctoritas est." To Him first, to Him above all others, God said on that day when He raised Him from the dead, and gave Him glory, "Thou art my Son, this day have I begotten Thee."

"*And the Prince of the kings of the earth.*"—A manifest reference to Ps. ii. 2, where the "kings of the earth" (compare Rev. vi. 15, for the same phrase used in the same sense), appear in open rebellion against the Christ of God; cf. Acts iv. 26; Ps. cx. 5; lxxxix. 27; Isai. lii. 15; Matt. xxviii. 18. Such a "*Prince of the kings of the earth*" He becomes in the exaltation which follows on and is most closely connected with his humiliation (Phil. ii. 9; Ps. lxxxix. 27); and shows Himself such at his glorious coming, as set forth in the later parts of this Book, "Lord of lords, and King of kings" (xvii. 14; xix. 16), breaking in pieces all of those "kings of the earth" who set themselves in battle array against Him, receiving the homage of all who are wise in time (Ps. ii. 10-12), and bring their glory and honour to lay them at his feet, and to receive them back at his hands (Rev. xxi. 24).

"*Unto Him that hath loved us, and washed us from our sins in his own blood.*"—The words are richer still in comfort, when we read, as we ought, *ἀγαπῶντι*, and not *ἀγαπήσαντι*: "*Unto Him that loves us*," whose love rests evermore on his redeemed. There is in the Greek theology an old and often-recurring play on the words *λύτρον* and *λουτρόν*, words so nearly allied in sound, and both expressing so well, though under images entirely diverse, the central benefits which redound to us through the sacrifice of the death of Christ. It is indeed older than this, and is implicitly involved in the etymology of Apollo, which Plato, whether in jest or in earnest, puts into the mouth of Socrates (*Cratylus*, 405 B.): *ὁ ἀπολούων τε καὶ ἀπολύων τῶν κακῶν*, these *κακά* being impurities of the body and of the soul. This near resemblance between *λύειν* and *λούειν* has given rise to a very interesting variety of readings here. Whichever reading we adopt, *λύσαντι* or *λούσαντι*, "*who released us*," or "*who washed us*," the words yield a beautiful meaning, as in either case they link themselves on to a whole circle of imagery already hallowed and consecrated by Scripture use. If we adopt *λύσαντι*, the passage then connects itself with all those which speak of Christ having given Himself as a *λύτρον* (Matt. xx. 28), as an *ἀντίλυτρον* for us (1 Tim. ii. 6; cf. 1 Pet. i. 18; Heb. ix. 12); as redeeming or purchasing us (Gal. iii. 13; iv. 5; Rev. v. 9; xiv. 3, 4); and somewhat more remotely with as many as describe the condition of sin as a condition of bondage, and Christ as having obtained freedom for us. If on the other hand we read *λούσαντι,* then the passage connects itself with such others as Ps. li. 4; Isai. i. 16, 18; Ezek. xxxvi. 25; Rev. vii. 14; as Acts xxii. 16; Ephes. v. 26; Tit. iii. 5; so, too, with all those which describe the *καθαρισμός,* the *καθαρίζειν,* as the end of Christ's death (1 John i. 7); and somewhat more remotely with as many as under types of the Levitical law set forth the benefits of this heavenly washing (Num. xix. 17-21). The weight of *external* evidence is so nearly balanced that it is very difficult to say on which side it predominates. For *λούσαντι,* the reading of the received text, adopted by our Translators, there is B, the Vulgate ("et *lavit* nos"), Bengel, Tischendorf, Tregelles; for *λύσαντι,* A, C, and among critical editions, Mill and Lachmann. But the *internal* evidence I confess appears to me very much in favour of retaining the reading of the received text, the poetic λούσαντι so agreeable to the poetic character of this Book, rather than the somewhat flat λύσαντι. Then it is quite true that redemption may be contemplated as a *λύειν ἐν τῷ αἵματι,* but by how much better right, and with how much livelier imagery as a *λούειν ἐν τῷ αἵματι,* and certainly Rev. vii. 14 points strongly this way.

Ver. 6. "*And hath made us kings and priests*

unto God and his Father."—Or rather, and according to the reading which must be preferred, "*And hath made us a kingdom* [ἐποίησεν ἡμᾶς βασιλείαν], *priests unto God and his Father*" ("Et fecit nos *regnum*, et sacerdotes Deo," Vulgate). There is a certain apparent inconcinnity in the abstract βασιλείαν joined with the concrete ἱερεῖς, but there can be no question about the reading, and the meaning remains exactly the same; except, indeed, that instead of the emphasis being equally distributed between the two words, the larger portion of it now falls on the first; and this agrees with the prominence given to the *reigning* of the saints in this Book (v. 10; xx. 4, 6; xxii. 5: cf. Dan. vii. 18, 22).—The royal priesthood of the redeemed (see Exod. xix. 6; 1 Pet. ii. 9) flows out of the royal priesthood of the Redeemer, a priest for ever after the order of Melchizedek (Ps. cx. 4; Zech. vi. 13). That the whole number of the redeemed shall in the world of glory have been made "*priests unto God*" is the analogon as regards persons to the new Jerusalem being without temple, in other words, being all temple, which is declared further on (xxi. 22); it is the abolition of the distinction between holy and profane (Zech. xiv. 20, 21) nearer and more remote from God, through all being henceforth holy, all being brought to the nearest whereof it is capable, to Him.

"*To Him be glory and dominion for ever and ever. Amen.*"—Cf. 1 Pet. iv. 11. A fuller doxology, being threefold, occurs iv. 9, 11; and a fuller yet, being fourfold, at v. 13; cf. Jude 25; and the fullest of all, the sevenfold doxology, at vii. 12; cf. 1 Chron. xxix. 11. A study of these, and a comparison of them with one another, would amply repay the pains bestowed upon it; above all, if it served to remind us of the prominence which the doxological element assumes in the highest worship of the Church, the very subordinate place which it oftentimes takes in ours. We can perhaps make our requests known unto God; and this is well, for it is prayer; but to give glory to God, quite apart from anything to be directly gotten by ourselves in return, this is better, for it is adoration; but it is rarer also, no less than better.

Ver. 7. "*Behold, He cometh with clouds.*"—The constant recurrence of this language in all descriptions of our Lord's second advent is very remarkable (Dan. vii. 13; Matt. xxiv. 30; xxvi. 64; Mark xiv. 62), and all the meaning of it will scarcely be attained till that great day of the Lord shall have itself arrived. This much seems certain, namely, that this accompaniment of clouds (it is *μετὰ τῶν νεφελῶν*) belongs not to the glory and gladness, but to the terror and anguish, of that day; as indeed the context of the present passage would indicate. The clouds have nothing in common with the light-cloud, the νεφέλη φωτεινή (Matt. xvii. 5), "the glorious privacy of light" into which the Lord was withdrawn for a while from the eyes of his disciples at the Transfiguration, but are rather the symbols of wrath, fit accompaniments of judgment: "Clouds and darkness are round about Him; righteousness and judgment are the habitation of his throne" (Ps. xcvii. 2; cf. xviii. 11; Nah. i. 3; Isai. xix. 1).

"*And every eye shall see Him, and they also which pierced Him, and all kindreds of the earth shall wail because of Him. Even so, Amen.*"—It will sometimes happen that a prophecy, severe in the Old Testament, by some gracious turn will be transformed from a threat to a promise in the New; thus, the "day of visitation" of St. Peter (1 Ep. ii. 12) is another from the "day of visitation" of the prophets,—that to be hoped for, this to be feared. But it is not so here. There is indeed a turn, yet not from the severe to the gracious, but the contrary. The words of the prophet Zechariah (xii. 10), on which this passage and John xix. 37 in common rest, are words of grace: "They shall look upon Me, whom they have pierced, and they shall mourn for Him." They express the profound repentance of the Jews, when the veil shall be at length taken from their hearts, and they shall behold in Jesus of Nazareth, whom they crucified, the Son of God, the King of Israel. But it cannot be denied that in their adaptation here they speak quite another language. They set forth the despair of the sinful world, of all the tribes of the earth (cf. Matt. xxiv. 30), when Christ the Judge shall come to execute judgment on all that obeyed not his gospel, who pierced Him with their sins; their remorse and despair, but give no hint of their repentance. The closing words, "*Even so, Amen*," are not to be taken as the prophet's devout acquiescence in the terribleness of that judgment-day,—a comparison with xxii. 20 might easily lead an English reader into this misunderstanding of them,—but as God's own seal and ratification of his own word.

Ver. 8. "*I am Alpha and Omega, the beginning and the ending, saith the Lord.*"—Cf. xxi. 6, where the words "*the beginning and the ending*" have a right to a place in the text; but not here; having been transferred from thence, without any authority at all. He who is "*Alpha and Omega*" (or better, "*Alpha and Ω*"), and thus indeed "*the beginning and the ending*," and "the first and the last" (i. 17; ii. 8), leaves no room for any other; is indeed the only I AM; and beside Him there is no God. Thus Clement of Alexandria (*Strom.* iv. 25): κύκλος γὰρ ὁ Υἱὸς πασῶν τῶν δυνάμεων εἰς ἓν εἱλουμένων καὶ ἑνουμένων· διὰ τοῦτο Ἄλφα καὶ Ω εἴρηται· and Tertullian, bringing out the unity of the Old and New Testaments, and the manner in which the glorious consummations of the latter attach themselves to the glorious commencements of the former (*De Monog.* v.): "Sic et duas Græciæ litteras summam et ultimam sibi induit Dominus, initii et finis concurrentium in se figuras; uti quemadmodum *α* ad *ω* usque volvitur, et rursus *ω* ad *α* explicatur, ita ostenderet in se esse et initii decursum ad finem, et finis recursum ad initium; ut omnis dispositio in Eum desinens, per quem cœpta est, per Sermonem scilicet Dei qui caro factus est, proinde desit quemadmodum et cœpit."

"*Which is and which was, and which is to come, the Almighty.*"—Cf. ver. 4. *Παντοκράτωρ*, which only occurs once in the New Testament (2 Cor. vi. 18) except in this Book, is a constant word in the Septuagint. "The Lord of Hosts" of the Hebrew is there sometimes *κύριος δυνάμεων*, or *στρατιῶν*, or *σαβαώθ*; but oftener, I think, *κύριος παντοκράτωρ*, as at Jer. iii. 19; Amos iii. 13; Hab. ii. 13. It is clear that the Old Testament uses of *παντοκράτωρ*, so very distinctly fixed as they are, must quite overrule and determine the New Testament employment of it; and thus the ingenious speculations of Gregory of Nyssa, and other Greek Fathers (see Suicer, s. v.), in which they seek a special meaning for it, and find it to express of God, that He holds all creation in his grasp, preserving it from that ruin and collapse which would at once overtake it, if not evermore sustained by his creative Word, prove nothing worth. This, grand an attribute as it is of the Godhead (Heb. i. 3), is assuredly not that which specially lies in *παντοκράτωρ*, for it is not that which it brought from the earlier Covenant.

Ver. 9. "*I John, who also am your brother.*" —The only other writer either in the Old Testament or the New who uses this style is Daniel—"I Daniel" (vii. 28; ix. 2; x. 2). It is one of the many points of resemblance, small and great, between this Book and that of Daniel. The *καί*, represented by "*also*" in our Version, and modifying this whole clause, should have no place in the text. It may have been suggested by 1 Pet. v. 1; and was probably inserted by some who esteemed ὁ ἀδελφὸς ὑμῶν too humble a title for one of the great pillars of the Church; and by that *καί* would make him to say, "who, being an Apostle, am *also* a brother."

"*And companion in tribulation, and in the kingdom and patience of Jesus Christ.*"—It has been sometimes asked, When was that prophecy and promise fulfilled concerning John, that he should drink of his Lord's cup, and be baptized with his Lord's baptism (Matt. xx. 22)? The fulfilment of this promise and prophecy as it regarded his brother James is plain; when the sword of Herod was dyed with his blood (Acts xii. 2). It was answered rightly by Origen long ago (*In Matt.* tom. xvi. § 6, *in fine*), Here—in this his banishment to Patmos; not thereby denying that there must have been a life-long θλῖψις for such an one as the Apostle John, but only affirming that the words found their most emphatic fulfilment now. Let us not fail to observe the connexion and the sequence —"*tribulation*" first, and "*the kingdom*" afterwards; on which Richard of St. Victor well: "Recte præmisit, *in tribulatione*, et post addit, *in regno*, quia si compatimur, et corregnabimus" (2 Tim. ii. 12; cf. Rom. viii. 17; 1 Pet. iv. 13). As yet, however, while the tribulation is present, the kingdom is only in hope; therefore he adds to these, as that which is the link between them, "*and patience of Jesus Christ;*" cf. Acts xiv. 22, where exactly these same three, the tribulation, the patience, and the kingdom occur. Ὑπομονή, which we have rendered "*patience*," is not so much the "patientia" as the "perseverentia" of the Latin; which last word Cicero (*De Invent.* ii. 54) thus defines: "In ratione bene considerată stabilis et perpetua mansio;" and Augustine (*Quæst.* lxxxiii. qu. 31): "Honestatis aut utilitatis causâ rerum arduarum ac difficilium voluntaria ac diuturna perpessio." It is indeed a beautiful word, expressing the *brave* patience of the Christian—*βασιλὶς τῶν ἀρετῶν,* Chrysostom does not fear to call it.

"*I was in the isle that is called Patmos, for the word of God, and for the testimony of Jesus Christ.*"—Patmos, now Patmo or Palmosa, one of the Sporades, a little rocky island in the Icarian Sea, S.-W. of Ephesus, a spot in itself utterly insignificant, would have remained unknown and almost unnamed, if this mention here had not given to it a name and a fame in the Church for ever. This its entire previous insignificance is slightly, yet unmistakably, indicated in the words "*that is called Patmos.*" St. John does not assume his readers to be familiar with it, any more than St. Mark, writing for those living at a distance from Palestine, with the Jordan (cf. Mark i. 5 with Matt. iii. 5). It is not so that a well-known island, Crete or Cyprus, is introduced (Acts xiii. 4). The deportation of criminals, or those accounted as such, to rocky and desolate islands was, as is well known, a common punishment among the Romans. Titus, according to Suetonius, banished some delators "in asperrimas insularum" (*Tit.* 8 ; cf. Juvenal, i. 73).

The unprejudiced reader will hardly be persuaded that St. John sets himself forth here as any other than such a constrained dweller in Patmos, one who had been banished thither "*for the word of God, and for the testimony of Jesus Christ.*" Those modern interpreters who find in these words no reference to any such suffering for the truth's sake, but only a statement on the writer's part that he was in the isle of Patmos for the sake of preaching the Word of God, or, as others, for the sake of receiving a communication of the Word of God, refuse the obvious meaning of the words, which moreover a comparison with vi. 9; xx. 4, seems to me to render imperative, for one which, if it also may possibly lie in them, has nothing but this bare possibility in its favour. It is difficult not to think that these interpreters have been unconsciously influenced by a desire to get rid of the strong testimony for St. John's authorship of the Book which lies in the consent of this declaration with that which early ecclesiastical history tells us about him, namely, that for his steadfastness in the faith of Christ he was by Domitian banished to Patmos, and only released at the accession of Nerva. The Apocalypse, it is worth observing by the way, has all internal evidence of having been thus written in time of persecution and by a confessor of the truth. The whole Book breathes the very air of martyrdom. Oftentimes slighted by the Church in times of prosperity, it is made much of, and its preciousness, as it were, instinctively discovered, in times of adversity and fiery trial. This Bengel has well observed: "In tribulatione fidelibus maxime hic liber sapit. Asiatica Ecclesia, præsertim a floridissimo Constantini tempore, minus magni æstimavit hunc librum. Africana Ecclesia, cruci magis obnoxia, semper hunc librum plurimi fecit." Tertullian may be quoted in proof of this assertion. How often does he seek, now to strengthen the faithful with the promises, and now to terrify the fearful with the threatenings, of this Book (*Scorp.* 12; *De Cor.* 15); and compare Cyprian, *De Exhort. Mart.* passim.

Ver. 10. "*I was in the Spirit on the Lord's day.*"—In one sense the faithful are always "*in the Spirit;*" they are "spiritual" (1 Cor. iii. 1, 15); are "led by the Spirit" (Rom. viii. 14); "walk in the Spirit" (Gal. v. 16, 25). But here, and at iv. 2; xxi. 10 (cf. Ezek. xl. 2, "in the visions of God"), the words are used in an eminent and peculiar sense; they describe not the habitual condition of faithful men, but an exceptional condition, differing from the other not in degree only, but in kind; a condition in which there is a suspension of all the motions and faculties of the natural life; that a higher life may be called, during and through this suspension, into a preternatural activity. It is the state of trance or ecstasy, that is, of standing out of oneself (θεία ἐξαλλαγὴ τῶν εἰωθότων νομίμων Plato calls it, *Phædrus*, 265 A, and on its positive side, ἐνθουσιασμός), so often described in Scripture as the condition of men to whom God would speak more directly (Acts x. 10; cf. xi. 5; xxii. 17); the antithesis to it, or the return out of it, being a γενόμενος ἐν ἑαυτῷ (Acts xii. 11); ἐν τῷ νοΐ (1 Cor. xiv. 14).[1] St. Paul exactly describes the experience of one who has passed through this state, 2 Cor. xii. 2-4. That world of spiritual realities is one from which man is comparatively estranged so long as he dwells in this house of clay; he has need to be transported out of himself, before he can find himself in the midst of and come into direct contact with it. Here we have the explanation of the fact that the Lord never was "in the Spirit," namely, because He was always "in the Spirit," because He always moved in that region as his proper haunt and home.

Separated in body from the fellowship of the faithful, the beloved Apostle was yet keeping with them the weekly feast of the resurrection on the day which the Lord had made for ever peculiarly

[1] Augustine (*Enarr. in Ps.* ciii. 11): "Illo orante [Acts x. 10] facta est illi mentis alienatio, quam Græci ecstasin dicunt; id est, aversa est mens ejus a consuetudine corporali ad visum quendam contemplandum, alienata a præsentibus." Cf. *in Ps.* lxvii. 28; *Quæst. in Gen.* l. 1, qu. 80; and *De Div. Quæst.* l. 2, qu. 1: "Mentis alienatio a sensibus corporis, ut spiritus hominis divino Spiritu assumptus capiendis atque intuendis imaginibus vacet."

his own. It was, as he is careful to declare to us, "*on the Lord's Day*," which occupied for the Church the place occupied by the Sabbath for the Jews, that he thus passed out of himself, and was drawn within the veil, and heard unspeakable words, and beheld things which, unless they had been shown by God, must have remained for ever hidden from mortal gaze. Some have assumed from this passage that ἡμέρα κυριακή was a designation of Sunday already familiar among Christians. This, however, seems a mistake. The name had probably its origin here. A little later we find ἡμέρα κυριακή familiar to Ignatius, as "Dominica solemnia" to Tertullian (*De Animâ*, c. 9; cf. Dionysius of Corinth, quoted by Eusebius, *H. E.* iv. 23, 8; Clement of Alexandria, *Strom.* vii. 12; Origen, *Con. Cels.* viii. 22). But though the name, "*the Lord's Day*," will very probably have had here its rise (the actual form of the phrase may have been suggested by κυριακὸν δεῖπνον, 1 Cor. xi. 20),—the thing, the celebration of the first day of the week as that on which the Lord brake the bands of death, and became the head of a new creation, called therefore sometimes ἀναστάσιμος ἡμέρα, this was as old as Christianity itself (John xx. 24-29; 1 Cor. xvi. 2; Acts xx. 7; *Ep. of Barnabas*, c. 15: ἄγομεν τὴν ἡμέραν τὴν ὀγδόην εἰς εὐφροσύνην: cf. Suicer, s. v. κυριακή). The strange fancy of some that ἡμέρα κυριακή means here "the day of the Lord," in the sense of "the day of judgment," intended as it is to subserve a scheme of Apocalyptic interpretation which certainly needs any support which it can any where find, has been abundantly refuted by Alford.

"*And I heard behind me a great voice, as of a trumpet.*"—The wondrous vision which the Seer shall behold does not break upon him all at once; he first hears behind him "*a voice, great as of a trumpet,*" summoning his attention, and preparing him for the still greater sight which he shall see. It is a "*great* voice," as the voice of the Lord must ever be (Ps. xxix. 3-9; lxviii. 33; Dan. x. 6; Matt. xxiv. 31; 1 Thess. iv. 16); a voice penetrating and clear, "*as of a trumpet;*" in which comparison there *may be* allusion, as Hengstenberg is sure there is, to the divinely-instituted rule of calling together by a trumpet the congregation of the Lord, when He had any thing to impart to them (Num. x. 2; Exod. xix. 16, 19; Joel ii. 1, 15; Matt. xxiv. 31; 1 Thess. iv. 16); although this to me does not seem very probable.

"*Saying, What thou seest, write in a book, and send it to the seven Churches which are in Asia; unto Ephesus, and unto Smyrna, and unto Pergamos, and unto Thyatira, and unto Sardis, and unto Philadelphia, and unto Laodicea.*"—The words,

"*I am Alpha and Omega, the first and the last,*" which in our Version follow immediately after "*Saying,*" have no right whatever to stand in the text. It is disputed whether the "*book*" which St. John is to write, and having written, to send to the seven Churches, is this whole Book of the Apocalypse, or only the seven shorter Epistles contained in chapters ii. and iii. Hengstenberg affirms the last; but against the great body of interpreters, and, as I am persuaded, wrongly. "*What thou seest*" must in that case be restrained to ver. 12-16 of this present chapter. All the rest, to the end of chap. iii., he will have *heard;* but will have seen nothing; and moreover ver. 19 is decisive that what he is to write of is more than that which he has then seen: "*Write the things which thou hast seen, and the things which are, and the things which shall be hereafter.*"

Doubtless it is not for nothing that seven Churches, neither more nor less, are here named. The reason of this lies deeper than some suggest, who will have these seven to include all the principal Churches of Asia; whatever others there were being merely annexed to these. But taking into account the rapid spread of the Gospel in the regions of Asia Minor as recorded in Scripture (Acts xix. 9; 1 Cor. xvi. 9), and in other historical documents of a date very little later, we cannot doubt that toward the end of the life of St. John there were flourishing and important Churches in many other cities of that region besides these seven; that if the first purpose of the great ascended Bishop of the Church had been to bring under spiritual review the whole Church of Asia, in this case Colosse, to which St. Paul addressed an Epistle, and Hierapolis, where was already the nucleus of a Church in the Apostle's time (Col. iv. 13), and where a little later Papias was bishop, and Miletus, the scene of apostolic labours (Acts xx. 17), and Tralles, called by Cicero "gravis, ornata et locuples civitas," to the Church in which city Ignatius wrote an epistle some twenty years later, as he did to that in Magnesia as well, these with others would scarcely have been passed by.[1] But what we may call the mys-

[1] There is an instructive chapter in Tacitus (*Annal.* iv. 55), throwing much light on the relative dignity and position, at a period a little earlier than this, of the chief cities in proconsular Asia. He is describing a contention which found place among eleven of them, which should have the honour of erecting a statue and temple to Tiberius. Among the eleven contending for this glorious privilege, which involved as well the maintaining as the founding of this cult, five out of our seven appear. Two, namely Philadelphia and Thyatira, do not enter the lists. Laodicea, with others not included in this seven, is set aside, as unequal in wealth and dignity to the task; Pergamum as having already a temple to Augustus, Ephesus as devoted to Diana, and others for various causes; till at length Smyrna and Sardis are the only competitors which remain. Of these the former is preferred, mainly on account of its greater devotedness in times past to the in-

tical or symbolic interest overbears and predominates over the actual. No doubt this actual was sufficiently provided for in another way, and these seven words of warning and encouragement so penetrated to the heart of things that, meeting the needs of these seven Churches, they also met the needs of all others subsisting in similar, or nearly similar conditions. Typical and representative Churches, these embodied, one or another of them, I will not say all the great leading aspects of the Church in its faithfulness or its unfaithfulness; but they embodied a great many, the broadest and the oftenest recurring.[1] The seven must in this point of view be regarded as constituting a complex whole, as possessing an ideal completeness. Christ, we feel sure, could not have placed Himself in the relation which He does to them, as holding in his hand the seven stars, walking among the seven golden candlesticks, these stars being the Angels of the Churches, and the candlesticks the Churches themselves, unless they ideally represented and set forth, in some way or other, the universal Church, militant here upon earth.

terests of the Roman State, when as yet the fortunes of Rome were not so completely in the ascendant as they were then.

[1] Grotius: "Sub earum nomine tacite comprehendit et alias Ecclesias, quia earum status et qualitates ad septem quasi genera possunt revocari, quorum exemplum præbent illæ Asiaticæ."

But this, which I have here rather assumed than proved, together with another question, namely, whether besides possessing this typical and representative character, these seven Epistles are not also historico-prophetical, do not unfold the future of the Church's fortunes to the end of time, seven *successive* stages and periods of its growth and history, has been so eagerly discussed, has, strangely enough, roused so much theological passion, that I am unwilling to treat the subject with the brevity which a place in this exposition would require. I must therefore refer the reader to an Excursus at the end of the volume, in which I have traced, rapidly indeed, but with some attempt at completeness, a sketch of the controversy, and have stated, and sought to justify, the conclusions on the points in debate at which I have myself arrived.

"*And I turned to see the voice that spake with me. And being turned, I saw seven golden candlesticks.*" *Λυχνία* is a word condemned by the Greek purists, who prefer λύχνιον (Lobeck, *Phrynichus*, p. 313). The "*seven candlesticks*"—the rendering is not a very happy one, though it is not very plain how it should be bettered—send us back, and are intended to send us back, to the seven-branched candlestick, or candelabrum, which bears ever the same name of λυχνία in the Septuagint (Exod. xxv. 31; cf. Heb. ix. 2; Philo, *Quis Rer. Div. Hær.*

44; Josephus, *B. J.* v. 5. 5); the six arms of which with the central shaft (*καλαμίσκοι*, Exod. xxv. 31; *κλάδοι*, Philo, *Vit. Mos.* iii. 9), made up the mystical seven, each with its several lamp (*λύχνος*, Zech. iv. 2). Nor is this the first occasion when that portion of the furniture of the tabernacle has had a higher mystical meaning ascribed to it. Already in the candlestick all of gold, which Zechariah saw (iv. 2), there was an anticipation of this image; being one of the many remarkable points of contact between his prophecies and the Apocalypse. Here, however, it is not one candlestick with seven branches which St. John beholds; but rather seven separate candlesticks. Nor is it without a meaning that the seven thus take the place of the one. The Jewish Church was one; for it was the Church of a single people; the Christian Church, that too is one, but it is also many; at once the "Church" and the "Churches." These may be quite independent of one another, the only bond of union with one another which they absolutely require being that of common dependence on the same Head, and derivation of life from the same Spirit; and are fitly represented by seven, the number of mystical completeness.

In the image itself by which the Churches are symbolized there is an eminent fitness. The candlestick, or lampstand, as we must rather conceive it here, is not light, but it is the bearer of light, that which diffuses it, that which holds it forth and causes it to shine throughout the house; being the appointed instrument for this. It is thus with the Church. God's word, God's truth, including in this all which He has declared of Himself in revealed religion, is light (Ps. cxix. 105; Prov. vi. 23); the Church is the light-bearer, light in the Lord (Ephes. v. 8), not having light of its own, but diffusing that which it receives of Him. Each too of the faithful in particular, after he has been illuminated (Heb. vi. 4), is a bearer of the light; "ye are the light of the world" (Matt. v. 14-16); "lights in the world, holding forth the word of life" (Phil. ii. 15). In accordance with this view of the matter, in the Levitical tabernacle the seven-branched candlestick stood in the Holy Place (Exod. xxvi. 35; xl. 4), which was the pattern of the Church upon earth, as the Holy of Holies was the pattern of the Church in heaven; and the only light which the Holy Place received was derived from that candlestick; the light of common day being quite excluded from it, in sign that the Lord God was the light thereof, that the light of the Church is the light of nature, but of grace.

These candlesticks are of gold (cf. Exod. xxv. 31; Zech. iv. 2), as so much else in this Book; "the *golden* girdle" (i. 13); "*golden* crowns"

(iv. 4); "*golden* vials" (v. 8); "*golden* censer" (viii. 3); "*golden* altar" (ibid.); "*golden* reed" (xxi. 15); "the city of pure *gold*" (xxi. 18); "the street of the city of pure *gold*" (xxi. 21). No doubt the preciousness of all belonging to the Church of God is indicated by the predominant employment of this the costliest and most perfect metal of all. A hint no doubt we have here of this, exactly as in the Ark and furniture of the Ark so much in like manner is of pure gold, the mercy-seat, the cherubim, the dishes, spoons, covers, tongs, snuff-dishes (Exod. xxv. 17, 18, 29, 38), the pot which had manna (Exod. xvi. 33),[1] every thing in short which did not by its bulk and consequent weight absolutely preclude this, and even that was for the most part overlaid with gold (Exod. xxv. 10, 11, 23, 24).[2] But the mere costliness of gold, that it was of all metals the rarest, and therefore the dearest, this was not the only motive for the predominant employment of it. Throughout all the

[1] This was a *golden* pot, as we learn from Heb. ix. 4; cf. LXX in loc., and Philo, *Cong. Erud. Gent.* § 18.

[2] Cocceius: "Aurum in figuris et symbolicis locutionibus significat id quod est omnium optimum, quod omnia perficit, et a nullo perficitur; sed in se est perfectissimum et purissimum, nullique mutationi obnoxium; quemadmodum aurum omnium metallorum perfectissimum est, et ab aliis non perficitur; sed quibus accedit ea perficit, et nec temporis, nec ignis, omnium destructoris violentiam injuriamque sentit."

ancient East there was a sense of sacredness attached to this metal, which still to a great extent survives. Thus "golden" in the Zend-Avesta is throughout synonymous with heavenly or divine. So also in many Eastern lands while silver might be degraded to profane and every-day uses of common life, might as money pass from hand to hand, "the pale and common drudge 'twixt man and man," it was not permitted to employ gold in any services except only royal and divine (see Bähr, *Symbolik*, vol. i. pp. 273, 282, 292).

Ver. 13. "*And in the midst of the seven candlesticks one like unto the Son of man.*"—Some translate "*like unto a son of man,*" that is to say, "like unto a man," the words merely for them expressing that He who was seen was in human shape, and, so far as the appearance warranted the conclusion, the sharer of a human nature (Ezek. xxxvii. 3, 16; xxxix. 1). The absence of the articles, however, does not require this either here or at xiv. 14; any more than *υἱὸς Θεοῦ* (Matt. xxvii. 54) demands to be translated "a son of God," or *πνεῦμα Θεοῦ,* "a Spirit of God." The beloved Apostle by this "*like unto the Son of man*" would express his recognition in this sublime appearance of Him whom he had once known on earth, the born of the Virgin Mary; and who even then had claimed to be executor of all judgment, because He was the Son of man (John v. 27).

"*Clothed with a garment down to the foot.*"—We are again reminded of Daniel's vision, where in like manner He whom the prophet saw was "clothed in linen" (x. 5), or, as it would be more rightly translated, "in a long linen garment." *Ποδήρης*, the "poderis" of ecclesiastical Latin, is properly an adjective here, with *χίτων* understood; cf. Wisd. xviii. 24: *ποδῆρες ἔνδυμα*, and Xenophon, *Cyrop.* vi. 2, 10: *ἄσπις ποδήρης*, a shield reaching down to the feet, such as the *θυρεός* (Ephes. vi. 16), and covering the whole person. The *long* robe is every where in the East the garment of dignity and honour (Gen. xxxvii. 3; Mark xiii. 38; Luke xv. 22)—the association of dignity with it probably resting originally on the absence of the necessity of labour; and thus of loins girt up, which it implied: see, on the other hand, 2 Sam. x. 4. The word nowhere else occurs in the New Testament, but several times in the Old; and designates there sometimes the long linen garment common to all the priests, the chetoneth, "the holy linen coat" (Lev. xvi. 4; Exod. xxxix. 27), sometimes the High Priest's "robe of the ephod" (Exod. xxviii. 31; Zech. iii. 4; Wisd. xviii. 24); *στολὴ δόξης*, as it is called, Ecclus. xlviii. 7. Yet these passages must not lead us, as they have led some, to regard this as a manifestation of Christ in his priestly character alone. The Rheims version indeed renders ποδήρης here "a *priestly* garment," but with no warrant for so doing. Any stately garment, any "vestis talaris," may be indicated by the word (Ecclus. xxvii. 8), as for instance, that worn by the Angel of the covenant (Ezek. ix. 2, 3). So too in Isaiah's magnificent vision (vi. 1), *He* was clothed with a ποδήρης, though the word does not there occur, whom the prophet beheld sitting as a King upon his throne, and whose train filled the temple. The ποδήρης, in fact, is quite as much a kingly garment as a priestly, even as Christ presents Himself here not only as the Priest, but the King, and, so far as there is any predominance, more the King than the Priest, ruling in the midst of his Church.

"*And girt about the paps with a golden girdle.*"—So we read of the Angels "having *their breasts* girded with golden girdles" (xv. 6); cf. Ovid: "cinctæque *ad pectora* vestes." The ordinary girding for one actively engaged was *at the loins* (1 Kings ii. 5; xviii. 46; Jer. xiii. 11; cf. Luke xii. 35; Eph. vi. 14; 1 Pet. i. 13); but Josephus (*Antt.* iii. 7, 2) expressly tells us that the Levitical priests were girt higher up, about the breast, or as it is here, "*about the paps*" (ἐπιζώννυνται κατὰ στῆθος)—favouring, as this higher cincture did, a calmer, more majestic movement (see Braun, *De*

Vest. Hebr. p. 402). The girdle, knitting up as it would do into a compact unity all the scattered forces of a man, is often contemplated as the symbol of strength and power (Isai. xxii. 21; Job xii. 18); and as nothing is so strong as righteousness and truth, therefore the prophet foretells of Messiah, "Righteousness shall be the girdle of his loins, and faithfulness the girdle of his reins" (Isai. xi. 5; cf. Ephes. vi. 14). The girdle here is "*golden;*" not merely with a golden clasp or buckle, as Hengstenberg, relying on 1 Macc. x. 89; xi. 58; xiv. 44, where such appears as the ensign of royalty, would have it; but all of gold; cf. xv. 7; and Dan. x. 5: "His loins were girded with fine gold of Uphaz." It is quite true that the curious girdle of the High Priest was not golden, but only wrought and interwoven with gold (Exod. xxviii. 8; xxxix. 5); but this with other departures in the present appearance of the Lord from the investiture of the High Priest only goes to confirm what was just asserted, namely, that we have to do with Him here not as the Priest only, but as also the King in his Church; for it is in this direction that all the variations tend.

Ver. 14. "*His head and his hairs were white like wool, as white as snow.*"—Cf. Dan. vii. 9: "The hair of his head was like the pure wool;" wool and snow being joined together on the score of their common whiteness both there and at Isai. i. 18. I must needs consider those interpreters as here altogether at fault who see in this whiteness of the Lord's hairs the symbol of age, the hoary head as of the Ancient of Days, which should inspire honour and respect. Augustine himself has not escaped this error (*Exp. ad Gal.* iv. 21): "Dominus non nisi ob antiquitatem veritatis in Apocalypsi albo càpite apparuit;" and Vitringa gives a reference to Lev. xix. 32. That it is an error a moment's reflection will convince. The white hairs of old age are at once the sign and the consequence of the decay of natural strength, in other words, of death commencing; the hair blanching because the blood refuses to circulate any longer in these extremities, as it will one day refuse to circulate in any part of the frame. Being then this, how can the white hairs, the hoary head which is the sign of weakness, decay, and the approach of death, be ascribed to Him who, as He is *from* everlasting, so also is He *to* everlasting? Even the Angel at the sepulchre is a νεανισκός, "a *young* màn" (Mark xvi. 5; cf. Zech. ii. 4); what then the Angel's Lord (cf. 2 Esdr. ii. 43, 47)?

"*And his eyes were as a flame of fire.*"—Cf. Dan. x. 6: "His eyes [were] as lamps of fire." This too has been understood by some, of the clear-sightedness of Christ, that all things are open and manifest to the eyes of Him with whom we have to do. Thus Vitringa: "Significant perspicaciam divinæ et puræ mentis omnia arcana pervadentis;" but Cocceius much better: "Significat hoc iram ἀπαραίτητον in adversarios." The other explanation is insufficient. "*His eyes were as a flame of fire*," does not say merely that He knows what is in man, that nothing can escape his searching penetrative glance; it expresses much more than this—the indignation of the Holy One at the discoveries of evil which He thus makes. These "*eyes of fire*," do not merely *look through* the hypocrite and the sinner, but *consume* him, him and his sins together, unless indeed he will suffer them to consume his sins, that so he may live. For indeed in the symbolism of Scripture, fire is throughout the expression of the divine anger; and seeing that nothing moves that anger but sin, of the divine anger against sin (Gen. xix. 24; Lev. x. 2; Num. xi. 1; xvi. 35; Ps. l. 3; xcvii. 3; 2 Kings i. 10, 12; Ezek. xxxviii. 22; xxxix. 6; Dan. vii. 9, 10; Luke ix. 54; 2 Thess. i. 8; Heb. x. 27; Jude 7; Rev. xx. 9). It need hardly be observed, as confirming this interpretation, that the eyes flashing fire are evermore the utterance, the outward tokens of indignation and wrath; thus Homer (*Il.* xiii. 474): ὀφθαλμὼ δ' ἄρα οἱ πυρὶ λάμπετον: cf. Virgil, *Æn.* xii. 101, 102. If any hesitation existed in ascribing this meaning to the symbol here, it must be removed by a comparison with xix. 11, 12. The whole imagery there is of Christ as a man of war coming forth in his anger to make war upon his enemies, and the "*eyes as a flame of fire*" are again ascribed to Him there.

Ver. 15. "*And his feet like unto fine brass, as if they burned in a furnace.*"—The ποδήρης, as the name sufficiently indicates, must have reached to the feet, but permitted them to be seen. They were no doubt bare; as were the feet of the Levitical priesthood ministering in the sanctuary. We are no where indeed expressly told of these that they ministered barefoot, but every thing leads us to this conclusion. Thus while all the other parts of the priestly investiture are described with the greatest minuteness, and Moses accurately instructed how they should be made, there is no mention of any covering for the feet. Then again the analogy of such passages as Exod. iii. 5; Josh. v. 15, and the fact that the *moral* idea of the shoe is that of a defence against the *defilements* of the earth, of which defilements there could be none in the Holy Place, all this irresistibly points this way. Plutarch's testimony to the contrary (*Symp.* iv. 6, 2), who ascribes, to the High Priest at least, buskins (κοθόρνους), cannot be regarded as of the slightest weight on the other side. Uncovered at all events the feet on the present occasion were; for St. John compares them to χαλκολίβανος—there is no reason why we should assume a neuter, *χαλκολίβανον,* as the nominative, which has very commonly been done—a word which we have translated "*fine brass.*" It occurs only here and at ii. 18; being, in all probability, of St. John's own composition; and has much perplexed, we may say has hitherto defied, interpreters to give any satisfactory explanation of it—to do more than guess at its etymology and its meaning.

It has been suggested, and the suggestion is as old as Arethas,—it is indeed older, for the Syriac and the Ethiopic versions rest upon it,—that we are to find *Λίβανος,* or Lebanon, in the latter part of the word, and that χαλκολίβανος means "brass of Mount Lebanon," such as was there found; or more generally "mountain-brass," "aurichalcum," as it is in the Vulgate; in the first syllable of which, as need hardly be observed, we are not to find "aurum," as though this mixed metal were of *gold* and brass, and the word designating it a hybrid, partly Latin, partly Greek, but *ὄρος,* "*ori*-chalcum" (*Æn.* xii. 87) = ὀρείχαλκος. So one quoted by Wolf: "Libanus pro monte quolibet, fortasse quod Libanus dederit ejusmodi genus metalli;" which it has been further sought to prove by putting together the promise to Asher, "Thy shoes shall be iron and brass" (Deut. xxxiii. 25), and the fact that Lebanon was within the borders of this tribe. It is hardly fair to urge against this etymology the objection that it violates the law which holds good in Greek composite words, namely, that the more important word should come last, and the merely qualitative first; which indeed holds good quite as much in our own language, in which "brass-mountain" would signify something very different from "mountain-brass." I say it is hardly fair to urge this, that the word should be rather λιβανόχαλκος than χαλκολίβανος, because the same objection may be urged against every other attempted explanation of the word, including that which seems to me the most probable of all. Another suggestion, first made by Salmasius, has found favour with Ewald, to the effect that this mysterious word is a somewhat euphonic form of χαλκοκλίβανος, brass of the κλίβανος, or furnace; it is scarcely likely to find favour with others, and is not worthy any serious notice. As little, I confess, does the solution of the riddle of this word, which Wordsworth has allowed and adopted, commend itself to me, namely, that the second part of the word is λίβανος, frankincense, brass of the colour of frankincense, that is, brass of a dark copper hue; for, to say nothing of the extreme unlikelihood of frankincense being sought to suggest what the colour was, this part of the description is thus put in direct opposition with all the rest. Every thing else is light, fire, of a white shining brightness; the feet must be so as well.

The explanation which satisfies this, as well as other conditions, and commends itself above any other, is one first proposed by Bochart (in a learned disquisition, *De Animal. S. Script.* pars ii. c. xvi. p. 883); and since adopted by Grotius, Vitringa, Hengstenberg, and others. Bochart sees in χαλκολίβανος, a hybrid formation, the combination of a Greek word and a Hebrew, χαλκός, and לִבֵּן = "albare," to make white; brass which in the furnace has attained what we call "*white* heat." In this word on a small scale, as in the Apocalypse itself on a larger, the two sacred tongues, Greek and Hebrew, will thus be wonderfully married. If this be the key of the word, it will then exactly correspond to, and the Seer will have intended to express by it, the "*burnished* brass" of the feet of the four living creatures (Ezek. i. 7; cf. ver. 27 and viii. 2), the "*polished* brass" of the feet of Him whom Daniel saw on the banks of Hiddekel (Dan. x. 6), neither "burnished" nor "polished" in those passages of our Translation exactly expressing the force of the original; which the LXX by ἐξαστράπτων in the first passage, στίλβων in the second (the Vulgate has well "candens" in both), had more precisely seized. If this be correct, the χαλκολίβανος will not be the "*fine*," or the "shining," but the "glowing," brass. This conclusion is very much strengthened by the epexegesis, "*as if they burned in a furnace;*" words of explanation immediately added by St. John, as probably knowing the difficulty which his readers would find in this unusual term. A further confirmation we may draw from a comparison with x. 1, where feet as "pillars *of fire*," which can only be feet as glowing or burning brass, are ascribed to the mighty Angel, who there appears. This grand and terrible image sets forth to us Christ in his power to tread down his enemies; at once to tread down and to consume them—"ut potentissimum in conculcandis hostibus" (Marckius).

"*And his voice as the sound of many waters.*"—Hitherto St. John has trodden closely on the footsteps of Daniel in his delineation of Him whom his eyes beheld; but grand as is the imagery which he offers ("the voice of his words [was] like the voice of a multitude," Dan. x. 6), the Seer of the New Testament, leaving this, draws now his comparison from another quarter, from Ezek. xliii. 2: "his voice was like a noise of many waters;" cf. Ezek. i. 24; Rev. xix. 6; Jer. l. 42; Isai. xvii. 12. We may note, I think, herein a special characteristic of this wonderful Book. Were it not that the term, "a mosaic," always seems to imply, or to suggest, something artificial, we might in many parts liken the Apocalypse to such a costly mosaic; the precious stones of which, wrought into novel combinations of beauty, have been brought from all the richest mines of the Old Testament and the New.—By this comparison of the voice of the Lord to "*the sound of many waters*," is not to be understood the "prædicatio Evangelii" (Vitringa), but the terribleness of the voice with which He will rebuke his foes within the Church and without.

Ver. 16. "*And He had in his right hand seven stars.*"—Cf. ver. 20; ii. 1; iii. 1. In what fashion we are to conceive the Lord as thus "*having in his right hand*" these "*seven stars*," has been often asked, and variously answered. Is it as so many jewelled rings on the fingers? The threatened rejection of the Laodicean Angel (iii. 16) would then find a remarkable parallel in Jer. xxii. 24: "Though Coniah, king of Judah, were the signet upon my right hand, yet would I pluck thee thence." But, not to mention other objections, the *seven* stars would ill distribute themselves on *five* fingers. Better therefore to regard them as a wreath or garland which He held in his right hand. "*The mystery of the seven stars*" we shall return to before long (ver. 20); and on two occasions shall have need to consider what is the spiritual signification of his having or holding these stars in his right hand (ii. 1; iii. 1); all which may therefore for the present be past over.

"*And out of his mouth went a sharp two-edged sword.*"—*Ῥομφαία*, sometimes *ῥομβαία*, in Latin 'rumpia' (Ennius, *Annal.* 14 [the passage has not reached us], Valerius Flaccus, vi. 96), is a Thracian word for a Thracian weapon (A. Gellius, x. 25; cf. Diefenbach, *Origines Europææ*, p. 409). It is properly the long and heavy broadsword (*ῥομφαία βαρυσίδηρος*, Plutarch, *Æmil. Paul.* 18; Livy, xxxi. 39), which the Thracians and other barbarous nations used; and as such to be distinguished from the *μάχαιρα*, the sacrificial knife, or short stabbing sword. The word, occurring six times in the Apocalypse, only occurs once besides in the New Testament (Luke ii. 35). This sword is "*two-edged*" here (*δίστομος*, cf. Heb. iv. 12, *μάχαιρα δίστομος* = *ἀμφίστομος* = *ἀμφήκης*, Homer, *Il.* x. 256), the sharpness of it being reckoned as its mouth; cf. Heb. xi. 34, *στόματα μαχαίρας*, and Judg. iii. 16; Ps. cxlix. 6; Prov. v. 4; Ecclus. xxi. 4. The phrase, "the *devouring* sword" (2 Sam. xviii. 8; Isai. i. 20; Jer. ii. 30) rests on the same image. Yet it is not a mere Hebraism; but finds its place in classical Greek poetry, and indeed in Greek prose as well; thus Euripides, *δίστομα φάσγανα*: and elsewhere, πέλεκυς δίστομος. As it is from the mouth that man's word proceeds, so this sword, not wielded in the hand, but proceeding from the mouth of the Son of God, is his Word (compare Isai. xlix. 2: "He hath made my mouth as a sharp sword"); but his Word, as it is also Spirit; "the sword of the Spirit, which is the Word of God" (Ephes. vi. 17; cf. Heb. iv. 12). They fall short of the full meaning of this emblem, who press mainly as the *tertium comparationis* here the penetrative searching power of the Word of God, amputating our vices, convincing us of our sins, as Tertullian (*Adv. Marc.* iii. 14); Cocceius: "Notatur vis verbi in conscientiam;" and Henry More (*Mystery of Iniquity*, ii. xiv. 6): "A prophetical symbol of that wonderful contrition of heart that the powerful Word of God makes when sincerely and seasonably evibrated against the enemies of his kingdom." The whole feeling, the whole sense of the passage with which we have here to do, requires that we should take this sword from the mouth as expressing rather the punishing than the convincing power of God's word. With this sword from his mouth He *fights* against his enemies and destroys them; compare ii. 12, 16; xix. 15, 21. The Word of the Lord is no empty threat, but having in readiness to avenge all disobedience; cf. Hos. vi. 5; Isai. xi. 4; 2 Thess. ii. 8; Wisd. xviii. 15,

16.—Shall we give any spiritual significance to the two-edgedness of this sword? Many have so done, Tertullian for instance (*Adv. Jud.*): "Bis acutus duobus Testamentis, legis antiquæ, et legis novæ;" and Augustine, *Enarr. in Ps.* cxlix. 6; and Richard of St. Victor: "Qui gladius utrâque parte dicitur acutus, quia in Veteri Testamento amputavit vitia carnalia, in Novo etiam spiritualia. Utrâque parte acutus est, quia qui foris in nobis amputat luxuriam carnis, intus resecat malitiam cordis. Utrâque parte acutus est, quia in his qui contemnunt quæ præcepit, corpus et animam punit. Utrâque parte acutus est, quia malos et a bonis discernit, et singulis quod merentur reddit."

"*And his countenance was as the sun shineth in his strength.*"—Of the Angel by the vacant tomb it is said, "His countenance was like lightning" (Matt. xxviii. 3; cf. Judg. xiii. 6); here the countenance of the Lord is compared to the sun "*in his strength*" (cf. x. 1), at his brightest and clearest, in the splendour of his highest noon, no veil, no mist, no cloud obscuring his brightness. When He shall appear, they that are his shall be like Him, for they shall see Him as He is; therefore of them too it can be said that in that day "they shall shine forth *as the sun* in the kingdom of their Father" (Matt. xiii. 43; cf. Wisd. iii. 7). No doubt if there had been any thing brighter than the sun, the Seer would have chosen it to set forth the transcendant and intolerable brightness of that countenance which he now beheld.

This description of the glorified Lord, which has now been brought to a conclusion, sublime as a purely mental conception, but intolerable, if we were to give it an outward form and expression, and picture Him with this sword proceeding from his mouth, these feet as burning brass, this hair white as wool, and the rest, may suggest a few reflections on the apocalyptic, and generally the Hebrew symbolism, and the very significant relations of difference and opposition in which it stands to the Greek. Religion and art for the Greek ran into one another with no very great preponderance of the claims of the former over the latter. Even in his religious symbolism the sense of beauty, of form, of proportion, overrules every other, and must at all costs find its satisfaction; so that the first necessity of the symbol is that it shall not affront, that it shall satisfy rather, the æsthetic sense. Rather than it should offend this, it would be moulded and modified even to the serious injury of the idea of which it was intended to be the exponent. But with the Hebrew symbolism it is altogether different. The first necessity there is that the symbol should set forth truly and fully the religious idea of which it is intended to be the vehicle. How it would appear when it clothed itself in an outward form and shape, whether it would find favour and allowance at the bar of taste, this was quite a secondary consideration; may be confidently affirmed not to have been a consideration at all; for indeed, with the one exception of the cherubim, there was no intention that it should embody itself there, but rather that it should remain ever and only a purely mental conception, the unembodied sign of an idea. I may observe, by the way, that no skill of delineation can make the cherubim other than unsightly objects to the eye. Thus in this present description of Christ, sublime and majestic as it is, it is only such so long as we keep it wholly apart from any external embodiment. Produce it outwardly, the sword going forth from the mouth, the eyes as a flame of fire, the hair white as wool, the feet as molten brass; and each and all of these images violate more or less our sense of beauty. Bengel, missing this important distinction, has sought to give a picture of the Lord Jesus according to this description, prefixing it to his German Commentary on the Apocalypse; a picture which is almost degrading, and only not deeply offensive to every feeling of reverence and awe, because we know that it was not so intended by this admirable man.[1]

[1] Others have done the same, though with quite a different object

The explanation of the difference does not lie altogether in the fact that the Greek created his symbol, and therefore could do what he would with his own; while the Hebrew received his from God, and could not therefore venture to touch it. It would have existed more or less without this distinction between the given and the invented, the inspired and uninspired. The unsightliness, often the repulsiveness, of the symbol, so long as it is judged merely by the laws of æsthetic beauty, is common to all the religions of the East. What an ugly sight is the Artemis multimammia of Ephesus, an Oriental deity, it need not be said, and not a Greek; what monstrous forms the Indian gods, with their hundred arms, present. At the same time we should altogether err if we accepted this as a mark of the inferiority of these nations to the Greeks. Inferiority in one sense no doubt it does indicate, a slighter perception of beauty, but superiority in other and more important matters, a deeper religious earnestness, a feeling upon their part that the essence was above the form, a convic-

and aim. I can perfectly remember seeing exposed in Carlisle's shop-window a blasphemous picture with the title, "The God of the Bible," constructed according to a similar scheme. Two or three days after, a Jew was brought before the magistrates, who in a righteous indignation had dashed his hand through the window, seized and destroyed it; and I do not think it appeared again.

tion that truth, such as they conceived it, was better than beauty, and that every thing else, as of lesser moment, was to be sacrificed to this. But now to return from this digression.

Ver. 17. "*And when I saw Him, I fell*[1] *at his feet as dead. And He laid his right hand upon me, saying unto me, Fear not.*"—This, as is evident, is no voluntary act of homage on the part of St. John, but an involuntary consequence of what he saw. Finding, as it does, its parallel in almost all manifestations of a divine, or even an angelic, presence, it must be owned to contain a mighty, because an instinctive witness for the sinfulness of man's nature; so that any very near revelation of ought which comes direct from heaven fills the children of men, even the holiest among them, with terror and amazement, yea, and sometimes with the expectation of death itself. Examples innumerable make plain that this holds equally true of good men and of bad (Gen. iii. 8; Exod. iii. 6; Judg. xiii. 6, 20, 22; 1 Chron. xxi. 20; Job xlii. 5, 6; Isai. vi. 5; Ezek. i. 28; iii. 23; xliii. 3; xliv. 4; Dan. viii. 17; x. 7, 8; Matt. xvii. 6; xxviii. 4, 5; Mark xvi. 5; Luke i. 12, 29; v. 8; xxiv. 5; John xviii. 6; Acts ix. 4; x. 4). The

[1] On this second aorist (ἔπεσα) with the termination of the first, an Alexandrian and afterwards a Byzantine form, see Lobeck, *Phrynichus*, p. 724, and Sturz, *De Dialecto Alexandrinâ*, p. 61.

unholy, and all flesh is such, cannot endure immediate contact with the holy, the human with the divine. Heathen legend consents here with Christian truth. Semele must perish, if Jupiter reveals himself to her in his glory, being consumed in the brightness of that glory; cf. Exod. xxxiii. 18, 20: "Thou canst not see my face; for there shall no man see Me, and live." For *every* man it is a dreadful thing to stand face to face with God. The beloved disciple, who had handled the Word of life, lain in his Lord's bosom in the days of his flesh, can as little as any other endure the revelation of his majesty, or do without that "*Fear not*," with which that Lord reassures him here. This same "*Fear not*" is uttered on similar occasions to Isaiah (vi. 7), to Daniel (x. 12), to the three at the Transfiguration, of whom John himself was one (Matt. xvii. 7). Nor is this reassurance confined to words only; the Lord at the same time lays his right hand upon him,—something parallel to which goes along with the "*Fear not*" of all the three cases just referred to (cf. Jer. i. 9); and from the touch of that strengthening hand the Seer receives strength again, and is set, no doubt, upon his feet once more (Ezek. i. 28; ii. 1, 2).

"*I am the first and the last.*"—This prerogative is three times claimed for the Lord Jehovah in Isaiah (xli. 4; xliv. 6; xlviii. 12); and in like manner three times in this Book (here, and ii. 8; xxii. 13). It is the expression of absolute Godhead: "I am the first and the last, and beside me there is no God" (Isai. xliv. 6). He is from eternity to eternity, so that there is no room for any other. All creation comes forth from Him (John i. 1-3), all creation returns to Him again, as from whom and by whom and to whom are all things. Not the semi-Socinian expositors alone, as Grotius and Wetstein, but others who lie under no such suspicion, Cocceius for instance, and Vitringa, have here gone astray, making "*first*" to mean the first in glory, and "*last*" the last in humiliation; "I am He who, being the foremost and first in all honour, became the lowest and last in dishonour, sounding the lowest depths of ignominy and shame." This, which itself is true (Phil. ii. 7, 8), is yet not the truth of this place. That truth is nobly expressed in the comment of a medieval theologian, Richard of St. Victor, more than once quoted already: "Ego sum primus et novissimus. Primus per creationem, novissimus per retributionem. Primus, quia ante me non est formatus Deus; novissimus, quia post me alius non erit. Primus, quia a me sunt omnia; novissimus, quia ad me sunt omnia; a me principio, ad me finem. Primus, quia Ego sum causa originis; novissimus, quia Ego judex et finis."

Ver. 18. "*I am He that liveth and was dead, and behold, I am alive for evermore. Amen.*"— Translate rather, "*And the living, and I became dead, and behold, I am living for evermore.*" Gain, as it appears to me, will thus accrue to every clause of the sentence. In the first place, *καί*, connecting this verse so closely with the one preceding, will have its rights, which are wholly overlooked in our Version. Then *ὁ ζῶν* expresses not so much that He, the Speaker, "lived," as that He was "the Living One," the Life (John i. 4; xiv. 6), *αὐτοζωή*, having life in Himself, and the fountain and source of life to others. It is true that in one sense it is the exclusive prerogative of the Father to have life in Himself, but a prerogative which He has communicated with the Son (John v. 26); of Him too it may be said, in the words of the Psalmist, *παρὰ Σοὶ πηγὴ ζωῆς* (Ps. xxxvi. 10, LXX.). To Him belongs *absolute* being (*ὄντως εἶναι*), as contrasted with the *relative* being of the creature, with the life which may be no life, seeing that it inevitably falls under the dominion of corruption and death, so soon as it is separated from Him, the source from which it was derived; for others may *share*, but He only *hath*, immortality (1 Tim. vi. 16), being *οὐσίᾳ ἀθάνατος, οὐ μετουσίᾳ* (Theodoret). All this is included in Christ's assertion here of Himself as *ὁ ζῶν*. Being thus The Living One, He goes on to say, "*I yet became* (ἐγενόμην) *dead;* I the source of all life stooped even to taste of death." Such is the second clause, and then follows the glorious third. "This state of death endured for Me but for an instant. I laid down my life that I might take it again. I drank of the brook in the way, and therefore have I lifted up my head (Ps. cx. 7); death having now in Me been so swallowed up in life, that *behold, I am living for evermore.*"

"*And have the keys of hell and of death.*"—We should read rather "*of death and of hell,*" for so all the best MSS. and Versions have it, while the reading of our Translation inverts the natural and logical order; for it is death which peoples hell or Hades; it is a king Death who makes possible a kingdom of the dead (vi. 8; xx. 13, 14); for by "*hell,*" or Hades, this invisible kingdom or dominion of the dead is intended, and that in all its extent, not merely in one dark province of it, the region assigned to the lost. Hengstenberg indeed affirms in his own confident way that "*death*" here means the second death, and as a consequence that "*hell*" or Hades, can mean only Gehenna; observing that in the New Testament this second death is alone set forth as an object of fear. But why is it that the other death, itself the outward sign and seal of God's extreme indignation against sin, has ceased to be an object of terror, has been robbed for the faithful of its sting? Why, except for that fact which we find proclaimed in these words, namely, that the Son of God has gone down into the dark realms of shadows and returned from it again—and not this only, but returned from it a conqueror, having overcome death, and burst, like another Samson (Judg. xvi. 3), the gates of the city of the grave which shut Him in; and in pledge of this having the keys of both, the absolute Lord who opens and shuts them at his will for all the children of men. For myself I cannot doubt, above all when I look at the words which immediately go before, that Christ sets Himself forth here as the overcomer of death natural; which it must always be remembered is rather death *unnatural;* for man was made for immortality (Gen. ii. 17), and death is the denial and reversal of the true law of his being (Rom. v. 12). He who is the Prince of life is indeed but saying here what already He had been bold to say, while the victory was yet unwon: "I am the Resurrection and the Life;" life, that is, in conflict with death, and overcoming it. The keys are the emblems of authority (cf. iii. 7); to have the keys is to have the power of Himself going in and out as He pleases, of admitting and excluding, shutting up and delivering others: cf. Deut. xxxii. 39, "I kill and I make alive;" and 1 Sam. ii. 6. The metaphor rests on the conception of Hades as a city with walls and gates; Christ had spoken in his earthly life of the *πύλαι Ἅιδου* (Matt. xvi. 18; cf. Isai. xxxviii. 10; Job xxxviii. 17).

Let me express here, before leaving this subject, the regret which all who have thoughtfully compared our Version with the original must feel that the one word "hell" covers there two words of such difference in meaning as *ᾅδης* and *γέεννα,* the first "Sheol," the gathering-place of all departed souls, the second the *λίμνη τοῦ πυρός* of this Book (xix. 20; xx. 10), the final abode of the lost. All must lament the manifold confusions which out of this have arisen; the practical loss indeed among our people of any doctrine about Hades at all. I have entered into this more at full elsewhere,[1] and have quite acknowledged the difficulty of taking any other course, so that it is much easier to note the fault than to suggest the remedy. The relations of *ᾅδης* to *γέεννα,* and also to *παράδεισος,* are well put in this extract from a funeral sermon of Jeremy Taylor: "The word *Αιδης* signifies indefinitely the state of separation, whether blessed or accursed; it means only 'the invisible place,' or the region of darkness, whither whoso descends

[1] *On the Authorized Version of the New Testament,* 2d edit. p. 20.

shall be no more seen. For as among the heathens the Elysian fields and Tartara are both ἐν ῞Αιδου,[1] so among the Jews and Christians *paradisus* and *gehenna* are the distinct states of Hades."[2]

Ver. 19. "*Write the things which thou hast seen, and the things which are, and the things which shall be hereafter.*"—It is certainly a piece of carelessness on the part of our Translators to have omitted, which none of the previous translators had done, the οὖν ("Write *therefore*"), about the right of which to a place in the text no question has been ever made. With what intention the illative particle is used, is not so easy to determine; perhaps it is best referred to what goes immediately before: "Seeing that I am this mighty One, the first and last, who was dead and am alive, do thou therefore write; for the things declared by Me are all steadfast and sure."

Ver. 20. "*The mystery of the seven stars which thou sawest in my right hand, and of the seven golden candlesticks. The seven stars are the Angels of the seven Churches, and the seven candlesticks*

[1] As witness the lines of the comic poet:

> καὶ γὰρ καθ' ῞Αιδην δύο τρίβους νομίζομεν,
> μίαν δικαίων, κατέραν ἀσεβῶν ὁδόν.

[2] A little work by König, *Die Lehre von Christi Höllenfahrt*, 1842, gives admirably the whole teaching of Scripture, and in an historic sketch that of the Church, concerning Hades.

which thou sawest are the seven Churches."—We may either regard the first sentence as governed by the "*Write*" of the verse preceding; so no doubt our Translators, who place only a comma at the conclusion of that verse; or else, placing a full-stop there, regard these words as a sort of nominative absolute, the *statement* of the "*mystery*," or spiritual riddle, of which the solution follows in the latter half of the verse. This distribution seems to me certainly preferable to the other. A "mystery" in the constant language of Scripture is something which man is capable of knowing, but only when it has been revealed to him by God (Matt. xiii. 11; Rom. xi. 25; Ephes. vi. 19; 1 Cor. xiii. 2), and not through any searching of his own. Thus, as has been well observed, *μυστήριον* and *ἀποκάλυψις* are correlative terms (Rom. xvi. 25); and as in the former clauses of the present verse there is the *μυστήριον,* so in the latter the *ἀποκάλυψις μυστηρίου.* From this, the revelation of the mystery, we learn that "*the seven stars are the Angels of the seven Churches.*" In all the typical language of Scripture stars are symbols of lordship and authority, ecclesiastical or civil. Thus a star is the symbol of the highest dominion of all; "There shall come *a star* out of Jacob" (Num. xxiv. 7); and the actual birth of Him whom Balaam prophesied of here, is announced by a star (Matt. ii. 2).

Faithful teachers are stars that shall shine for ever (Dan. xii. 3); false teachers are wandering stars (Jude 13), or stars which fall from heaven (Rev. viii. 10; vi. 13; xii. 4). But "*the Angels of the seven Churches*" have given occasion to much discussion and dispute; and only when we know exactly what they mean, shall we feel perfectly sure that we have interpreted the "*stars*" aright; or rather that we have apprehended aright the interpretation of them given here by the Spirit.

Some, then, have understood by the "*Angels*" the *heavenly* messengers who bear this name. They urge that often elsewhere in this Book as the word "Angel" recurs, it is never in any other sense; therefore that in these we are to recognize the guardian Angels over the several Churches, "their Angels;" that if single persons had thus their Angels (Matt. xviii. 10; cf. Acts xii. 15), much more the same might be predicated of Churches (Dan. xii. 1). Thus Origen (*Hom.* xiii. *in Luc.*): "Si audacter expedit loqui Scripturarum sensum sequenti, per singulas Ecclesias bini sunt Episcopi, alius visibilis, alius invisibilis; ille visui carnis, hic sensui patens. Et quomodo homo, si commissam sibi dispensationem bene egerit, laudatur a Domino, si male culpæ et vitio subjacet, sic et Angelus." And again (*Hom.* xx. *in Num.*): "Secundum ea quæ Johannes in Apocalypsi scribit, unicuique Ecclesiæ generaliter Angelus præest, qui vel collaudatur pro bene gestis populi, vel etiam pro delictis ejus culpatur. In quo etiam stupendi mysterii admiratione permoveor, quod intantum Deo cura de nobis est, ut etiam Angelos suos culpari pro nobis et confutari patiatur. Sic enim cum pædagogo traditur puer, si forte minus dignis, nec secundum paternam nobilitatem imbutus appareat disciplinis, continuo culpa ad pædagogum refertur, nec ita puer a patre ut pædagogus arguitur." Cf. Jerome (*In Mich.* vi. 1, 2), who has evidently copied this passage.

The preoccupation of an obvious objection is in the words just quoted ingeniously attempted, but not successfully accomplished. Indeed the objection is one which it is impossible to surmount: this, namely, How could *holy* Angels be charged with such delinquencies as are laid to the charge of some of the Angels here (ii. 4; iii. 1, 15)? See some good observations on this point in Augustine (*Ep.* 43, § 22): "Angelo Ecclesiæ Ephesi scribe; Quod si de Angelo superiorum cœlorum, et non de præpositis Ecclesiæ vellet intelligi, non consequenter diceret: Sed habeo adversum te, quod caritatem primam reliquisti. Hoc de superioribus Angelis dici non potest, qui perpetuam retinent caritatem, unde qui defecerunt et lapsi sunt, diabolus est et angeli ejus."

This then of the "*Angels*" meaning *heavenly* Angels may certainly be dismissed. Even all which Alford has urged in its favour will be unable, I am persuaded, to procure any wide acceptance for it. The Angel must be some person or persons in the Church on earth, not one overlooking it from heaven. I say some person *or persons*, not as myself thinking it possible that he can represent a plurality, but having in view explanations which by some have been offered, and on which something will have to be said.

But if some human person in the Church, who but the chief shepherd, in other words, the bishop? To whom else would all which we here in these Epistles find ascribed to the Angel apply? For myself, I cannot but think that the argument for the existence of the episcopate in the later apostolic times, and that as a divinely recognized institution, which may be drawn from the position of the Angels in the several Churches, and from the language in which they are addressed, is exceedingly strong. The Angel in each Church is one; but surely none can suppose for an instant that there was only one presbyter, or other minister serving in holy things, for the whole flourishing Church of Ephesus, or of Smyrna; and that we are in this way to account for the single Angel of the several Churches. Thirty years before this time St. Paul had uttered his parting words at Miletus to the elders of the Ephesian Church (Acts xx. 17), and certainly addressed them even then as many (ver. 25). Taking into account what we know of the spread of the Christian faith in these parts during the intermediate time, it is probable that their number was at this time largely increased. And yet now, with this large number of presbyters, there is only one Angel in each of these Churches. What can he be but a bishop?—a bishop too with the prerogatives which we ascribe to one. His preëminence cannot be explained away, as though he had been merely a ruling elder, a *primus inter pares*, with only such authority and jurisdiction as the others, his peers, may have lent him. For the great Bishop of souls who is here on his spiritual visitation, every where holds the Angel responsible for the spiritual condition of his Church; for the false teaching which he has not put down, for the false teachers whom he has not separated from the communion of the faithful,—in short, for every disorder in doctrine or discipline which has remained unrepressed. But Christ could not so deal with them, could not charge them personally with these negligences and omissions, unless upon the ground that they had been clothed with power and authority sufficient to have prevented them, so that these evils could only have existed through their neglect and allowance.

By what has been just said it is not intended in the least to affirm that bishops were commonly called Angels in the primitive Church, or called so at all, except with a more or less conscious reference to the use of the word in the Apocalypse. There is a certain mysteriousness, and remoteness from the common language of men, in the adoption of this term, and such there is intended to be. It belongs to the enigmatic symbolic character of the Book, elevated in its language throughout above the level of daily life. Those to whom this title is ascribed are herein presented to the Church as clothed with a peculiar dignity, and are herein themselves reminded that they stand before One, whose ministries of grace and love they should be swift to fulfil on earth, even as those whose names they bear are swift to fulfil them in heaven. There is then a certain, though very partial right in what Origen taught; and "Angel" *is* a heavenly title here; but a heavenly title which has been borrowed by earth, which has been transferred and applied to men; a transfer not without its analogies in the Old Testament (Eccles. v. 5; Mal. ii. 7; iii. 1); and rendered more easy by the fact that Angel is a name not designating the personality, but the office, of those heavenly beings by whom it properly is borne.

It is not to be supposed that those who believe the government of the Church to have been presbyterian at the first, and who see in the episcopate a result of declension from apostolic purity, should accept these conclusions. At the same time they are far from being at one in the ways by which they have sought to evade the argument for primitive episcopacy which we believe that we are here justified in finding.

Thus some affirm that the Angel represents and stands for not any single person, but the whole body of the προεστῶτες, the collective presbytery, contemplated and addressed not as many, but as one. So for the most part the early anti-episcopal Protestants, Brightman for example; and even Hengstenberg has not disdained to fall back on this unworthy subterfuge; the mere statement of which involves its condemnation. Vitringa (*De Synag. Vet.* p. 911) with more candour mentions this only to reject it, and finds a clear testimony here for the superior dignity of one in these several Churches; though naturally the episcopate which he thus recognizes, is of the mildest form, of the Usherian type; and Beza in like manner glosses τῷ ἀγγέλῳ, *i. e.* προεστῶτι; though, curiously enough, he considers that the upgrowth of the tyrannous hierarchy of

Rome is evidence sufficient that, however there were προεστῶτες in these apostolic Churches, it was never intended of God that such should always continue in the Church.

But there is a poorer evasion even than this; which has lately been revived by Ebrard. It rests on an entirely gratuitous assumption, on the fiction, namely, that the seven Churches had sent their messengers to St. John at Patmos, therefore called the "*Angels*," or messengers (cf. Luke ix. 52) "*of the Churches*." These in these Epistles are now successively addrest, that they may bring back his word, or rather the word of Christ, to those Churches from which they had been deputed. But in answering a letter by a messenger, you write *by*, you do not usually write *to*, him; nor is it easy to see where is the correspondency between such messengers, subordinate officials of the Churches, and stars; or what the mystery of the relation between them then would be; or how the Lord should set forth as an eminent prerogative of his, that He held the seven stars, that is, the seven messengers, in his right hand (ii. 1). The scheme breaks down at every point, and among many lame and feeble shifts must needs be regarded as the lamest and feeblest of all. I again repeat my conviction that in these Angels we are to recognize the bishops of the several Churches. So many difficulties, embarrassments, improbabilities attend every other solution, all which disappear with the adoption of this, while no others rise in their room, that, were not other interests, often no doubt unconsciously, at work, it would be very hard to understand how any could have ever arrived at a different conclusion.

I will take the opportunity of a pause here between this, the Introduction to the seven Epistles, and the seven Epistles themselves, to say a few needful words on the mystery of the number seven; which only I have left unsaid so long, because unwilling to interrupt the exposition by any thing in the shape of a dissertation; not to say that I found it difficult to attach to any one of those important sevens which have already occurred, considerations which properly belonged to them all.

Even the most careless reader of the Apocalypse must be struck with the manner in which almost every thing there is ordered by sevens. Thus, besides the seven Churches, and their seven Angels, we have already in this first chapter the seven Spirits (ver. 4), the seven candlesticks (ver. 12), the seven stars (ver. 16); and then further the seven lamps of fire (iv. 5), the seven seals (v. 1), the seven horns and seven eyes of the Lamb (v. 6), the seven heavenly Angels and the seven trumpets (viii. 2), the seven thunders (x. 3), the seven heads of the dragon, and the seven crowns upon these heads (xii. 3), the same of the beast rising out of the sea (xiii. 1), the seven last plagues (xv. 1), the seven vials (xv. 7), the seven mountains (xvii. 9), the seven kings (xvii. 10); not to speak of other recurrences, not so obvious, of this number seven as the signature of the Book; as, for instance, the distribution of it into seven visions, the sevenfold ascription of glory to the Lamb (v. 12), and to God (vii. 12).

But indeed the recurrence, and, as I shall seek to show, the symbolic dignity of the number seven runs through the whole of Scripture from first to last,—to say nothing of the echoes of this sense of its significance which abound in every religion of heathendom;[1] and if it is more strongly marked in the Apocalypse than in any other book of Scripture, it is only that this, like so much else, has culminated here. Should it be asked, What is the special significance, and what the sacredness and peculiar dignity of seven, of what is it the signature, the answer is not very hard to give. A careful induction from all the passages where this number cannot be regarded as fortuitous, but is evidently of Divine ordinance and appointment (I call fortuitous such sevens as occur, Acts xix. 14; xx. 6), will leave no

[1] "Die allgemeine Heiligkeit der Siebenzahl haben die Alten schon in allen Beziehungen bemerkt." Creuzer, *Symbolik*, vol. ii. p. 161, where see a large collection of the literature on the subject.

doubt that it claims throughout Scripture to be considered as the covenant number, the sign and signature of God's covenant relation to mankind, and above all to that portion of mankind with which this relation is not potential merely, but actual, namely the Church.

The evidences of this reach back to the very beginning. We meet them first in the hallowing of the seventh day, in pledge and token of the covenant of God with man (Gen. ii. 3; cf. Ezek. xx. 12), as indeed in the binding up of seven in the very word Sabbath.[1] So too circumcision, being the sign of a covenant, is accomplished on the eighth, or after seven days (Gen. xvii. 12; Lev. xii. 3). And as seven is the signature of God's covenant with man, so of all man's covenants with his fellows, resting as these do and must, on the anterior covenant with God; thus of treaties of peace (Gen. xxi. 20), of marriages (Judg. xiv. 12). Nor should it be left unnoticed that the word seven is again bound up in the Hebrew word signifying an oath, or a covenant confirmed with an oath. Seven

[1] It was therefore a true instinct of hatred against a divine institution which led those who in the first French Revolution proclaimed the abolition of the Christian religion, to make war also on the Christian week, the distribution of time by sevens, and to substitute that by decades in its stead. They felt that here was a witness for God in the world, a witness that He was the measurer out of our times to us, which must not be allowed to survive.

is the number of sacrifice, by aid of which the covenant once established, is continually maintained in its first vigour and strength, and the relations between God and man, which sin is evermore disturbing, and threatening to bring to an end, are restored (2 Chron. xxix. 21; Job xlii. 8; cf. Num. xxiii. 1, 14, 29). It is the number of purification and consecration, as the fruits of the sacrifice (Lev. iv. 6, 17; viii. 11, 33; xiv. 9, 51; xvi. 14, 19; Num. xix. 12, 19), of forgiveness (Matt. xviii. 21, 22; Luke xvii. 4). Then, again, seven is the number of every grace and benefit bestowed upon Israel; which is thus marked as flowing out of the covenant and a consequence of it. The priests compass Jericho seven days, and on the seventh day seven times, that all Israel may know that the city is given into their hands by their God; and that its conquest is a direct and immediate result of their covenant relation to Him (Josh. vi. 4, 15, 16). Naaman is to dip in Jordan seven times, that he may acknowledge the God of Israel the author of his cure (2 Kings v. 10). It is the number of reward to those that are faithful in the covenant (Deut. xxviii. 7; 1 Sam. ii. 5); of punishment to those who are froward in the covenant (Lev. xxvi. 21, 24, 28; Deut. xxviii. 25; 2 Sam. xii. 8; xxiv. 13), or to those who injure the people in it (Gen. iv. 15, 24; Ps. lxxix. 12; Exod. vii. 25); or again of punishment, regarded in the light of a making of amends, a readjusting of the disturbed balances of justice, and so a restoring of harmony between the sinner and the outraged law of God (Prov. vi. 31). All the feasts, as must be obvious to every one, are ordered by seven, or else by seven multiplied into seven (7 × 7), and thus made intenser still. Thus it is, not to recur again to Sabbath, the mother of all feasts, with the Passover (Exod. xii. 15, 16), the feast of weeks (Deut. xvi. 9), of tabernacles (Deut. xvi. 13, 15), the sabbath-year (Lev. xxv. 2, 3; Deut. xv. 1), and the jubilee (Lev. xxv. 8).[1]

Further we may observe that wherever God is at work in the history of other nations outside of the covenant, while yet He would make it plainly to appear that it is for Israel's sake, and having respect to the covenant, that He is so working, this signature of seven in his dealing with those nations is never wanting. Thus it is the number of the years of plenty and of the years of famine, in sign that these were sent not so much for Egypt's sake, as for Israel's, and as conducing to the divine preparation through which the chosen people were to pass (Gen. xli. 26, 27). Seven times pass over Nebuchadnezzar, that he may learn in his abasement how that the God of his Jewish captives is indeed the King over all the earth (Dan. iv. 16, 23, 25).

[1] See Philo, *De Septenario*, passim.

But it would be endless to go through all passages in proof; it would need to quote or refer to a great part of Scripture. I prefer leaving to the student of God's Word to fill up the sketch which I have drawn, and to find for himself further confirmation of what has been asserted here.

But if it should be further asked, *Why* has seven been selected for this, what are the grounds of its adoption to this high dignity and honour, the answer does not seem very far to seek. I am indeed aware that in all speculations upon numbers we may very profitably lay to heart the wise caution of Fuller,[1] clothed, as is ever the case with his wisdom, in witty words: "For matter of numbers fancy is never at a loss, like a beggar never out of his way, but hath some haunts where to repose itself. But such as in expounding of Scripture reap more than God did sow there, never eat what they reap thence, because such grainless husks, when seriously threshed out, vanish all into chaff." And yet I feel very sure that in this matter we need not dread lest we should be threshing barren ears, with only chaff for our pains.

To the question then asked above it may be replied by first calling attention to the fact that the number seven results from the combination of three and four. But can it be shown that these in Scrip-

[1] *A Pisgah Sight of Palestine*, b. iii. c. 6.

ture have severally any symbolic significance of their own? Assuredly yes. Three, the signature of God; four, that of the world; and thus seven, or these numbers brought into contact and relation, the token and signature of the covenant between these two.

That three is the number of God, of the ever-blessed Trinity, this of itself needs no proof. And it is so recognized in Scripture. There are vestiges of this in the Old Testament, in the *Trisagion* of Isai. vi. 3; in the blessing as from three distinct persons, Num. vi. 24-26; in the prominent position assumed there by the Angel of the Covenant, hereafter to be acknowledged as the second Person of the Trinity, in the often mention not of God, but *the Spirit* of God, hereafter to be acknowledged as the third (Gen. i. 2; Ps. li. 11). These footprints of the Trinity are purposely more or less obscure, and only clear when they are read in the light of a later revelation; for the office of the Church of the Old Testament was to guard the truth of the unity of the Godhead, not to declare the Trinity; which indeed, so long as polytheism was not overcome, but still had its roots even in the minds of the chosen people itself, could not yet have been safely declared. Here is explanation amply sufficient, of the reserve with which the number three is employed in the Old Testament as the signature of Deity; the reason why this is only perfectly plain and clear in the New.

Four, the next number to three, and growing immediately out of it, is the signature of the world —of the world, not indeed as a rude undigested mass, but as a *κόσμος*, as the revelation, so far as nature can be the revelation, of God. Four is stamped every where on this the organized world. Thus, not to speak of the four elements, the four seasons, neither of which are recognized in Scripture, we have there the four winds (Ezek. xxxvii. 9; Matt. xxiv. 31; Rev. vii. 1); the four corners of the earth (Rev. vii. 1; xx. 8); the four living creatures, emblems of all creaturely life (Rev. iv. 6), and each of these with four faces and four wings (Ezek. i. 5, 6); the four beasts coming up from the sea, and representing the four great world-empires which in the providence of God should succeed one another (Dan. vii. 3); the four metals composing the image which sets forth the same phases of empire (Dan. ii. 32, 33); the four Gospels, or the four-sided Gospel (*εὐαγγέλιον τετράγωνον*, as one called it of old), in sign of its designation for all the world; the sheet tied at the four corners (Acts x. 11; xi. 5);[1] the four horns, the sum total of the

[1] Augustine (*Enarr. in Ps.* ci. *Serm.* iii.): "Discus qui quatuor lineis continebatur orbis terrarum erat in quatuor partibus. Has quatuor partes sæpe Scriptura commemorat, orientem et occidentem,

forces of the world as arrayed against the Church (Zech. i. 18); the enumeration, wherever this is wished to be exhaustive, of the inhabitants of the world by four, kindreds, tongues, peoples, and nations (Rev. v. 9; cf. vii. 9; x. 11; xi. 9; xiv. 6; xvii. 15).

There are reasons then amply sufficient why seven, being thus, as it is, made up of three and four, should be itself the signature of the covenant. No mere accident or caprice dictated the selection of it. And if this number of the covenant, then we can account for its constant recurrence in this Book; for admitting, as few would refuse to do, that the idea of God's covenant with his Church as the key to all history, comes to its head in the Apocalypse, it is nothing wonderful that this Book should be more markedly ordered by seven, and have this number stamped upon it even more strongly, than any other portion of Scripture.[1]

aquilonem et meridiem. Ideo quia totus orbis per Evangelium vocabatur, quatuor Evangelia conscripta sunt."

[1] On this whole subject of the symbolic worth and dignity of numbers in Scripture, see Bähr, *Symbolik des Mos. Cultus*, vol. i. pp. 128-209; and a good article by Kurtz, in the *Theoll. Stud. u. Krit.* 1844, pp. 315-370.

EPISTLE TO THE CHURCH OF EPHESUS.

REV. ii. 1–7.

Ver. 1. "*Unto the Angel of the Church of Ephesus write.*"—Before proceeding to consider this the first Epistle in the series, it may be well worth while to call the attention of the reader to the symmetry, to what we should call in human composition, the remarkable art, to be traced in the construction of them all; quite justifying the words of Henry More: "There never was a book penned with that artifice as this of the Apocalypse." They are all constructed precisely on the same scheme. They every one of them contain—

α. A command in exactly the same form to the Seer that he should write to the Angel of the Church.

β. One or more glorious titles which Christ claims for Himself, as adding weight and authority to the message which He sends; these titles being in almost every case drawn more or less evidently from the attributes ascribed to Him, or claimed by Him, in the manifestation of Himself which has just gone before (i. 4-20).

γ. The actual message from Christ to the Angel of the Church, declaring his intimate knowledge of its condition, good, or bad, or mixed, with a summons to steadfastness in the good, to repentance from the evil—all this brought home by the fact that He was walking up and down in the midst of his Churches, having in readiness to punish, and having in readiness to reward.

δ. A promise to the faithful, to him that should overcome—the heavenly blessedness being presented under the richest variety of the most attractive, and often the most original, images.

ε. Finally, the whole is summed up with an exhortation which shall give an universal character to these particular addresses, a summons to every one with a spiritual ear that he should give earnest heed to the things, which were indeed spoken to all. In the addresses to the four last Churches the position of δ and ε is reversed.

On comparing these Epistles one with another, we may observe that in two Churches, namely Smyrna and Philadelphia, the great Shepherd and Bishop of souls finds matter only for praise; in two, Sardis and Laodicea, with very smallest exception in the former, only for rebuke. In three of the Churches, in Ephesus, Pergamum, and Thyatira, the condition is a mixed one, so that with some things to praise, there are also some, more in one, fewer in another, to condemn. It will thus be perceived at once what far-looking provision is made in the selection of these particular Churches to be addressed, as in the scheme of the addresses to them, for the most varied instructions; for reproof, for praise, for reproof and praise mingled together and tempered by one another; for promises and threatenings. The spiritual condition of the several Churches gives room and opportunity, nay, constitutes a necessity, for each and all of these.

Ephesus, the chief city of Ionia, "Asiæ lumen," πρώτη τῆς *Ἀσίας*, as the Ephesians themselves styled it, asserting in this style for Ephesus that primacy which Smyrna and Pergamum disputed with it, had now so far outstripped both its competitors that it was at once the civil and ecclesiastic centre of that Asia with which we have to do. Wealthy, prosperous, and magnificent, a meeting-place of oriental religions and Greek culture, and famous on many grounds in heathen antiquity, it was chiefly famous for the celebrated temple of Diana, one of the seven wonders of the world, about which we read so much, Acts xix. (cf. Creuzer, *Symbolik*, vol. ii. p. 515). But Ephesus had better titles of honour than these. It was a greatly favoured city. St. Paul laboured there during three years (Acts xx. 31); he ordained Timothy to be bishop there (1 Tim. i. 3; cf. Eusebius, *H. E.* iii. 4); Aquila, Priscilla, Apollos (Acts xviii. 19, 24, 26), Tychicus (Ephes. vi. 21), all contributed to build up the Church in that city. And if we may judge from St. Paul's Epistle to the Ephesians, and from his parting address to the elders of that Church (Acts xx. 17-38) nowhere does the word of the Gospel seem to have found a kindlier soil, to have struck root more deeply, or to have borne fairer fruits of faith and love. St. John too had made it the chief seat of his ministry, his metropolis, during the closing years of his protracted life; from whence he exercised a wide, though not wholly unquestioned, jurisdiction (see 3 Ep. 9, 10) over the whole of "*Asia.*" How early that ministry there began it is impossible to say, the date of his withdrawal from Jerusalem being itself uncertain, and uncertain also whether he at once chose Ephesus for the middle point of his spiritual activity. From a Church to which so much was given, much would be required. How far it had profited as it ought by these signal advantages, how far it had maintained itself at those spiritual heights to which it had once attained, will presently be seen.

"*These things saith He that holdeth the seven*

stars in his right hand."—The title is borrowed from i. 16: "*He had in his right hand seven stars;*" cf. i. 20, where "*the mystery of the seven stars*" is unfolded. It is only when all the titles furnished by chap. i. 4-20 are exhausted, that the Lord seeks them from any other quarter. At the same time there is a significant alteration here. At i. 16 it is ὁ ἔχων, "*He that hath;*" here more emphatically it is ὁ κρατῶν, "*He that holdeth.*" The variation is not without intention; ὁ κρατῶν (cf. ii. 25; iii. 11) is stronger than ὁ ἔχων, "*He that holdeth*" than "*He that hath.*" He *holds* these stars in his grasp,—words full of comfort for them, if only they are true to Him; none shall pluck them out of his hand (John x. 28), none shall harm them in the delivery of their message (Matt. x. 30; Acts xviii. 9, 10); or if the malice of their enemies is so far permitted that they are able to kill the body, they shall only in this way prepare for them an earlier and a speedier passage to glory (Acts vii. 56, 60; Rev. xi. 7, 12); but words which are full of fear for the unfaithful, for the idol shepherds (Zech. xi. 17), who feed themselves and not the flock (Ezek. xxxiv. 1-10). Them too He holds in his grasp, and none can deliver them from his hand.

"*Who walketh in the midst of the seven golden candlesticks.*"—"*Who walketh*" is new. The Seer had indeed already beheld the Lord "*in the midst of the seven candlesticks*" (i. 13), but not "*walking*" in their midst, the word expressing the unwearied activity of Christ in his Church (cf. Lev. xvi. 12), moving up and down in the midst of it; beholding the evil and the good; evermore trimming and feeding with oil of grace the golden lamps of the sanctuary. Marckius: "Ad innuendam clarius perpetuitatem actûs et curam Christi contra conatus oppositos Satanæ." It is impossible not to admire the appropriateness of these titles, expressing as they do the broader and more general relations of Christ to his Church, for the first Epistle in this series; which constitutes, as this and a thousand other tokens declare, not an accidental aggregate, but a divinely-ordered complex, with all its parts mutually upholding and sustaining one another.

Ver. 2. "*I know thy works.*"—This is a formula which introduces all the seven Epistles. "*Works*" therefore are not, as some interpreters would understand them, *good* works; for Christ uses this language where there were no works which He could count good (iii. 15); as little are they *bad* works (iii. 8); but the word is used with the same freedom here as in other parts of Scripture, now for those (John vii. 21; 1 Cor. iii. 14); and now for these (1 Cor. iii. 15; Tit. i. 16). "*I know thy works*" has another intention than to express either praise or blame. It declares rather the omniscience of Him who walks up and down among the candlesticks of gold, whom nothing escapes (Amos iv. 13; Ps. xi. 4, 5; John ii. 24, 25; Heb. iv. 13; Rev. ii. 23; Acts i. 24; xv. 8); being words of comfort and strength for all them who, amid infinite weaknesses, are yet able to say, "Search me, O Lord, and know my heart; try me, and know my thoughts, and see if there be any wicked way in me" (Ps. cxxxix. 23, 24), or with St. John, "Lord, Thou knowest all things, Thou knowest that I love Thee" (John xxi. 17); but words of fear for every one who would fain keep back any thing in his outer or inner life from the Lord. All is open and manifest before Him with whom we have to do; and this in these words He declares.

"*And thy labour and thy patience.*"—There was an earlier Angel of this same Church of Ephesus, on whom St. Paul had urged that he should not fail in this labour and patience (2 Tim. ii. 25, 26); and Christ's commendation here shows that the holy lesson had been laid to heart by him who had now stept into his place. The κόπος, occasioned probably by the earnest resistance which it was necessary to oppose to the false teachers in the Ephesian Church, would naturally fall chiefly on the bishop and presbyters—above all, on the first.

—*Κόπος* and *κοπιάω* are frequently used in reference both to apostolic and ministerial labours (Rom. xvi. 12; 1 Cor. xv. 10; Gal. iv. 11); *κόπος* often in connexion with *μόχθος* (1 Thess. ii. 9; 2 Thess. iii. 8; 2 Cor. xi. 27); the latter perhaps marking the toil on the side of the magnitude of the obstacles which it has to surmount, as the derivation *μόγις*, and the possible connexion with *μέγας*, seems to suggest (Ellicott); the former alluding to the toil and suffering which in these labours strenuously and faithfully performed is involved. For indeed this word *κόπος*, signifying as it does not merely labour, but labour *unto weariness*, may suggest some solemn reflections to every one who at all affects to be working for his Lord, and as under his great taskmaster's eye. This is what Christ looks for, this is what Christ praises, in his servants. But how often does labour, which esteems itself labour for Him, stop very short of this, take care that it shall never arrive at this point; and perhaps in our days none are more tempted continually to measure out to themselves tasks too light and inadequate, than those to whom an office and ministry in the Church has been committed. Indeed, there is here to them an ever-recurring temptation, and this from the fact that they do for the most part measure out their own day's task to themselves. Others in almost every other calling have it measured out to them; if not the zeal, earnestness, sincerity which they are to put into the performance of it, yet at any rate the outward limits, the amount of time which they shall devote to it, and often the definite amount of it which they shall accomplish. Not so we. We give to it exactly the number of hours which we please; we are for the most part responsible to no man; and when labourers thus apportion their own burdens, and do this from day to day, how near the danger that they should unduly spare themselves, and make their burdens far lighter than they should have been. We may well keep this word κόπος, and all that it signifies, namely labour unto weariness, in mind; and remember ever that it is this which the Lord praises and allows.

"*And how thou canst not bear them which are evil.*"—Christ has good things to say of the Church of Ephesus, and He, who rejoices in the truth, dwells on these good things first. It is well worth while to observe here the graciousness of the Lord, that He puts thus in the foremost place all which He can find to approve; and only after this has received its mead of praise, notes the shortcomings which He is also compelled to rebuke. Many graces had decayed at Ephesus; of this we may be sure; seeing that the grace of all graces, namely love, had decayed (ver. 4); but in the midst of this decay there survived an earnest hatred of certain evil-doers and evil deeds. The κακοί here are not exactly equivalent to the κακοὶ ἐργάται of Phil. iii. 2. These last are the *prominent* workers of mischief in the Church, false apostles, false prophets, and the like; but the κακοί will include the whole rabble of evil-doers as well. It is not a little remarkable that the grace or virtue here ascribed to the Angel of the Ephesian Church and still more strongly at ver. 6, should have a name in classical Greek, μισοπονηρία (Plutarch, *Quom. Am. ab Adul.* 12), the person of whom the grace is predicated being μισοπόνηρος, while neither of these words, nor yet any equivalent to them, occurs in the New Testament. Φιλάγαθος it has (Tit. i. 8), but nowhere μισοπόνηρος, nor any adequate substitute for it. It is the stranger, as this hatred of evil, purely as evil, however little thought of, or admired now, is eminently a *Christian* grace (Rom. xii. 9; cf. Ps. cxxxix. 21). The sphere in which the Angel of Ephesus had the chief opportunity of manifesting this holy intolerance of evil-doers was, no doubt, that of Church-discipline, separating off from fellowship with the faithful those who named the name of Christ, yet would not depart from iniquity (2 Tim. ii. 19). The infirmities, even the sins, of *weak* brethren, these are burdens which we may, nay, which we are commanded to, bear (cf. Gal. vi.

2, where the same word βαστάζειν is used); it is otherwise with *false* brethren (Ps. cxix. 115; cix. 21, 22; 1 Cor. v. 11).

"*And thou hast tried them which say they are apostles, and are not, and hast found them liars.*"—We translate by the same word the πειράζειν here and the δοκιμάζειν of 1 John iv. 1. What this Angel at Ephesus had done, and effectually done, St. John there bids those to whom he is writing that they should do, namely, prove the spirits of those who came to them claiming to teach as with authority, and to bring a direct message from God (cf. 1 Thess. v. 21; 1 Tim. iv. 1). The touchstone which he there gives, the Ithuriel's spear which should compel each heretic to start up and show himself in his proper shape, is the acknowledgment or denial that Jesus Christ was come in the flesh (ver. 2, 3). At the same time we must not regard this as so absolutely *the* touchstone, but that other times and other conditions of the Church might demand other tests. Thus, in the fourth century and during the Arian conflict the *Homoousion* was that by which the spirits were to be tried. And when our Lord, warning against false prophets, lays down this rule, "Ye shall know them by their fruits" (Matt. vii. 16), He adds a further test by which all such may be detected. By what methods the Angel of this Church had tried these pretenders to the apostolate, and discovered the falsehood of their claims, we are not told; but probably by a union of both these tests. If these false prophets were, as is generally assumed, the chiefs and leaders of the Nicolaitan wickedness, which is presently named by its name (ver. 6), then doctrinally he will have tried them by the touchstone of Christ's true humanity, whether they would confess this or deny it;—we may be sure that they had that in common with all other Gnostics, which led them to the denial of it; —and practically, by the fruits which they bore; which, being works of shame and darkness, avouched that the workers of them were not, and could not be, sent of Him who is Light, and in whom is no darkness at all. And even were they not precisely identical with the Nicolaitans, on which there will be something to say at ver. 6, these tests would not the less effectually have accomplished this work.

We must not press the word "*apostles*," as though it implied a claim on their parts to have seen and been immediately sent by the Lord Jesus Christ, which was necessary for an Apostle in the highest sense of the word (Acts i. 21, 22; 1 Cor. ix. 1), nor even by the mother Church at Jerusalem. It was now too late for either. St. John alone of living men could claim the first prerogative, and Jerusalem had long ago been destroyed. As little are these "*which say they are apostles*" identical in the actual form of their resistance to the truth with those "false apostles, deceitful workers," who every where sought to hinder the labours of St. Paul, and every where denied the apostolic authority which he claimed (2 Cor. x. 11). Those and these had indeed this in common, that they alike opposed the truth; but those were Judaizers, seeking to bring back the ceremonial law and the obligations of it, see Acts xv. 1, and Galatians, passim; these do not judaize, but heathenize, seeking to throw off every yoke, to rid themselves not of the ceremonial law only, but also of the moral; and to break down every distinction separating the Church from a world lying in the wicked one.[1]

Ver. 3. "*And hast borne, and hast patience, and for my name's sake hast laboured, and hast*

[1] This intolerance of error, this resolution to hold fast the precious deposit of the truth, to suffer nothing to be added to it, nothing to be taken from it, nothing to be altered in it, was still the mark and glory of the Ephesian Church at a date somewhat later than this. It is a remarkable testimony to this which Ignatius, writing not many years after, bears, and it admirably agrees with the testimony which the Lord Himself bears here to its zeal for doctrinal purity (*ad Ephes.* vi.): *αὐτὸς μὲν οὖν Ὀνήσιμος ὑπερεπαινεῖ ὑμῶν τὴν ἐν Θεῷ εὐταξίαν, ὅτι ἐν ὑμῖν οὐδεμία αἵρεσις κατοικεῖ· ἀλλ' οὐδὲ ἀκούετέ τινος πλέον ἤπερ Ἰησοῦ Χριστοῦ λαλοῦντος ἐν ἀληθείᾳ.* And again, c. ix. *ἔγνων δὲ παροδεύσαντάς τινας ἐκεῖθεν, ἔχοντας κακὴν διδαχήν· οὓς οὐκ εἰάσατε σπεῖραι εἰς ὑμᾶς, βύσαντες τὰ ὦτα, εἰς τὸ μὴ παραδέξασθαι τὰ σπειρόμενα ὑπ' αὐτῶν.*

not fainted."—There is a good deal of filling up by transcribers here, and more than one phrase to be omitted. The following version will represent more truly the original as it stands in the best critical editions: "*And hast patience, and didst bear for my name's sake, and hast not grown weary.*" It is not hard to see the inducements which led transcribers in the last clause of the verse to change καὶ οὐ κεκοπίακας into κεκοπίακας καὶ οὐ κέκμηκας. They took the verb κοπιάω only in the sense of "to labour;" but how could it be said in praise of the Ephesian Angel that he had not laboured; above all when his κόπος only one verse before was the especial object of the Lord's commendation, as indeed it is throughout the Epistle? so they changed the word to what we have in the received text and in our Version; "*thou hast laboured, and hast not fainted.*" But κοπιάω is not only to labour, but implying, as we have seen it does, strenuous and exhausting labour, will often mean farther, to grow weary with labour (thus John iv. 6; Matt. xi. 28: κοπιῶντες καὶ πεφορτισμένοι); and it is this for which the Lord here praises the Angel and in him the Church at Ephesus, that it had borne the burden and heat of a long day's toil without fainting under, or waxing weary of it. This recurrence to the κόπος of the verse preceding is very instructive, though it is hard, if not impossible, to reproduce it in English. "Thou knowest what *κόπος* is, without knowing what *κοπιᾶν* is;" and that this is not accidental seems evident from the exactly similar recurrence of *βαστάζειν* in both verses; "There are things which thou canst not bear, and things which thou canst bear; thou canst not bear the wicked, such false brethren as name the name of Christ only to bring shame upon it; thou hast something of the spirit of him who declared, 'He that telleth lies shall not tarry in my sight' (Ps. ci. 10), but thou canst bear my reproach, my cross;" cf. Luke xiv. 27, where the same word *βαστάζειν* is used as here; so also John xix. 17. Wetstein: "Eleganter opponuntur: *οὐ δύνῃ βαστάσαι* et *ἐβάστασας*. Ferre potes molestias propter Christum et vexationes; at non potes ferre pseudapostolos."

Ver. 4. "*Nevertheless I have somewhat against thee, because thou hast left thy first love.*"—*Ἔχω κατὰ σοῦ*: cf. for the same phrase Matt. v. 23; Mark xi. 25; and for a similar, Col. iii. 13. This is one of three occasions (see ver. 14, 20) on which Christ has to make a like exception, and to dash his praise with blame. In neither, however, of the other cases is the blame so severe as here, the "*somewhat,*" which appears in part to mitigate the severity of this judgment, having nothing corresponding with it in the original. It is indeed not a "*somewhat,*" which the Lord has against the

Ephesian Church; it threatens to grow to be an "every thing;" for see the verse following, and compare 1 Cor. xiii. 1-3. The great passage on "*first love*" is Jer. ii. 2: "I remember thee, the kindness of thy youth, the love of thine espousals, when thou wentest after me in the wilderness, in a land that was not sown,"—words which set forth the first warmth of gratitude, the first devotion of heart on the part of Israel to its Redeemer and Lord (Exod. xiv. 31; xv. 1), when it seemed as if the flood-tides of a thankful love would never ebb, but would bear it triumphantly over every obstacle which it might meet in its path. Such a "*first love*" of the Bride to the heavenly Bridegroom, and in Him to all that are his, dwelt largely in the Ephesian Church when St. Paul wrote his Epistle to it; he gives God thanks for their love unto all the saints (i. 15); he draws them without a misgiving into the deepest mysteries of human love and divine (v. 23-33). The suggestion that this leaving of the first love can refer to the abating of any other love but that to God and Christ, grows out of an entire ignorance of the whole spiritual life, the ways by which it travels, and the dangers to which it is inevitably exposed, and which, alas! only too often prove fatal to it.

On the question, *When* the Apocalypse was composed, we have a certain amount of implicit evidence here, in this reproach with which the Lord reproaches the Ephesian Angel; such as has its value in confirming the ecclesiastical tradition which places it in the reign of Domitian, as against the more modern view which assumes it to have been written in the time of Nero. It has been well observed that in St. Paul's Epistle to the Church of Ephesus there are no signs, nor even presentiments, of this approaching spiritual declension with which the great Searcher of hearts upbraids it here. Writing to no Church does he treat of higher spiritual mysteries. There is no word in the Epistle of blame, no word indicating dissatisfaction with the spiritual condition of his Ephesian converts. He warns them, indeed, in his parting charge given at Miletus of dangers threatening them no less from within than from without (Acts xx. 29, 30); but no word indicates that they by any fault of theirs were laying themselves open to these. Those who place the Apocalypse in the reign of Nero hardly allow ten years between that condition and this—too brief a period for so great and mournful a change. It is inconceivable that there should have been such a letting go of first love in so brief a time. No: that which we have here described marks, as Hengstenberg has excellently said, the rise of another generation—a condition analogous to that of the children of Israel, when Joshua and the elders who had seen the great wonders in Egypt were gathered to their fathers (Josh. xxiv. 31). With their departure another order of things commences. A second generation rises up rather with the traditions of earnest religion than the living power of it. The forms, which were once instinct with life, still survive; but the life itself has, not indeed altogether, but in good part, departed from them. Place the Apocalypse under Domitian, and thirty years will have intervened since St. Paul wrote his Epistle to Ephesus—exactly the period which we require, exactly the life of a generation; the outlines of the truth are still preserved; but the truth itself is not for a second generation what it was for the first; apparently there is nothing changed; while yet in fact every thing is changed. How often has something of this kind repeated itself in the Church.[1]

[1] There is a passage in Bishop Burnet's *History of his own Times*, which has always seemed to me to throw considerable light on this picture of the Ephesian Church, active, zealous of good works, resolute to maintain a form of sound words, the truth once delivered, and yet with its inner principle of love so far decayed. He is describing the state of the Protestant communities of Switzerland, Germany, and Holland, and of the French Protestant refugees who had found shelter among them from the dragonades, the "mission bottée" as it is so facetiously called by some Roman Catholic writers, of Louis XIV. His words, written in the year 1680, are as follows: "I was indeed amazed at the labours and learning of the ministers among the Re-

Ver. 5. "*Remember therefore from whence thou art fallen, and repent, and do the first works.*"—There are ever goads in the memory of a better and a nobler past, goading him who has taken up with meaner things and lower, and urging him to make what he has lost once more his own; as, to take an extreme instance, it is the prodigal's recollection of the bread enough and to spare in his father's house, which makes the swine's husks and the famine even among them, so intolerable to him. And therefore is it that this Ephesian Angel is bidden to remember the glorious heights of grace, the heavenly places whereon, though yet on earth, he once walked with Christ during the fervency of his first

formed. They understood the Scriptures well in the original tongues, they had all the points of controversy very ready, and did thoroughly understand the whole body of divinity. In many places they preached every day, and were almost constantly employed in visiting their flock. But they performed their devotions but slightly, and read their prayers, which were too long, with great precipitation and little zeal. Their sermons were too long and too dry. And they were so strict, even to jealousy, in the smallest points in which they put orthodoxy, that one who could not go into all their notions, but was resolved not to quarrel with them, could not converse much with them with any freedom." Speaking of the French refugees from the dragonades, he says: "Even among them there did not appear a spirit of piety and devotion suitable to their condition, though persons who have willingly suffered the loss of all things rather than sin against their consciences, must be believed to have a deeper principle in them, than can well be observed by others."

love. Perhaps the desire shall thus be kindled in him to scale these heights again. In this "*from whence thou art fallen*," an allusion may possibly lie to Isai. xiv. 12, "How art thou fallen from heaven, O Lucifer, son of the morning."—"*And*, as thou rememberest, *repent, and do the first works.*" Christ does not say "Feel thy first feelings;" that perhaps would have been impossible, and even if possible, might have had but little value in it; but "*Do the first works*," such as thou didst in the time of thy first devotedness and zeal. Not the *quantity*, but the *quality*, of his works was now other and worse than once it had been.

"*Or else I will come unto thee quickly, and will remove thy candlestick out of his place, except thou repent.*"—The "*quickly*" is wanting in most MSS., and has probably found its way here from ver. 16; iii. 11; xxii. 7, 12, 20. The removing of the candlestick from a place implies the entire departure of Christ's grace, of his Church with all its blessings, from that spot, with the transfer of it to another; for it is removal of the candlestick, not extinction of the candle, which is threatened here—judgment for some, but that very judgment the occasion of mercy for others. And so it has been. The Churches of Asia are now no more, or barely and hardly exist; but the grace of God, withdrawn from them, has been bestowed elsewhere. The seat of the Church has been changed, but the Church itself still survives. The candlestick has been removed, but the candle has not been quenched; and what the East has lost the West has gained. How awful the fulfilment of the threat has been in regard of Ephesus every modern traveller thither has borne witness. One who lately visited the place found only three Christians there, and these sunk in such ignorance and apathy as scarcely to have heard the names of St. Paul or St. John.

Ver. 6. "*But this thou hast, that thou hatest the deeds of the Nicolaitans, which I also hate.*"—Very beautiful is the tenderness of the Lord in thus bringing forward a second time some good thing which He had found at Ephesus. Having been compelled to speak sharp severe words, He yet will not leave off with these; but having wounded, He will, so far as it is safe to do so, also heal.[1] It is no small

[1] On this mingling of praise, so far as truth will allow, with the necessary blame, and the leaving off not with blame, but with praise, Plutarch has much to say in his delightful treatise, "*How to discern a Flatterer from a Friend*," which is full of instruction on the true spirit of Christian rebuke. On this, which the Lord so notably practises here, namely the not leaving off with rebuke, but if possible with praise, he beautifully says (c. 37): Ἐπεὶ τοίνυν, ὥσπερ εἴρηται, πολλάκις ἡ παῤῥησία τῷ θεραπευομένῳ λυπηρὰ ὑπάρχει, δεῖ μιμεῖσθαι τοὺς ἰατρούς. οὔτε γὰρ ἐκεῖνοι τέμνοντες, ἐν τῷ πονεῖν καὶ ἀλγεῖν καταλείπουσι τὸ πεπονθὸς, ἀλλ' ἐνέβρεξαν προσηνῶς καὶ κατῃόνησαν· οὔτε οἱ νουθετοῦντες ἀστείως, τὸ πικρὸν καὶ δηκτικὸν προσβαλόντες ἀποτρέχου-

praise to love that which Christ loves, and to hate that which Christ hates, and this praise the Lord will not withhold from the Angel of Ephesus.

But the Nicolaitans, whose deeds were the object of the earnest hate of Christ's servant, as also of his own, who were they? It is not an easy question to answer. Was there, in the first place, any sect existing at the time when these words were uttered, which actually bore this name? I am disposed to think there was not. The other names of this Book, Egypt, Babylon, Sodom, in agreement with its apocalyptic character, are predominantly mystical and symbolic; and in all probability this is so as well; while the key to the right understanding of it is given us at ii. 14, 15; where those "*that hold the doctrine of Balaam*" (ver. 14) are evidently identical with those "*that hold the doctrine of the Nicolaitans*" (ver. 15). We are here set upon the right track. It is probable that we hardly rate high enough the significance of Balaam as an Anti-Moses, and therefore as an Antichrist, in the Old Testament. But without entering more into this, it may be observed that his name, according to the best etymology, signifies "Destroyer of the people" ("qui absorpsit populum," from בֶּלַע and עָם), and Νικόλαος (*νικᾶν τὸν λαόν*) is no more than a greciz-

σιν, ἀλλ' ὁμιλίαις ἑτέραις καὶ λόγοις ἐπιεικέσιν ἐκπραΰνουσι καὶ διαχέουσιν. Cf. c. xxxiii.

ing of this name,—such alternation, or duplication, presenting a word, now in its Greek, now in its Hebrew aspect, being altogether in the character of the Book, Greek in language, but Hebrew in form and spirit, and several times recurring in it; thus, *'Απολλύων* and *'Αβαδδών* (ix. 11); *Διάβολος* and *Σατανᾶς* (xii. 9; xx. 2); *ναί* and *ἀμήν* (i. 7). The genesis of the name, which, so understood, will almost exactly correspond to Armillus (= *ἐρημόλαος*), the name by which the final Antichrist, who shall seduce the Christians to their ruin, is known among the Jews (see Eisenmenger, *Entd. Judenth.* ii. 705, sqq.), may be accounted for in this way. The Nicolaitans, as we have seen, are the Balaamites; no sect bearing the one name or the other; but those who in the New Dispensation repeated the sin of Balaam in the Old, and sought to overcome or destroy the people of God by the same temptations whereby Balaam had sought to overcome them before. But it was into the fleshly sins of heathenism that he had sought to lead them, to introduce these among the people of God, to draw them to eat idol meats and to commit fornication (Num. xxv. 1–9; xxxi. 16); and this the leading character of his wickedness must be also of theirs.

The Nicolaitans then, or Balaamites, are no sect that in early times bore one of these names or the other; but those who after the pattern of Balaam's sin sought to introduce a false freedom, the freedom of the flesh, into the Church of God. These were the foremost tempters of the Church in the later apostolic times when the Apocalypse was written, and in the times immediately succeeding. The first great battle which the Church had to fight was with Jewish legalism; this came to its head historically, and found its condemnation, in the Council of Jerusalem (Acts xv. 1–31), dogmatically in St. Paul's Epistle to the Galatians, those who refused to accept the Church's decisions on the matter gradually forming themselves more and more into a schismatical heretical body, not any longer within, but henceforth without, the Church's pale. But this danger overcome, St. Paul lived to see before the close of his ministry the rise of another, of exactly the opposite error—that, namely, of heathen false freedom and libertinism; while in the later writings of the New Covenant, in the Epistle of St. Jude, in the second of St. Peter, and in the Apocalypse of St. John we find these libertine errors full blown. They all speak of lawless ones (2 Pet. ii. 16), who abused St. Paul's doctrine of grace (iii. 16), who promised liberty to others, being themselves the servants of corruption (ii. 19), who turned the grace of God into lasciviousness (Jude 4); or, as these Nicolaitans, would fain entice the servants of God to eat idol meats and commit fornication. It is not indeed a little remarkable, as attesting the identity of those whose works the Lord here declares that He hates with them whom his Apostles denounce, that Balaam, whose name as we have seen is the key-word to the name which these Nicolaitans bear, and to the works which they do, is set forth both by St. Peter (ii. 15) and St. Jude (ver. 11) as the seducer in whose path of error these later seducers were themselves running and persuading others to run.

But it may be urged against this view of the matter that we find actual Nicolaitans in the second century. Doubtless we do so. That there existed in the second and third centuries a sect of antinomian Gnostics, who bore this name, has been denied by some; but on grounds quite insufficient. Irenæus (i. xxvi. 3) is probably in error when he makes the founder of this sect to have been Nicolas, the proselyte of Antioch, of whom such honourable mention is made in the Acts (vi. 3, 5); and who, if this were true, must afterwards have miserably fallen away from the faith; while yet the fault of Irenæus is probably no more than that he too lightly admitted the claim which they made to Nicolas, as the author of their heresy. It is certainly difficult to see what authority any statement of his would retain with us, if we felt at liberty to set aside his distinct assertion of such a sect as existing in his own time.

But still more explicit are the references made to them by Tertullian (*De Præsc. Hær.* 46). It cannot be said of him, as it sometimes is of Irenæus, that he knows nothing about them except what he has drawn from these passages of Scripture; for he gives an account of their doctrines, not merely libertine, but Gnostic, at considerable length. Clement of Alexandria also (*Strom.* ii. 20) speaks without hesitation of the Nicolaitans (οἱ φάσκοντες ἑαυτοὺς Νικολάῳ ἕπεσθαι) as a body existing in his day; and compare iii. 4, where he records their unbridled excessive lusts. He indeed entirely acquits Nicolas the deacon from having had any share in the authorship of this heresy, giving no credit to this boasted genealogy of theirs. The *Apostolic Constitutions* (vi. 8) do the same. With such distinct notices of Nicolaitans existing in the second century, it seems a piece of unwarranted scepticism to deny the historic existence of such a sect. At the same time, there is no need to suppose that they were the spiritual descendants of actual Nicolaitans, of libertines I mean, bearing this name, in the times of the Apostle. Rather, springing up at a later day, one of the innumerable branches of the Gnostic heresy, they assumed this name which they found ready made for them in the Apocalypse.[1]

[1] The fullest collection of all passages of antiquity bearing on the

It may seem indeed, at the first showing, almost inconceivable that a sect, professing to stand even in the remotest relation to Christianity, should appropriate to itself a name so branded with infamy as in Holy Scripture is this. But we must remember that with many of the Gnostics this was a relation of absolute and entire opposition to nearly all of the Scripture; and the history of these daring fighters against God would supply many parallel instances of blasphemous impiety. Thus, not to speak of the Ophites, there were the Cainites (Tertullian indeed identifies them and the Nicolaitans, *De Præsc. Hær.* 33), all whose saints and heroes were those whom the Scripture had marked with deepest reprobation, the list beginning with Cain and ending with Judas Iscariot (Tertullian, *De Præsc. Hær.* 47). When too we keep in mind the intense antagonism of the antinomian Gnostics to John as a judaizing Apostle, contradistinguished from Paul, who with their own Marcion was to sit, Paul on the right hand, and Marcion on the left hand, of Christ in his kingdom, being those for whom this was reserved of the Father (Matt. xx. 23; Origen, *in Luc. Hom.* 25), assuredly there will seem nothing strange that a name which John branded with worst dishonour, they who gloried in

Nicolaitans which I know is to be found in Stern's *Commentar über die Offenbarung*, 1854, pp. 141-145.

their shame should assume as one of chiefest honour;—just as in an infidel publication of the present day which has sometimes come under my eye, there are letters signed in blasphemous earnest with the signature of "Antichrist."

One point still remains. Is the hating the deeds of the Nicolaitans of this verse identical with not being able to "*bear them which are evil*" of ver. 2? or, being a grace growing out of the same holy impatience of evil, is there for all this a certain difference between them, so that while that was rather a hatred of error in doctrine, of departure from the faith once delivered, an unmasking of them that said they were apostles, and were not, this is more a hatred of evil *done*, of *the deeds* of the Nicolaitans? In other words, is the Lord here recurring to the good thing which He has already found and praised in Ephesus? or is this new praise, and the recognition of a further grace? Most expositors take for granted that Christ here returns to the praise which He has already uttered, that the Nicolaitans therefore are identical with "*them that are evil*" of the former verse. I cannot think it; but must see here not the repetition of praise bestowed before, which seems somewhat flat, but a further merit which Christ is well pleased to find and to acknowledge in his Church at Ephesus. The *deeds* of the Nicolaitans were, no doubt, the crowning wickedness there, the bitter fruit growing out of that evil root of false doctrine; but whether in root or fruit this evil was equally hated by the Angel and Church of Ephesus.

Ver. 7. "*He that hath an ear, let him hear what the Spirit saith unto the Churches.*"—These words recur in each of the Epistles; with only this difference, that in the former three they occur *before*, in the latter four *after*, the final promise. Is there any meaning in this change of place? It is difficult to believe that there is not. The Apocalypse is a work of such consummate art, a device of such profound wisdom, that one is slow to assume any thing accidental in it, any departure from a rule which has been once admitted, without a meaning. At the same time I must own that I have never seen any satisfactory explanation of this. That in every case the words usher in, or commend, truths of the deepest concernment to all, there can be no doubt. This we might confidently argue from the very form of the exhortation; but we further gather it from a comparison of the passages, all of them of deepest significance, where the same summons to attention recurs (Matt. xi. 15; xiii. 9, 43; Mark vii. 16; Rev. xiii. 9); so that Irving (*Expos. of the Revelation*, vol. i. p. 354) has perfect right when he affirms, "This form always is used of radical and as it were of generative truths, great principles, most precious promises, most deep fetches from the secrets of God, being as it were eyes of truth, seeds and kernels of knowledge." These words then proclaim to us that they are matters of weightiest concernment to the whole Church of God, which Christ is uttering here.

But let us look a little closer at them, and see what other lessons this summons, in the form which it here takes, is capable of yielding. And first the "*ear*" here is not a *natural* ear, and this therefore a summons to every man, for every man has such a natural ear, to attend to the words now spoken; but rather the words are an equivalent to the *ὁ δυνάμενος χωρεῖν χωρείτω* of Matt. xix. 12, and imply that, spiritual truth needing a spiritual organ for its discernment, only he will be able to hear to whom God has given the hearing ear (Deut. xxix. 4), whose ear He has wakened (Isai. l. 4, 5); of others it is true, "their ear is uncircumcised, and they *cannot* hearken" (Jer. vi. 10). And yet for all this the words are in another sense addressed to every one, inasmuch as he who has not this hearing ear, who discovers from the failure of these words of Christ to reach the depths of his spirit, that he has it not, is implicitly bidden to seek it of Him, who can alone give it to any, and who would be well pleased to give it to all. But secondly we are taught by these words how absolute is the identity between the workings of the Son and the Holy Ghost; how truly the Spirit is the Spirit of the Son, as of the Father. Christ has been speaking throughout; but now without a word of explanation, what *He* speaks is declared to be what the Spirit speaks. It is the Spirit who declares these things to the Churches. And in that phrase, "*the Churches*," we are further reminded of the universal character which this Epistle and those that follow it possess. It might seem that all which had hitherto been uttered had been uttered only to one Church, to that of Ephesus; nor is it meant in the least to deny this primary destination, that all the reproofs, encouragements, warnings, promises which it contained were designed for Ephesus; but they are not limited to it. Christ will allow of no such limitation. In a form somewhat more solemn He virtually repeats what He once spoke in the days of his flesh, "What I say unto you, I say unto all;" for, standing as He does at the central heart of things, in his particular there ever lies involved an universal; and therefore is it that heaven and earth may pass away, but his words can never pass away.

"*To him that overcometh will I give to eat of the tree of life, which is in the midst of the Paradise of God.*"—It is deeply interesting and instructive to observe how in this, and probably in every other case, the character of the promise corresponds to the character of the faithfulness displayed. They who have abstained from the idol meats, from the sinful dainties of the flesh and world, shall, in return, "*eat of the tree of life;*" or, as it is in the Epistle to Pergamum, "*of the hidden manna*" (ii. 17); the same law of correspondency and compensation being found, as I have said, to reign in most, if not all of the other promises as well. They who have not feared those who can kill the body only, who have given, where need was, their bodies to the flame, shall not be hurt by the second death (ii. 11). They whom the world has not vanquished, shall have dominion over the world (ii. 26, 27). They who keep their garments here undefiled, shall be clad in the white and shining garments of immortality there (iii. 4, 5). They who overcome Jewish pretensions (and the earnest warnings of the Epistle to the Hebrews, show us that this for some was not done without the hardest struggle) shall be made free, not of an earthly, but of an heavenly, Jerusalem (iii. 12). The only Church in which any difficulty occurs in tracing the correlation between the form of the victory and the form of the reward, is the last.

But this much said by way of general introduction to all the promises, the promise here may well claim closer attention. "*To him that overcometh,*"

The image of the Christian as a conqueror, an overcomer, is frequent with St. Paul (2 Tim. ii. 5; 1 Cor. ix. 24, 25); but such phrases as *νικᾶν τὸν κόσμον, νικᾶν τὸν πονηρόν*, or simply *νικᾶν* as here, nowhere occur in his Epistles—the only passage in them which in the least resembles these, or where the word is used to express the moral victory over sin and temptation, is Rom. xii. 21. This use of *νικᾶν*, with that single and partial exception, is exclusively St. John's; and the frequent recurrence of it on the one side in his Gospels and Epistles, and on the other in the Apocalypse (thus compare John xvi. 32; 1 Ep. ii. 13, 14; v. 4, 5, with Rev. ii. 11, 17, 26; iii. 5, 12, 21; xii. 11; xxi. 7), constitutes an interesting point of contact between the language of this Book and of those others whereof he was the author as well; and for those who need such arguments, as argument for the identity of the author of those and of this.

It is very noteworthy, and this "*I will give*," recurring as it does so constantly in all these Epistles, bids us to note, how absolutely without reserve or qualification Christ assumes for Himself throughout them all, the distribution of rewards, as supreme and sole *μισθαποδότης* (Heb. xi. 6) in the kingdom of glory (ii. 10, 17, 26, 28; iii. 21; cf. xxi. 6, and 2 Tim. iv. 8). Elsewhere St. Paul has said, "The gift *of God* is eternal life" (Rom.

vi. 22); here it appears eminently as the gift of Christ. And his "*I will give*," though still in the future, is sure. It has nothing in it of the δώσω of that ever promising but never performing king of Macedon; who, having ever this same δώσω on his lips, but never the δῶρον in his hands, acquired the name of Doson, fastened as no honourable distinction upon him who never crowned the promise with the performance.

In "*the tree of life*" there is manifest allusion to Gen. ii. 9. The use of *ξύλον*, the dead timber in classical Greek, for *δένδρον*, the living tree, there as here is Hellenistic; not indeed exclusively confined to the Septuagint and the New Testament, being found in the Alexandrian poets, Callimachus for instance, as well; indeed, there is an anticipation of it in Herodotus, iii. 47. The tree which disappeared with the disappearance of the earthly Paradise, reappears with the reappearance of the heavenly, Christ's kingdom being in the highest sense "the restitution of all things" (Acts iii. 21). Whatever had been lost through Adam's sin is won back, and that too in a higher shape, through Christ's obedience. That the memory of "*the tree of life*" had not in the mean time perished, we gather from such passages as Prov. iii. 18; xi. 30; xiii. 12; xv. 4.[1] To eat of the tree of life is a fig-

[1] The Rabbis, of course, know a great deal about this "*tree of*

urative phrase to express participation in the life eternal; cf. Gen. iii. 22; Ezek. xlvii. 12;[1] Rev. xxii. 2, 14; 2 Esdr. ii. 12; vii. 53; and Ecclus. xix. 19: "They that do the things that please Him shall receive the fruit of the tree of immortality." Compare the words of the Christian Sibyl:

> Οἱ δὲ Θεὸν τιμῶντες ἀληθινὸν ἀέναόντε
> Ζωὴν κληρονομοῦσι τὸν αἰῶνος χρόνον, αὐτοὶ
> Οἰκοῦντες Παραδείσου ὁμῶς ἐριθήλεα κῆπον,
> Δαινύμενοι γλυκὺν ἄρτον ἀπ' οὐρανοῦ ἀστερόεντος.

We meet with echoes and reminiscences of this "tree of life" in the mythologies of many nations; or if not actual reminiscences of it, yet reachings out after it, as in the Yggdrasil of our own northern mythology (see Grimm, *Deutsche Mythol.* p. 756); and still more remarkable in the Persian Hom. This is the king of trees, is called in the Zend-Avesta the Death-destroyer; it grows by the fountain of Arduisur, in other words, the waters

life." Its boughs overshadow the whole of Paradise. It has five hundred thousand fragrant smells, and its fruit as many pleasant tastes, not one of them resembling the other (Eisenmenger, *Entdecktes Judenthum*, vol. ii. p. 311).

[1] Lucian's words (*Ver. Hist.* ii. 14), in his account of the Island of the Blest, sound very much like a scoff at this: αἱ μὲν ἄμπελοι δωδεκάφοροί εἰσι, καὶ κατὰ μῆνα ἕκαστον καρποφοροῦσι.

of life; while its sap drunken confers immortality (Creuzer, *Symbolik*, vol. i. p. 187, and often).

For the words, "*which is in the midst of the Paradise of God,*" there can be no doubt that we should read simply, "*which is in the Paradise of God.*" Transcribers brought their "*in the midst*" from Gen. ii. 9. *Παράδεισος* is a word whose history is well worth tracing. The word and thing which it designated are both generally said to be Persian; though this is now earnestly denied by some, who claim for it a Semitic origin (see Tuch, *Genesis*, p. 68). As is well known, it was first naturalized in Greek by Xenophon, who designated by it the parks or pleasure-gardens of Persia, in which wild beasts were kept, or stately trees grown (*Hell.* iv. 1. 15; *Cyrop.* i. 4. 11), being at once the "vivarium" and the "viridarium" of the Romans. Classical Latin did not know the word 'paradisus' (see A. Gellius, ii. 20. 4, and the long circumlocution by which Cicero, *De Senect.* 17, is compelled to express the thing). Where the Septuagint employs *παράδεισος*, it is commonly to designate the garden of Eden (Gen. ii. 8; iii. 1; Ezek. xxviii. 13), though sometimes employing it for any stately garden of delight whatever (Isai. i. 30; Jer. xxix. 5; Eccl. ii. 5): *ἐποίησα μοι κήπους καὶ παραδείσους*). The word, when it appears in the New Testament, has taken a great spring. The ideal beauty of that dwelling-place of our first parents, perhaps also the fact that it had now vanished from the earth, has caused the name "Paradise" to be transferred to that region and province in Hades, or the invisible world, where the souls of the faithful are gathered, waiting for their perfect consummation and bliss. "Their [the Jews'] meaning therefore was this; that as paradise, or the garden of Eden, was a place of great beauty, pleasure, and tranquillity, so the state of separate souls was a state of peace and excellent delights" (J. Taylor). It is in this sense that Christ allowed and employed the term, when to the dying thief He said, "This day shalt thou be with Me in Paradise" (Luke xxii. 43).[1] But even this is not all. The word takes a higher meaning yet; for this inferior Paradise is not to be confounded with the heavenly Paradise, "the Paradise *of God*," as it is here called, "the third heaven," where is the presence and glory of God (2 Cor. xii. 2, 4).[2] We may thus trace παράδεισος passing through a series of meanings, each one higher than the last; from any garden of delight,

[1] The most interesting passages in the Fathers on Paradise as this middle state, are Tertullian, *De Animâ*, 55 (his book *De Paradiso* has not reached us); and Origen, *De Princ.* ii. 11. 6.

[2] There is much about both Paradises, the upper and the under, as the Jews were wont to call them, in Eisenmenger, *Entdecktes Judenthum*, vol. ii. pp. 260-320.

which is its first meaning, it comes to be predominantly applied to the garden of Eden, then to the resting-place of separate souls in joy and felicity, and lastly, to the very heaven itself; and we see eminently in it, what we see indeed in so many words, how revealed religion assumes them into her service, and makes them vehicles of far higher truth than any which they knew at first, transforming and transfiguring them, as in this case, from glory to glory.

This "*tree of life*," with the privilege of eating of its fruits, as belonging to the faithful overcomer, reappears at the close of this Book (xxii. 2, 14). Indeed it is very interesting to note, and here will be a fit opportunity for noting, the fine and subtle bands which knit one part of the Apocalypse to another, the marvellous art, if we may dare to use an earthly word speaking of a heavenly fact, with which this Book is constructed. Especially these seven Epistles, which at first sight might appear, which to some have appeared, to hang loosely on the rest, to be but slightly attached, do yet on nearer examination prove to be bound to it by the closest possible bands. There is not one of the promises made to the faithful in these second and third chapters, which does not look on to, and perhaps first finds its explanation in, some later portion of the Book. Thus the eating of the tree of life, at

xxii. 2, 14, 19; deliverance from the second death (ii. 11) receives its solemn commentary, xx. 14; xxi. 8; the writing of the new name of ii. 17 reappears xiv. 1; the dominion over the heathen of ii. 26 at xx. 4; the morning star of ii. 28 at xxii. 16; the white garments of iii. 5 at iv. 4; vii. 9, 13; the name found written in the book of life of iii. 5 at xiii. 8; xx. 15; the New Jerusalem and the citizenship in it of iii. 12 at xxi. 10; xxii. 14; the sitting upon the throne of iii. 21 at iv. 4.[1]

There is one thing more to observe before leaving this promise,—namely the large amount of evidence in favour of a very interesting reading,—"*in the Paradise of my God*" (τοῦ Θεοῦ μου). It is not hard to understand the motives which led to

[1] Very beautifully Bengel on this matter, though his words refer not to the seven Epistles only, but to the whole Book: "Partes hujus libri passim inter se respiciunt. Omnino structura libri hujus prorsus artem divinam spirat; estque ejus quodam modo proprium, ut res futuras multas, et in multitudine varias, proximas, intermedias, remotissimas, maximas, minimas, terribiles, salutares, ex veteribus prophetis repetitas, novas, longas, breves, easque inter se contextas, oppositas, compositas, seque mutuo involventes et evolventes, ad se invicem ex intervallo parvo aut magno respicientes, adeoque interdum quasi disparentes, abruptas, suspensas, et postea de improviso opportunissime sub conspectum redeuntes, absoluto compendio complectatur; atque his rebus, quæ complectitur liber, structura libri exacte respondet. Itaque in omnibus suis partibus admirabilem habet varietatem, spirasque pulcerrimas, simulque summam harmoniam, per ipsas anomalias, quæ illam interpellare videntur, valde illustratam."

the omission of this *μου*—the fear namely of Arian conclusions, or others dishonourable to the divinity of Christ, which may probably have influenced transcribers. Such fears are altogether superfluous, as Arethas long ago observed. This Scripture does but say what innumerable others say as well. The Lord after his resurrection could speak of "*my* Father and *your* Father, *my* God and *your* God" (John xx. 17); and compare in this very Book, "the temple of *my* God," "the name of *my* God," "the city of *my* God" (iii. 12); while St. Paul does not scruple to speak of the God, as well as the Father, of our Lord Jesus Christ (Ephes. i. 17).

II.

EPISTLE TO THE CHURCH OF SMYRNA.

Rev. ii. 8–11.

Ver. 8. "*And unto the Angel of the Church in Smyrna write.*"—The next in order to Ephesus of the seven Churches is Smyrna, the next in the natural order as it is also in the spiritual, lying as it does a little to the north of that city. Smyrna, *ἄγαλμα τῆς Ἀσίας*, as it has been called, was one of the fairest and noblest cities of Ionia; most favourably placed upon the coast to command the trade of the Levant, which equally in old and modern times it has enjoyed. In early ecclesiastical history Smyrna is chiefly famous as the Church over which Polycarp presided as bishop. This Church must have been founded at a very early date, though there is no mention of it either in the Acts or the Epistles of St. Paul. Knowing as we do that at a period only a little later than this, Polycarp was bishop there, a very interesting question presents itself to us, namely, whether he might not have been bishop now; whether he may not be the Angel to whom this Epistle is addrest. There is much to make this probable; and the fact, if it were so, would throw much light on the character of the Epistle, and beautifully account for that key-note of martyrdom to which it is set; while the difficulties which some find in this, rest mainly on the erroneous assumption that the Apocalypse was composed under Nero or Galba, and not under Domitian. It is true indeed that we have thus to assume an episcopate of his, which lasted for more than seventy years; for "the good confession" of Polycarp did not take place till the year 168, while the Apocalypse was probably written in 96. Let us see, however, how far ecclesiastical history will bear us out in this. As early as 108 Ignatius on his way to his Roman martyrdom found Polycarp the bishop or Angel of the Church of Smyrna (*Mart. Ign.* 3), addressing to him a letter which, despite of all which has been said against it, must still be considered genuine. We have only to extend his episcopate twelve years *a parte ante*, and he will have been Angel of Smyrna when this Epistle was addrest to that Church.

Is there any great unlikelihood in this? His reply to the Roman Governor, who tempted him to save his life by denying his Lord, is well known —namely that he could not thus renounce a Lord whom for eighty and six years he had served, and during all this time had received nothing but good from Him (*De S. Polyc. Mart.* 9; Eusebius, *H. E.* iv. 15). But these "eighty and six years" can scarcely represent the whole length of his life, for Irenæus (*Adv. Hær.* iii. 3. 4; cf. Eusebius, *H. E.* iv. 14) lays such a stress on the extreme old age which Polycarp had attained, that, great as this age is, we must yet esteem the number of his years to have been greater still. They represent no doubt the years since his conversion. Counting back eighty-six years from the year 168, being that of his martyrdom, we have A.D. 82 as the year when he was first in Christ. This will give us fourteen years as the period which will have elapsed from his conversion to that when this present Epistle was written, during which time he may very well have attained the post of chiefest honour and toil and peril in the Church of Smyrna. Tertullian indeed distinctly tells us that he was consecrated bishop of Smyrna by St. John (*De Præsc. Hæret.* 32); and Irenæus, who declares to us that he had himself in his youth often talked with Polycarp, declares the same (Eusebius, *H. E.* iv. 14; cf. iii. 36; Jerome, *Catal. Script.* s. v. *Polycarpus;* Jacobson, *Patt. Apostoll.* p. 564; and Röthe, *Die*

Anfänge d. christl. Kirche, p. 429). There are then very sufficient reasons for thinking it at least possible, to me it seems probable, that to Polycarp himself the words which follow were first spoken.

"*These things saith the first and the last, which was dead, and is alive.*"—Being addressed, as this Epistle is, to a Church exposed, and hereafter to be still more exposed, to the fiercest blasts of persecution, it is graciously ordered that all the attributes which Christ here claims for Himself should be such as would encourage and support his servants in their trials and distress. Brightman: "Titulos sibi sumit [Christus] qui præsenti rerum conditioni conveniunt. Unde varium suæ gloriæ radium in singulis Epistolis spargit, pro variâ fortunâ quâ sunt Ecclesiæ." For these titles of Christ, "*the first and the last*," and "*which was dead, and is alive*," or rather, "*who became dead, and lived again*," see i. 17, 18. *Ἔζησεν* here is not "vixit," but "revixit" (cf. Ezek. xxxvii. 3; John v. 25; Rev. xiii. 14); death having been for Him only the passage to a more glorious life. How then should his servants fear them who could kill the body, and then had nothing more which they could do? how should they doubt of committing their souls to One, who had so triumphantly redeemed his own?

Ver. 9. "*I know thy works, and tribulation,*

and poverty; but thou art rich."—For the first clause see what has been said already on ver. 2; the words of themselves express neither praise nor blame. The "*tribulation*" refers out of all doubt to the affliction which the Church of Smyrna endured at the hands of its Jewish and heathen persecutors and oppressors, *θλίβειν* and *θλῖψις* being constant words to express this (1 Thess. iii. 4; Heb. xi. 37; Acts xx. 23; Rev. i. 9, and often). So too their "*poverty*" will probably have come upon them through the spoiling of their goods (Heb. x. 34), and the various wrongs in their worldly estate which the profession of the faith of Christ will have brought with it.

"*But thou art rich.*"—How much better this, poor in the esteem of the world, but rich before Christ, than the condition of the Laodicean Angel, rich in his own esteem, but most poor in the sight of Christ (iii. 17). There can, of course, be no doubt that "*rich*" here means rich *in grace* (cf. Rom. viii. 32; Col. ii. 3; 1 Tim. vi. 18), having treasure in heaven (Matt. vi. 20; xix. 21; Luke xii. 21), as the same word *πλούσιος* expresses in a similar, but yet a far higher sense, rich *in glory* elsewhere (2 Cor. viii. 9). These words, to which James ii. 5-7 furnishes a remarkable parallel, constitute a very beautiful parenthesis, declaring as they do the judgment of heaven concerning this

Church of Smyrna, as contradistinguished from the judgment of earth. Men saw nothing there save the poverty, but He who sees not as man seeth, saw the true riches which this seeming poverty concealed, which indeed the poverty, rightly interpreted, *was;* even as He too often sees the real poverty which may lie behind the show of riches; for there are both poor rich-men and rich poor-men in his sight.

"*And I know the blasphemy of them which say they are Jews, and are not, but are the synagogue of Satan.*"—The most important question which presents itself here is, In what sense shall we take the term "*Jews*"? by "*those which say they are Jews, and are not,*" shall we understand Jews literally so called, who, being the natural seed of Abraham, claimed also to be the spiritual; or accepting "*Jews*" here as the designation of the true circumcision not made with hands, that is, of Christians, shall we see in these, some who claimed to be Christians, but whose right to belong to his Church Christ here denies? The former appears to me the preferable interpretation. The analogy of such passages as Rom. ii. 28, 29; ix. 6; Phil. iii. 2, 3, seems to point this way.[1] Then again

[1] There is a long discussion in one of Augustine's letters (*Ep.* cxcvi. § 6-16), how far Christians, as the true circumcision, might rightfully be called Jews.

these opposers and blasphemers were evidently persecutors to bonds and death of the faithful at Smyrna; but, extreme shame and disgrace as some of the heretical sects were bringing on the true Church at this time, there is no tittle of evidence that they had the power or the desire to persecute it with the weapons of outward persecution. It was otherwise, however, with the Jews literally so named. What their '*blasphemy*' against Jesus of Nazareth, against the Lord of glory, but known to them as "the hanged one," was, and still is, we know only too well (see Eisenmenger, *Entdecktes Judenthum*, vol. i. pp. 61-188). While too the opposition of the heathen was still languid and occasional, the jealousy of Rome being hardly awakened, the fierceness of *their* enmity, the eagerness with which *they* sought to arouse that of the heathen, almost every page in the Acts declares (xiii. 50; xiv. 2, 5, 19; xvii. 5; xxiv. 2; 1 Thess. ii. 14); and many a page of early ecclesiastical history no less. Moreover, this blasphemy and malignant antagonism of the Jews against the truth displayed itself in bitterest enmity against this very Church of Smyrna. We learn from that precious document, the Epistle of the Church of Smyrna recording the martyrdom of Polycarp, that Jews joined with heathens in crying out in the amphitheatre that the Christian bishop should be cast to the lions; and when there was a difficulty about this, that he should be burned alive; which being granted, the Jews, as was their wont (ὡς ἔθος αὐτοῖς), were foremost and forwardest in bringing logs for the pile; they, too, doing all that lay in their power to hinder the remains of the martyr from being delivered to his followers for burial (ch. 12, 13, 17).

In the words which follow, "*but are the synagogue of Satan*," I find another proof that Jews, literally so called, are intended. To them belonged the synagogue, to Christians the Church. Throughout all the New Testament συναγωγή is only once used for a Christian place of assembly (Jam. ii. 2), never for the body of the faithful in Christ Jesus. With this one exception, capable of an easy explanation (see my *Synonyms of the New Testament*, § 1), the word is abandoned to the Jews. And that of theirs, which might have been the Church of the living God, is now "*the synagogue of Satan*"—a hard saying, a terrible word, but one which they, once the chosen people of the Lord, had wrought with all their might to deserve. Nothing else indeed was possible for them, if they would not be his people indeed; they could not be as the heathen, merely *non*-Christian, they must be *anti*-Christian. The measure of their former nearness to God was the measure of their present distance from Him. In the height to which they were lifted up was included the depth to which, if they did not continue at that height, they must inevitably fall. And this, true for them, is true also for all.—As nothing is accidental in this Book, so it is worth remarking that as we have here "*the synagogue of Satan*," so presently "*the throne of Satan*" (ii. 13), and then lastly, "*the depths of Satan*" (ii. 24); "*the synagogue of Satan*" representing the Jewish antagonism to the Church, "*the throne of Satan*" the heathen, and "*the depths of Satan*" the heretical.

Ver. 10. "*Fear none of those things which thou shalt suffer.*"—The great Captain of our salvation never keeps back or conceals what those who faithfully witness for Him may have to bear for his name's sake; never entices recruits into his service, or seeks to retain them under his banner, by the promise that they shall find all things easy and pleasant there. So far from this, He says of Paul at the outset of his apostolic career, "I will show him how great things he must suffer for my name's sake" (Acts ix. 16; cf. Matt. x. 16-31; Luke ix. 23; John xvi. 1, 23; Ezek. ii. 3-7; Jer. i. 19); and in like manner He announces to the Angel of Smyrna that bonds, and tribulation, and death itself, are before him and before others, as many as at Smyrna shall continue faithful to the end. But for all this they are *not* to fear. Presently He will declare to them *why* they should not fear; but first he further unrolls in their sight the scroll of their sufferings.

"*Behold, the devil shall cast some of you into prison, that ye may be tried.*"—Ὁ διάβολος (= κατήγωρ, Rev. xii. 10), a name given to Satan by the Alexandrian translators with reference to the work of accuser ascribed to him, Job i. 2; Zech. iii. 1, 2. How well under him the Jews played the secondary *rôle* of διάβολοι, first against the Lord Himself, and then against his servants, appears in the Gospels (Luke xxiii. 2; John xix. 12), in the Acts (xvii. 5-8; xxiv. 2), and in all the early Church history. From a multitude of passages in Justin Martyr's *Dialogue with Trypho*, and Origen's answer to Celsus (iii. 1; vi. 27), it is clear that they were the authors of the calumnies against the Christians with which the malice of the heathen was stimulated and fed.

The manner in which this persecution of the saints is here traced to the direct agency of Satan, is very well worthy of note. We sometimes assume that Christians were persecuted, because the truth for which they bore witness affronted the pride, the prejudices, and the passions of men; and this is true; but we have not so reached to the ground of the matter. There is nothing more remarkable in the records which have come down to us of the early persecutions, and in this point they singularly illustrate the Scripture before us, than the sense which the confessors and martyrs, and those who afterwards narrate their sufferings and their triumphs, entertain and utter, that these great fights of affliction through which they were called to pass, were the immediate work of the Devil, and no mere result of the offended passions, prejudices, or interests of men. The enemies of flesh and blood, as mere tools and instruments, are nearly lost sight of by them in a continual reference to Satan as the invisible but real author of all. And assuredly they had right. So we might boldly say, even if we had not the warrant of such Scriptures as this. Thus, who that reads that story of the persecution of the saints at Lyons and Vienne, A.D. 177, happily preserved for us by Eusebius (*H. E.* v. 1) in the very words of the survivors, that wondrous tale of persistent inventive cruelty on the part of the heathen, overmatched by a superhuman patience on the part of the faithful, but must feel that here there is infinitely more than a conflict of bad men with good? There is rather on the one side an outbreak from the bottomless pit, the might and malice of the Devil, making war against God in the person of his saints; on the other, such a victory over Satan as could only have been surpassed when Christ Himself beheld him fall like lightning from heaven. This reference to the Devil as the primary author of all assaults upon the Church, the sense of which speaks out so strikingly in these *Acta Martyrum* of the Gallic martyrs, hardly speaks out less strongly in others; thus see the *Ep. de S. Polycarpi Mart.* iii. 17, 19; *Mart. Ignat.* 7.

From the fact that our Translators have rendered ἵνα πειρασθῆτε, "*that ye may be tried*," we may certainly conclude that they contemplated these πειρασμοί rather as the gracious *trials* of God (cf. Jam. i. 2, 3; 1 Pet. i. 7) than the *temptations* of the Devil. Yet assuredly this is not so; and Tyndale and Cranmer, who translate, "*to tempt you*," are to be preferred; so Marckius: "Ut tentemini; non simplici probatione constantiæ, quo pacto Deus tentat suos, sed incitatione ad malum et infidelitatem, quo pacto Deus neminem tentat." *Temptation* from the Devil, not *trial* or proof from a Heavenly Father's hand, is that which, according to this word of the Lord, was in store for them. It is indeed perfectly true that the same event is oftentimes both the one and the other—God sifting and winnowing the man to separate his chaff from his wheat, the Devil sifting and winnowing him in the hope that nothing else but chaff will be found in him. It is quite true also that πειράζειν is used in both senses; sometimes in a sense closely bordering upon that of δοκιμάζειν, and then ascribed to God, who, as the supreme δοκιμαστὴς τῶν καρδιῶν, tempts and makes trial of his servants to show them what of sin, of infirmity, of unbelief is in themselves; and showing them this, to leave them holier than before this temptation He found them (Heb. xi. 17: cf. Gen. xxii. 1; Exod. xv. 25; Deut. xiii. 3). At the same time πειράζειν is much oftener used of tempting *by the Devil*, solicitation on his part *to evil* (Matt. iv. 1; 1 Cor. x. 13; Gal. vi. 1; 1 Thess. iii. 5; Heb. ii. 18; Jam. i. 13); and the words going immediately before, "*Behold the Devil will cast some of you into prison*," are decisive that the Lord is here warning his servants, as He did in the days of his personal ministry upon earth, against fierce assaults of their ghostly enemy which were close at hand, that so by watchfulness and prayer they might be able to stand in the evil day that was so near (Luke xxii. 32).

The temptations of imprisonment He especially adduces here. In the records of the Church's early conflicts with the heathen, we constantly find the prison doing its work; those who endured torture bravely being returned to prison, that so it might be seen whether hunger and thirst, darkness and chains, would not be effectual in breaking down by little and little the courage and the steadfastness which had resisted manfully the first onset of the foe. Sometimes it would prove so. The Church's early story, furnishing in the main a glorious commentary on these words, furnishes a mournful commentary as well. When temptations such as the Lord here speaks of arrived, it would be ever seen that there were many weak brethren, and some false brethren; and the Church, rejoicing over the steadfastness of multitudes among her children, had yet to mourn over the faltering infirmity of some, and the bold apostasy of others (Eusebius, *H. E.* v. 1. 10; Cyprian, *De Laps.* 1, 2).

"*And ye shall have tribulation ten days.*"—For ἕξετε Lachmann and others have received into the text ἔχητε, which then equally with πειρασθῆτε will depend on ἵνα. These "*ten days,*" during which the tribulation of Smyrna shall endure, have been very variously interpreted, some understanding by them a very long period (cf. Gen. xxxi. 41; Job xix. 3; Num. xiv. 22); and some a very short (Gen. xxiv. 55; Num. xi. 19). Those who interpret in the former sense have very commonly seen here allusion to the ten persecutions which the Church is often said to have passed through, during the three hundred years of its conflict with heathen Rome. It has been objected that this enumeration of exactly ten persecutions is merely an arbitrary one; that, if we include in our list only those which had some right to be called general, as extending over the whole Roman empire, the persecutions would not be so many; if all those which reached any one Church or province, they would be many more. But, setting this objection aside, I am persuaded we must look for something very different here from an announcement of the great length of time over which the persecution would extend; the "*ten days*" declare rather the shortness of time within which all this tyranny would be overpast. I conclude this from the fact that only so will the words fall in with the whole temper and spirit of this verse, which is encouraging and consolatory throughout. Here, as so often elsewhere, the briefness of a trial is urged as a motive for the patient endurance of it (cf. Isai. xxvi. 20; liv. 8; Ps. xxx. 5; Matt. xxiv. 22; 2 Cor. iv. 17; 1 Pet. i. 6; v. 30).

"*Be thou faithful unto death, and I will give thee a crown of life.*"—More than one of the early Fathers have written an "*Exhortatio ad Martyrium*," but what are they all as compared with this? It needs hardly be observed that this "*unto death*" is an intensive, not an extensive, term. Christ does not mean, "to thy life's end," contemplating life under the aspect of time; but "to the sharpest and worst which the enemy can inflict upon thee, even to death itself." Dare and endure, the words would say, the worst which evil men can threaten and inflict, even death itself (Matt. x. 22; xxiv. 13; Ecclus. iv. 28). Marckius: "Quam exigit [fidelitatem] usque ad mortem, non tam terminum temporis notans, quanquam et ad metæ nostræ finem sit perseverandum, quam quidem gradum mali, in quo fidelitas nostra demonstranda est, ut mortem ipsam in causâ fidei et pietatis subire non detractemus." For the words of the promise which follow, "*and I will give thee a crown of life*," compare 2 Esdr. ii. 42-47, which, however, it can hardly be doubted is the interpolation of some later Christian hand (see Lücke, *Offenb. d. Johan.* p. 155, 2d edit.).

This "*crown of life*," always remaining essentially the same, is not the less designated by a rich variety of images. Here, and with St. James (i. 12), it is "*a crown of life*;" with St. Paul, "a crown *of righteousness*" (2 Tim. iv. 8; cf. Plutarch, *Philop. et Flam.* 3: δικαιοσύνης καὶ χρηστότητος στέφανος); with St. Peter, "a crown *of glory*" (1 Ep. v. 4); with Isaiah, "a crown *of beauty*" (lii. 3, στέφανος κάλλους, LXX.; with which compare διάδημα τοῦ κάλλους, Wisd. v. 17); in the *Mart. S. Polycarpi*, "a crown *of incorruption*" (ἀφθαρσίας, xvii. 19; cf. Eusebius, *H. E.* v. 1; μέγας τῆς ἀφθαρσίας στέφανος); with Ignatius, "a crown *of conflict*" (ἀθλήσεως, *Mart.* 5, with probable reference to 2 Tim. ii. 5). Whether Lucian intended a sneer at these glorious promises of the Scripture, when he introduces the impostor Peregrinus, who had been among the Christians, though he died a Cynic, to declare his intention of adding, by a voluntary death, a golden crown to a golden life (χρυσῷ βίῳ χρυσῆν κορώνην ἐπιθεῖναι, *De Mort. Pereg.* § 33), may be questionable. That he has many such scoffs at the promises of Scripture, as at its miracles and other facts, no one who has at all studied the matter will be disposed to deny.

One may pause to consider here, Is this crown the *diadem* of royalty, or the *garland* of victory, "Krone" or "Kranz"? I believe the former. It is quite true that στέφανος is seldom used in this sense, much oftener διάδημα (see my *Synonyms of the New Testament*, § 23); yet the "golden crowns" (στέφανοι) of chapter v. can only be royal crowns (cf. ver. 10); στέφανος too is the word which all the Evangelists employ of the crown of thorns, evidently a caricature of royalty, which was planted on the Saviour's brows. Did we indeed meet these words "*a crown of life*" in the Epistles of St. Paul, we should be justified in saying that in all probability the wreath or garland of the victor in the games, the "crown" in this sense was intended. St. Paul was familiar with the Greek games, and freely drew his imagery from them (1 Cor. vii. 24-27; Phil. iii. 12; 1 Tim. vi. 12); does not fear to contemplate the faithful under the aspect of runners (θεόδρομοι, as Ignatius, *ad Philad.* c. ii., calls them) and wrestlers in the games. His universal, Hellenic as well as Jewish, education, exempted him from any scruples upon this point. Not so, however, the Christians of Palestine. These Greek games were strange to them, or only not strange, as they were the objects of their deepest abhorrence; as witness the tumults and troubles which accompanied the first introduction of them by Herod the Great at Jerusalem, recorded at length by Josephus (*Antt.* xv. 8. 1-4). Tertullian's point of view, who styles them (*Scorp.* 6) "contentiosa solemnia et superstitiosa certamina Græcarum et religionum et voluptatum," would very much have been theirs. And then, to me at least, decisive on this point is the fact, that nowhere else in the Apocalypse is there found a single image drawn from the range of heathen antiquity. The Book moves exclusively in the circle of Jewish imagery—either sacred or cabalistic; derived in largest part from the depths of the temple service. The palms in the hands of those who stand before the throne (vii. 9) may seem an exception to the universality of this rule; but really are far from so being. It is quite true that the palm was for Greek and Roman a token of victory, but this "palmiferens company," to use Henry More's words, these happy palmers, do not stand before the throne as conquerors,—Tertullian's exposition, "albati et *palmis victoriæ insignes*" (*Scorp.* 12.), being at fault,—but as those who keep the true feast of tabernacles, the feast of rest, of all the weary toil in the wilderness accomplished and ended; and as such, and to mark them for what they are, they bear, according to the injunctions of the Old Testament, the branches of palms in their hands (Lev. xxiii. 40; cf. Neh. viii. 15; 2 Macc. x. 7; John xii. 13; Josephus, *Antt.* xiii. 13. 5); see some beautiful remarks on this point in Hengstenberg, in part anticipated by Vitringa. I must needs then believe, that these are royal *crowns*, not victorious *garlands*, which the Lord is promising here.

Ver. 11. "*He that hath an ear to hear, let him hear what the Spirit saith unto the Churches; He that overcometh shall not be hurt of the second death.*"—This "*second death,*" setting forth the "vita non vitalis," the death in life of the lost, as contrasted with the life in death of the saved, is a phrase peculiar to the Apocalypse (cf. xx. 6, 14; xxi. 8); but is not uncommon in the later Jewish theology; indeed frequent in the Chaldee Paraphrase. Vitringa: "Phrasis nata haud dubie in scholâ sanctorum virorum qui fidem et spem Ecclesiæ post reditum ex exilio Babylonico explicarunt." But though the *word* is not on the lips of the Lord during his earthly life, He does not shrink from proclaiming the fearful *thing*. The *δεύτερος θάνατος* of this Book is the *γέεννα* of Matt. v. 29; Mark ix. 43-49; Luke xii. 5. The phrase is itself a solemn witness against the Sadduceeism and Epicureanism, which would make the natural death the be-all and end-all of existence. As there is a life beyond this present life for the faithful, so a death beyond the death which falls under our eye for the wicked. "Vita damnatorum mors est," is the fearful gloss of Augustine on these words.[1]

So much has been idly written upon names, not a little most idly on the names of these seven Churches, and the mystical meanings which they contain, that one shrinks from any seeming fellowship in such foolish and unprofitable fancies; and yet it is difficult not to remember here that *σμύρνα*, the name of this suffering Church which should give out its sweetness in persecution and in death, is a subform of *μύῤῥα* (Lobeck, *Pathol.* p. 241); and that myrrh, an aromatic gum of Arabia, served for embalming the dead (John xix. 39; cf. Herodotus,

[1] Philo too, though he does not know this phrase, "*the second death*," has a terrible commentary upon it (*De Præm. et Pœn.* 12): *ἄνθρωποι μὲν γὰρ πέρας τιμωριῶν εἶναι νομίζουσι θάνατον· ἐν δὲ τῷ θείῳ δικαστηρίῳ μόγις ἐστὶν οὗτος ἀρχή.* And going on to ask what is the punishment of the ungodly, he answers, *ζῆν ἀποθνήσκοντα ἀεὶ, καὶ τρόπον τινὰ θάνατον ἀθάνατον ὑπομένειν καὶ ἀτελεύτητον*, with more which I cannot quote.

ii. 40, 86), went up as incense before the Lord (Exod. xxx. 23), was one of the perfumes of the bridegroom (Ps. xlv. 8), and of the bride (Cant. iii. 6); all which Vitringa has excellently urged: "Myrrha itaque nobis hic symbolice figurat graviores Ecclesiæ afflictiones, *amaras* equidem et ingratas carni, *πρὸς τὸ παρόν,* quod ad tempus præsens, sed ex quibus fructus provenit vere *salutaris.* Solet enim eas Deus suâ providentiâ Ecclesiæ immittere, ut electos et electorum fidem præservet a *corruptione*, et illos hoc etiam medio veluti *condiat* ad immortalitatem, et *fragrantiam* iis conciliet egregiam virtutum Christianarum, quarum exercitium persecutiones Ecclesiæ solent suscitare."

III.

EPISTLE TO THE CHURCH OF PERGAMUM.

Rev. ii. 12–17.

Ver. 12. "*And to the Angel of the Church in Pergamos write.*"—A word or two may fitly find place here on the name of this city, as it appears in our Authorized Version. In the first place, why do our Translators, writing "*Pergamos,*" and not "*Pergamus,*" retain a Greek termination for it, and for it alone? 'Assos' (Acts xx. 13, 14) is not a parallel case, for the Romans wrote 'Assos' as frequently as 'Assus;' and always 'Chios,' which therefore is quite correct (Acts xx. 15). But if '*Pergamos,*' then, by the same rule, 'Ephesos,' 'Miletos,' and many more. And even against '*Pergamus,*' though more correct than '*Pergamos,*' there would still be something to object. Instances of the feminine, ἡ Πέργαμος (Ptolemy, i. 2), are excessively rare (see Lobeck, *Phrynichus*, p. 422); while the neuter, τὸ Πέργαμον in Greek. and 'Pergamum' in Latin, occurs innumerable times (Xenophon, *Anab.* vii. 8. 8; Polybius, iv. 48. 2; Strabo, xiii. 4; Pliny, *H. N.* v. 33). I shall speak throughout of the city under this its more usual designation. It was another illustrious city of Asia; ἐπιφανὴς πόλις Strabo calls it (xiii. 4); "longe clarissimum Asiæ Pergamum," Pliny (*H. N.* v. 33). Although of high antiquity, its greatness, splendour, and importance did not date very far back. It only attained these under the successors of Alexander. One of these made Pergamum the capital of his kingdom—the same kingdom which a later of his dynasty, Attalus the Second, bequeathed to the Romans. It was famous for its vast library; for splendid temples of Zeus, of Athene, and of Apollo; but most of all for the worship of Æsculapius (Tacitus, *Annal.* iii. 63; Xenophon, *Anab.* vii. 8. 23), the remains of whose magnificent temple outside the city still remain.

"*These things saith He which hath the sharp sword with two edges.*"—Compare i. 16.

Ver. 13. "*I know thy works, and where thou dwellest, even where Satan's seat is.*"—This may not sound, at the first hearing, a reassuring word; and yet indeed it is eminently such. None of the peculiar difficulties and dangers which beset the Church at Pergamum are concealed from Christ. We indeed ask now, and it is not easy to give a satisfactory answer to the question, Why should Pergamum more than any other corrupt heathen city have been "*Satan's seat*," or "*Satan's throne*;" for as θρόνος is constantly in this Book translated "*throne*" when applied to the powers of heaven, it should be so also when applied to the hellish caricature of the heavenly kingdom; to the kingdom which the rulers of the darkness of this world seek to set up over against the kingdom of light. The question has been variously answered. Some have supposed that allusion is here to the fane of Æsculapius, Θεὸς Σωτήρ he was called, where lying miracles of healing were vaunted to be performed, Satan seeking by the aid of these to counterwork the work of the Gospel. The explanation is quite insufficient. All which we can securely conclude from this language is, that from one cause or another, these causes being now unknown, Pergamum enjoyed the bad preëminence of being the head-quarters in these parts of the opposition to Christ and his Gospel. Why it should have thus deserved the name of "*Satan's throne*," so emphatically repeated a second time at the end of this verse, "*where Satan dwelleth*," must remain one of the unsolved riddles of these Epistles. Some circumstances, of which no historical notice has reached us, may have especially stirred up the fanaticism of the heathen there.

"*And thou holdest fast my name, and hast not denied my faith, even in those days wherein Anti-*

pas was my faithful martyr, who was slain among you, where Satan dwelleth."—There is a multitude of small variations of reading here, though none seriously affecting the sense. There was probably an anacoluthon in the sentence originally, which transcribers would not let be; but tried by various devices to palliate or remove. It is evident from the testimony borne here to the Pergamene Church, that many there, probably the Angel himself, had shown an honourable steadfastness in the faith; had been confessors of it; though possibly only one, Antipas, had resisted, or had been called to resist, unto blood. Eusebius (*H. E.* iv. 15) records several martyrs who at a somewhat later day were at Pergamum faithful to death, and received a crown of life. Attalus also, it may be mentioned, who did so valiantly in the persecutions of Lyons and Vienne, and won a foremost place in that noble company of martyrs, was a Pergamene (*Ib.* v. 1, 14, 38, 47).

Of Antipas, except from the glorious record which the Lord bears to him here, we know absolutely nothing. It is difficult to understand the silence of all ecclesiastical history respecting so famous a martyr, one singled out by Christ to such honour as this; for silent in regard of him ecclesiastical history must be confessed to be; that which Tertullian (*Scorp.* 12) and other early writers tell us about him, being merely devised *in fugam vacui*, and manifestly drawn from the passage before us. They *know* nothing about him except what they find here. Later Latin martyrologies, of course, know a great deal; according to these he was bishop of Pergamum, and by command of Domitian was shut up, Perillus-like, in a brazen bull, afterwards made red-hot; this being his passage to life. Hengstenberg has a curious explanation of this name, though it is not perfectly original; he has derived at least the hint of it from Aretius. Pressing the fact that almost all other names, he would say all, are symbolic in this Book, as Jezebel, Balaam, Egypt, Sodom, he urges that this must be symbolic too. But Ἀντίπας, what is it but a word formed on the same model as Ἀντίχριστος; and as this is made up of ἀντί and Χριστός, so Ἀντίπας of ἀντί and πᾶς, and Antipas is one who for Christ's sake has dared to stand out *against all*, an ἀντίκοσμος; cf. Jer. xx. 10; xv. 10, "Woe is me, my mother, that thou hast borne me a man of strife and a man of contention *to the whole earth*," which must be the character and condition of an eminently godly man set in the midst of a world which lieth in the wicked one (Jam. iv. 4; Acts iv. 19; v. 29). A later commentator contemptuously dismisses this with the observation that Ἀντίπας is only an abbreviation of Ἀντίπατρος, as Νικόμας of Νικομήδης,

Μηνᾶς of *Μηνόδωρος*, and the like. I am certainly not disposed to rate this higher than an ingenious fancy, a *lusus* of the critic's art, but see little or no force in this argument against it. Antipas, once formed, enters into all the rights which its new form confers upon it, irrespective of the process by which it may have attained this form. But it is not worth while to vindicate from a bad objection that which will not commend itself a whit the more, even after this objection is set aside.

Ver. 14. "*But I have a few things against thee, because thou hast there them that hold the doctrine of Balaam, who taught Balac to cast a stumbling-block before the children of Israel, to eat things sacrificed unto idols, and to commit fornication.*" —Those "*that hold the doctrine of Balaam*" are, I am persuaded, identical with the Nicolaitans of ver. 6, 15; indeed the latter verse seems to leave no doubt on the matter. The mention of him as the tempter and seducer would of itself sufficiently explain what was the nature of the sins to which he tempted and seduced (Num. xxv. 1-9; xxxi. 15, 16); but the sins are here expressly named. First, however, something may be said on the words ὃς ἐδίδασκε τῷ Βαλάκ, which we, and I believe rightly, have rendered, "*who taught Balac.*" Hengstenberg indeed, and Bengel before him, on the strength of this dative, a *dativus commodi* as they regard it, united with the fact that διδάσκειν habitually governs an accusative of the person who is the object of the teaching (thus ver. 20 in this very chapter), have urged that we ought to translate "*who taught for Balac*," that is, in the interests of Balac, to please him; and, in confirmation of this, they press that there is no hint in Scripture of Balaam having suggested *to Balac* to put these temptations in the way of the children of Israel; the parting of the two is recorded Num. xxiv. 25, nor is there any reason, they say, to suppose that they ever met again; it was to the Moabitish women themselves, to Balac's people, but not to Balac himself, that Balaam suggested the placing these stumbling-blocks in their way. I am persuaded that this is a mistake. The construction proposed is much too artificial for the Apocalypse; the dative after διδάσκειν is the penetrating of a Hebrew idiom through the forms of the Greek language; and there is nothing at Num. xxxi. 16 to compel us to understand that Balaam's communication with the daughters of Moab was immediate, and not through the intermediation of the king. Thus see Josephus, *Antt.* iv. 6. 6, who assumes this last to have certainly been the case; and cf. Vitringa, *Obss. Sac.* l. iv. c. ix. § 29.

There are two words which claim here special consideration, σκάνδαλον and εἰδωλόθυτον. Σκάνδαλον, a later form of σκανδάληθρον (Aristophanes,

Acharnan. 686), and σκανδαλίζω (there is no σκανδαληθρίζω, see *Rost und Palm*), occur only, I believe, in the sacred Scriptures, the Septuagint and the New Testament, and in such writings as are immediately dependant upon these (see Suicer, s. v.); being almost always in them employed in a tropical sense; Judith v. 1; Lev. xxix. 14 are exceptions. Σκάνδαλον is properly a trap (joined often with παγίς, Josh. xxiii. 13; Ps. cxl. 9; Rom. xi. 9), or more precisely that part of the trap on which the bait was laid, and the touching of which caused the trap to close upon its prey; then generally any loop or noose set in the path, which should entangle the foot of the unwary walker and cause him to stumble and fall; σκάνδαλον=πρόσκομμα (Rom. xiv. 13) and σκανδαλίζειν=προσκόπτειν (Matt. iv. 6; Rom. ix. 32); and next any stone, or hindrance of any kind (Hesychius explains it by ἐμποδισμός), which should have the same effect (1 Pet. ii. 7). Satan, then, as *the* Tempter is the great placer of "scandals," "stumbling-blocks," or "offences," in the path of men; his sworn servants, a Balaam or a Jeroboam (1 Kin. xiv. 16), are the same consciously. All of us unconsciously, by careless walking, by seeking what shall please ourselves rather than edify others (1 Cor. viii. 10), are in danger of being the same; all are deeply concerned with the warning of Matt. xviii. 7.

Εἰδωλόθυτον is a New Testament word to express what the heathen sacrifices were, as they presented themselves to the eye of a Christian or a Jew, namely things offered to idols.[1] The Gentiles themselves expressed the same by *ἱερόθυτον* (which word occurs 1 Cor. x. 28, according to the better reading, St. Paul there assuming a Gentile to be speaking, and using, if not an honourable, yet at any rate a neutral word), or by *θεόθυτον,* which the Greek purists preferred (Lobeck, *Phrynichus*, p. 139). It will be worth while here to consider under what plea any who even named the name of Christ could consent to eat of these idol-meats, and yet claim to retain allegiance to that name. We may be quite sure that as many of the stock of Abraham as joined themselves to the Church of Christ were not so much as tempted to this sin; their whole previous education, all that they had learned to abhor or to hold dear, was for them a sufficient safeguard against it (Num. xxv. 2; Ps. cvi. 28; Dan. i. 8; Tob. i. 10, 11). It was otherwise with the converts from the heathen world; with the Gentile Christian,

[1] It is a notable example of the extreme inconsistency of our Version in rendering the same word in different places, that *εἰδωλόθυτα* is rendered in four different ways; it is "meats offered to idols" (Acts xv. 29), it is "things offered to idols" (Acts xxi. 15), it is "things that are offered in sacrifice unto idols" (1 Cor. viii. 4), it is "things sacrificed unto idols" (Rev. ii. 14).

gathered in, it may be, to the Church of Christ out of some corrupt Greek city. Refusal to partake in the idol-meats was for him refusal to partake, not merely in the idolatry which he had renounced, but in very much else which he was not at all so well prepared to renounce; it involved abstinence from almost every public, every private festivity, a withdrawal in great part from the whole social life of his time; for sacrifice had bound itself up in almost every act of this social life. We have a singular evidence of this in the fact that "to kill" and "to sacrifice" had in Greek almost become identical; *θύειν*, which had originally meant the latter, meaning the former now. The poor, offering a slain beast, after the priest and the altar had received their shares, would sell the remainder in the market; the rich would give this which remained over away. From one cause or another, there was a certainty at many entertainments of meeting these sacrificial meats, there was a possibility of meeting them at all. The question therefore was one which, like that of caste at the present day in India, would continually obtrude itself, which could not be set aside.[1]

Already we find at the Council of Jerusalem

[1] See an excellent Essay on this subject in Stanley's *Commentary on the First Epistle to the Corinthians*, with this title, *The sacrificial feasts of the heathen*, vol. i. pp. 149–152.

the Apostles resolving that among the few "necessary things" (Acts xv. 28) which must be absolutely demanded of the Gentile converts, abstinence from "the pollutions of idols" (ver. 20), or, as in the more formal decree it is expressed, "meats offered to idols" (ver. 29), was one. Some two years later various cases of conscience have occurred exactly in that Church where beforehand we might have looked for them, namely at Corinth, and St. Paul has been called upon to settle them. Some it would seem there, who boasted of their γνῶσις, affirmed that they saw through the whole heathen idolatry that it was a fraud and a lie; to them an idol was nothing; what fear then that they should become partakers with the idol through partaking of the idol meats? and these, in the assertion of their liberty, sat openly at meat in the very idol temple itself (1 Cor. viii. 10). So too at a somewhat later date, in Justin Martyr's *Dialogue with Trypho*, the Jew Trypho makes it a charge against the Christians that many of them partook of idol sacrifices, affirming that they were in no way injured by them (c. 35); to whom the Christian Father replies that these Marcionites, Valentinians, and the rest, usurped the name of Christ, but that the Catholic Church repudiated them utterly, in no way acknowledged them for children of hers. From Irenæus (i. 6. 3) we learn that they not merely thus ate of the idol meats, boasting that they were not defiled by them, but took a foremost share in the celebration of the heathen festivals. Others, in an opposite extreme and excess of scrupulosity, were exceedingly troubled lest the meat they innocently bought in the market, or partook of at the house of a heathen friend, might not have been offered in sacrifice, and so they unknowingly defiled (1 Cor. x. 25, 27). All will no doubt remember the wonderful wisdom and love with which St. Paul deals with these various cases, strengthening and guiding the weak, rebuking and restraining the proud. Some, however, of these latter continued to allow themselves in these dangerous liberties, degenerating easily into scandalous excesses; although, after such decisions, first of the Council at Jerusalem, and afterwards of St. Paul, not any longer *within* the bosom of the Church, but without it; and one may see in the Nicolaitans the legitimate spiritual descendants of those Gnostics (Gnostics at least in the bud) who were not brought back to humbler, more loving, more self-denying courses by the earnest remonstrances of St. Paul.

Ver. 15. "*So hast thou also them that hold the doctrine of the Nicolaitans, which thing I hate.*"— As Balac had Balaam, a false prophet and seducer, "*so hast thou also,*" wanting that earnest hatred of evil which would make such a presence and such a teaching intolerable to thee, "*them that hold the doctrine of the Nicolaitans;*" and then Christ adds, "*which thing I hate,*" reminding him how ill it became him not to hate that which was hated of his Lord. In this matter at least the Angel of Ephesus had more of the mind of Christ than he had (ver. 6). What Christ hated, that Angel hated too.

Ver. 16. "*Repent; or else I will come unto thee quickly, and will fight against them with the sword of my mouth.*"—Out of this feebleness of moral indignation against evil it had come to pass that the Angel had not testified with sufficient energy against the Nicolaitans and their doctrine; he could not say with Paul, "I am pure from the blood of all men" (Acts xx. 26). But now repenting and faithfully witnessing against their errors, he would either recover them for the truth, or else drive them wholly from the communion of the Church—in either case a gain. If he do not repent, the Lord will come quickly, and fight against him and them with the sword of his mouth. We have, I am persuaded, another allusion here to the history of Balaam, namely to Num. xxxi. 8 (cf. Josh. xiii. 22): "Balaam also, the son of Beor, they slew with the sword;" this sword of the children of Israel being indeed the sword of God; cf. Num.

xxii. 31. Vitringa: "Verba hæc manifeste respiciunt historiam Bileami: in quâ habemus, primo quidem, Angelum Domini *stricto ense* se Bileamo, populo Dei maledicere meditanti, in viâ opposuisse, et, si in instituto perseveraret, exitium illi minatum esse; deinde Bileamum, et Israelitas qui consilium illius secuti fuerant, jussu Dei gladio periisse."

In that, "*I will fight against them*," it might seem at first sight as if there was only a threat for these ungodly workers; and not for the Angel who had been faithful in the main, nor for the better portion of the Church. But it is not so. When God has a controversy with a Church or with a people, the *tribulation* reaches all, though the *judgment* is only for his foes. The gold and the dross are cast alike into the fire, though it is only the dross that is consumed therein. The holy prophet is entangled outwardly in the same doom with the ungodly king (Jer. xxxix. 4; xliii. 6; Matt. xxiv. 20, 21). There may be, there assuredly will be, on the part of the faithful, a separation from the sin—there is seldom a separation from the suffering—of such a time. This suffering is for all. It is well that it should be so; that there should be nothing in the usual course of God's judgments to flatter the selfish hope of avoiding a share in the woe. Enough for any to escape the woe within the woe, namely, the sense of this suffering as the utterance of the extreme displeasure of God.

Ver. 17. "*He that hath an ear, let him hear what the Spirit saith unto the Churches; To him that overcometh will I give to eat of the hidden manna.*"—There can, I think, be no doubt that allusion is here to the manna which at God's express command Moses caused to be laid up before the Lord in the Sanctuary (Exod. xvi. 32-34; cf. Heb. ix. 4). This manna, as being thus laid up in the Holy Place, obtained the name of "*hidden*," "occultatum," or "reconditum," as Cocceius presses that it should be rendered, not "occultum;" for it is not κρυπτόν in the original, but κεκρυμμένον; not therefore "latens manna" as in Tertullian, but "absconditum" as in the Vulgate. It is true that many commentators, as Hengstenberg, omit any reference to this, and some expressly deny that there is any such; but Vitringa rightly: "Ducit autem phrasis nos manifeste ad cogitandum de mannâ illo, quod ex jussu Dei in urnâ reponendum erat in sacratissimo Tabernaculi conclavi, per divinam providentiam ab omni corruptione præservandum; . . . . quod manna vere symbolum fuit Christi virtute obedientiæ suæ in cœlum translati, et ibi delitescentis, usque quo Ecclesia ipsius luctam suam in his terris absolverit." The question, what we shall exactly understand by this "*hidden manna*," and the eating of it, has not always been answered with precision. Origen very characteristically understands by it the inner mystical sense of Scripture as contrasted with the outward form and letter (*Hom.* 9 *in Exod.*): "Urna mannæ reposita, intellectus Verbi Dei subtilis et dulcis." For the Mystics it is in general that graciousness of God which can only be known by those who have themselves actually tasted it; thus one of these: "Hujus spiritualis et occulti mannæ sapor latet in occulto, nisi gustando sentiatur." I take it, however, that this "*hidden manna*" represents a more central benefit even than these; moreover, like all the other promises of these Epistles, it represents a benefit pertaining to the future kingdom of glory, and not to the present kingdom of grace. I would not indeed affirm that this promise has not prelibations which will be tasted in the present time; for the life eternal commences on this side of the grave, and not first on the other; and here in the wilderness Christ is the bread from heaven, the bread of God, the true manna, of which those that eat shall never die (John vi. 31-33, 48-51). Nay, more than this; since his Ascension He is in some sort a "*hidden manna*" for them now. Like that manna laid up in the Sanctuary before the Testimony, He too, withdrawn from sight, but in a human body, and bearing our flesh, is yet exempted from the law of corruption under which all other children of men have lain (Exod. xvi. 20, 33, 34; Acts ii. 27, 31). But this promise of feeding on "*the hidden manna*" is misunderstood, or at any rate is scanted of its full meaning, unless we look on to something more and higher than this. The words imply that, however hidden now, it shall not remain hidden evermore; and the best commentary on them is to be found at 1 Cor. ii. 9;[1] 1 John iii. 2. The seeing Christ as He is, of the latter passage, and through this beatific vision being made like to Him, is identical with this eating of the hidden manna; which shall, as it were, be then brought forth from the sanctuary, the Holy of Holies of God's immediate presence, where it was withdrawn from sight so long, that all may partake of it; the glory of Christ, now shrouded and concealed, being then revealed to his people.

There has been, and there will be again, occasion to observe, that in almost all these promises there is a peculiar adaptation of the promise to the self-denial by which it will have been won. Witsius notes this here, and draws out very beautifully the inner sweetness of this promise (*Miscell. Sacra*, vol. i. p. 692): "Eas [profanas epulas] si quis gen-

[1] Alcuin: "Apte ergo illa satietas celestis gloriæ manna [absconditum?] vocatur, quia juxta Pauli vocem nec oculus vidit, nec in cor hominis ascendit, quæ præparavit Deus diligentibus se."

erosâ fidei constantiâ, una cum omnibus blandientis seculi deliciis atque illiciis fortiter spreverit, sciat se satiatum iri suavissimis divinæ tam gratiæ quam gloriæ epulis, quorum suavitatem nemo rite æstimare novit, nisi qui gustavit. Propterea autem *mannæ absconditæ* comparantur, id est, illi quæ in urnâ aureâ in abdito loco asservanda, coram facie Jehovæ seposita fuit, I. Quia quod præcipuum est in illâ dulcedinis Christi participatione reservatur cum Christo in cœlis (Col. iii. 3; 2 Tim. i. 12). II. Quia mundanorum hominum nemo dulcedinem hujus novit (Joh. xiv. 17); immo ne ipsi fideles quidem antequam experiantur (1 Joh. iii. 2). III. Quia communio ista non in diem est, uti manna quotidiana, sed perpetua, uti illa quæ seposita coram Domino a putrefactione et vermibus immunis erat (Joh. vi. 27), et propterea profanis Pergamensium epulis immensum anteferenda."

"*And will give him a white stone, and in the stone a new name written, which no man knoweth saving he that receiveth it.*"—"*White*" is every where the colour and livery of heaven; and nowhere with a greater or so great an emphasis, or with so frequent iteration, as in this Book. Thus of the Son of God we were told, "His head and his hairs were *white* like wool, as *white* as snow" (i. 14). Then besides this "*white* stone" we have "*white* raiment" (iii. 5), "*white* robes" (vii. 9), "a *white* cloud" (xiv. 14), "fine linen clean and *white*" (xix. 8, 14), "*white* horses" (xix. 11, 14), "a great *white* throne" (xx. 11). With these passages compare Dan. vii. 9; Matt. xvii. 2; xxviii. 3; Mark ix. 3; xvi. 5; John xx. 12; Acts i. 10. The sense of the fitness of white to serve as a symbol of absolute purity speaks out in many ways; it would do so singularly in the Latin "castus," if Döderlein's suggestion that "castus" is a participle of "candeo" could be allowed. It may be well to observe that this "*white*" as the colour of heaven, is not the mere absence of other colour, not the dull "albus," but the bright "candidus;" glistering white—as is evident from many passages; for instance, from a comparison of Matt. xxviii. 3 and Luke xxiv. 4 with John xx. 12; of Rev. xx. 11 (λευκὸς θρόνος) with its original in Daniel vii. 9 (θρόνος αὐτοῦ φλὸξ πυρός); and from those passages just now referred to, which relate to the Transfiguration. It is the character of intense white to be shining; thus "niteo" (= "niviteo") is connected with "nix;" λευκός with "lux," see Donaldson, *New Cratylus*, § 269. We may note too how λευκός and λαμπρός are used as convertible terms, Rev. xix. 8, 14; while at Acts x. 30, λευκῇ and λαμπρᾷ are different readings; and at Cant. v. 11, the Septuagint has λευκός, and Symmachus λαμπρός.

And as "*white*," so also "*new*" belongs eminently to this Book; being one of the key-words of it; He who is the giver of this revelation every where setting forth Himself as the only renewer of all which sin had made old; the author of a new creation even in the midst of a decaying and dying world; and thus we have besides the "*new* name" here (cf. iii. 12), the "*new* Jerusalem" (iii. 12), the "*new* song" (v. 9), the "*new* heaven and the *new* earth" (xxi. 1), and finally "all things *new*" (xxi. 5); with all which we may profitably compare Ps. xxxii. 3; cxliii. 10; Isai. xlii. 10; lxii. 2; lxv. 17; Jer. xxxi. 31; Ezek. xi. 19; xxxvi. 26.

But though it is not difficult to fix the symbolic significance of "*white*" and "*new*" in this Book, it must be freely admitted that we still wait an entirely satisfactory explanation of this "*white stone*" with the "*new name*" written in it. The greater number of expositors, especially the older ones, start from a point to which no objection can be made, namely, that there was in ancient times something festal, fortunate, of good omen, in white pebbles or beans. Thus the Greek phrase λευκὴ ἡμέρα, or λευκὸν ἦμαρ (Æschylus, *Pers.* 305), is commonly derived from a custom ascribed to the Scythians or Thracians, of indicating each happy day which they spent with a white stone placed in an urn, each unhappy with a black. After death, as those or these preponderated in number, their lives were counted happy or miserable (Pliny, *H. N.* vii. 41; the Younger Pliny, *Ep.* vi. 11; Martial ix. 53: "Dies nobis Signandi melioribus lapillis"). Or there is another explanation of the "white day," connecting it still with the white stone or bean, I mean that given by Plutarch in his *Life of Pericles*, c. 64; I quote the translation of North. At the siege of Samos, fearing that his soldiers would be weary with its length, "he divided his army into eight companies, whom he made to draw lots, and that company which lighted upon the white bean, they should be quiet and make good cheer, while the other seven fought. And they say that from thence it came that when any have made good cheer, and taken pleasure abroad, they do yet call it a white day, because of the white bean."

But how, it may be asked, is all this brought to bear on the promise of the "*white stone*" to the faithful here? The earliest attempt to find help in this quarter is that of the Greek commentator Andreas. He sees allusion in these words to the white pebble, by placing which in the ballot-box the Greek judges pronounced the sentence of acquittal (*ψῆφοι σώζουσαι* they were therefore called), as by the black of condemnation; a custom expressed in the well-known lines of Ovid (*Metam.* xv. 41, 42):

"Mos erat antiquus, niveis atrisque lapillis,
His damnare reos, illis absolvere culpæ."

But, not to speak of a grave fault, of which I shall presently speak, common to this and almost every other explanation of these words which is offered, this one is manifestly inadequate; the absolving pebble was not *given to* the acquitted, as this is to the victor, nor was there any name written upon it.

Others see allusion to the *tessera* (it too was called ψῆφος) which the conquerors at the Olympic or other solemn games (the ὀλυμπιονῖκαι, ἱερονῖκαι) received from the master of the games; which ψῆφος gave ever after to him who received it certain honorary distinctions and privileges, as for example, the right of free access to the public entertainments. So Arethas, Gerhard (*Loci Theoll.* vol. ii. p. 327), and others; while Vitringa is obliged to confess that he can only explain the symbol by combining together these two customs of the absolving pebble, and the *tessera* given to the victor in the games; which two in the higher interpretation must be blended into one: "Ut tamen verum fatear, probabile videri possit Dominum orationem suam hoc loco ita temperâsse, ut non ad simplicem aliquem ritum, apud Græcos receptum, hic loci alluserit, sed phrasin suam mutuatus sit a duobus illis ritibus supra commemoratis, inter se compositis, qui licet diversi fuerint generis, in tertio tamen, quod dicitur, inter se conveniebant."

But all these explanations, and others which it would be tedious to enumerate, even if they were more satisfactory, and they appear to me most unsatisfactory, are affected with the same fatal weakness, namely, that they are borrowed from *heathen* antiquity, while this Book moves exclusively within the circle of sacred, that is, of Jewish, imagery and symbols; nor is the explanation of its symbols in any case to be sought beyond this circle. All which on this matter was said in respect of the "*crown of life*" (ii. 10) finds its application here. It is true that Hengstenberg, whose interpretation I have not yet mentioned, avoids this mistake, but at a cost which leaves his as valueless as the others. For him the "*white stone*" has no significance of its own, no independent value, being introduced merely for the sake of the "*new name*" which is written upon it, and that it may serve as a vehicle for this name, the substrate on which that is superinduced, and as such entirely subordinate to it. Few, I am persuaded, reading the words of the promise, with the emphasis which the Lord lays on the twice-repeated mention of the stone, and noting the independent place which it occupies as itself a gift, whatever other gifts might be associated with it, will be content to acquiesce in this, or to regard as a solution, what is in fact merely an evasion, of the difficulty which the words present.

But to return. The first necessary condition of any interpretation which should be accepted as satisfactory being this, that it should be sacred and not heathen, at the same time this is not the only one. There appear to me two other necessary conditions, the non-fulfilment of which is fatal to any exposition; the fulfilment of them, on the contrary, not being itself a proof that the right interpretation has been seized; but only a *conditio sine quâ non*, and up to a certain point implying a probability that this has been attained. Besides thus being Jewish or sacred, and not heathen or profane, which I believe is the universal law of all Apocalyptic symbolism, the solution must in this particular instance refer to the wilderness period of Jewish history, in the same way as the "*hidden manna*" does. I must ask the reader to suspend his demand for a proof of this assertion till we have reached the very last of the promises, when the course and order of them all will be considered. And, in the second place, it must be capable of being brought into some unity with that other promise of eating of the hidden manna; there must be some bond of connexion between the two. I conclude this not merely from the natural fitness of things, but from the analogy of all the other promises made to the other Churches. In every other case the promise is either absolutely single, as at ii. 7, 11; iii. 21; or single in its central idea, as at ii. 26-28; iii. 5, 12, which I shall have the opportunity of showing. Which thing being so, it is very improbable that the present should be an exception to the rule, and that here two entirely disparate promises should be arbitrarily linked together.

The only solution I know which fulfils all these conditions, is one proposed by Züllig.[1] It has found no favour whatever, having been indeed wrought out by him in a manner of itself sufficient to insure its rejection. Fully acknowledging my obligation to him for the original suggestion of it, and for some of the arguments by which it is supported, I must yet claim to set it forth independently of him, nor is he in any respect responsible for my statement of it.

Starting then from a reconsideration of the word ψῆφος, this, it may be observed, is sometimes used in the later Greek for a *precious* stone; thus ψῆφος δακτυλική, the gem in a seal-ring. Neither is there in the epithet λευκός, not "albus" but "candidus," anything which renders this unlikely here, but rather the contrary; a diamond, for instance, being of the purest glistering white. The

[1] *Offenb. Johannis*, vol. i. pp. 408-454.

ψῆφος λευκή then may be, not what we commonly begin with taking for granted it must be, a white pebble, but a precious stone shining white, a diamond. But may not the mysterious Urim and Thummim have been exactly this? First, let me observe, by way of preoccupying a difficulty on the threshold, that whatever this may have been, it was not two things, but two names for one and the same thing (see Bähr, *Symbolik d. Mos. Cult.* vol. ii. pp. 109, 110); often therefore called only the Urim (Num. xxvii. 21; 1 Sam. xxviii. 6). Sparing my readers the learning which might easily be transcribed to any amount from the many elaborate treatises devoted to the question what this Urim and Thummim was, let me state the conclusions to which those who have studied the matter most profoundly have arrived. They are agreed that it was some precious thing which the High Priest bore within the *Choschen* or square breastplate of judgment, this being doubled back upon itself, to the end that like a purse it might contain the treasure committed to it (Exod. xxviii. 15-30; Lev. viii. 8), and with all its costly jewellery and elaborate workmanship existing for this object, quite as much as the ark for the tables of the law. But what precious thing this Urim was is shrouded in mystery; only as that in the purse, that for which the purse was made, is likely to have been *more* precious than the purse itself, if that was set with its twelve precious stones, each with the name of a tribe engraven on it, in this we are led to look for a stone rarer and more costly than them all; and it is certainly very noticeable that among the twelve stones of the breastplate the diamond does not appear; for the mention of it in our Version (Exod. xxviii. 18) is confessedly a mistake;—as though this stone had been reserved for a higher honour and dignity still.

Then further, no one knows, probably no one ever knew, what was written on the Urim; except indeed the High Priest; who, consulting it that he might in some way obtain through it lively oracles from God, in matters which greatly concerned the weal or woe of the people, could not have remained ignorant of this. It is generally conjectured, however, to have been the holy Tetragrammaton; the ineffable name of God. I need hardly ask the reader who has followed me thus far to note how well this agrees with the words before us, "*and in the stone a new name written, which no man knoweth saving he that receiveth it.*" Many indeed are led away from the right interpretation of these last words, by referring this "*receiveth it,*" to the "*name,*" and not to the "*stone;*" "*saving he that receiveth this name,*"—when, as I feel sure, we ought to understand it, "*saving he that receiveth this stone.*" They assume the overcomer's own name to be that written on this stone; and draw from these words an intimation that, just as the mystery of regeneration is known only to the new-born, so the yet higher glory of heaven only to him that is partaker of it (1 Cor. xiii. 9); which all is most true, and a new name is often used to express a new blessedness (Isai. lxii. 2; lxv. 15); but yet it is not the truth, I am persuaded, of the present words. The "*new name*" here is something even better than this. It is the new name of God or of Christ, "*my new name*" (iii. 12), some revelation of the glory of God, only in that higher state capable of being communicated by Him to his people, and which they only can understand who have actually received; for it is a knowing which is identical with a being.

How excellently well the promise, so understood, matches with the other promise of the hidden manna, which goes hand in hand with it. I said at the outset of this inquiry, that there ought to be an inner bond between the two parts of the promise, and such, according to this interpretation, there is. "*The hidden manna*" and the "*white stone*" are not merely united in time, belonging both to the wilderness period of the history of God's people; but they are united as both representing high-priestly privileges, which the Lord should at length impart to all his people, kings and priests to God, as He will then have made them all. If any should eat of "*the hidden manna*," who but the High Priest, who alone had entrance into the Holy Place where it was laid up? If any should have knowledge of what was graven on the Urim, who but the same High Priest, in whose keeping it was, and who was bound by his very office to consult it? The mystery of what was written there, shut to every other, would be open to him. In lack of any more satisfying explanation of the "*white stone*;" with the "*new name*" written upon it, I venture to suggest that the key to it may possibly be here.

IV.

EPISTLE TO THE CHURCH OF THYATIRA.

Rev. ii. 18-29.

Ver. 18. "*And unto the Angel of the Church in Thyatira write.*"—The Roman road from Pergamum to Sardis left Thyatira, as we are told by Strabo (xiii. 4), a little to the left; St. John is led in the Spirit by the same route which he may often in time past have travelled in the course of his apostolic visitations. Thyatira, a city of no first-rate dignity, was a Macedonian colony (Strabo, xiii. 4); and it may be looked at as a slight and unintentional confirmation, in a minute particular, of the veracity of the Acts, that Lydia, a purple-seller of Thyatira, is met exactly in the Macedonian city of Philippi (Acts xvi. 14), being precisely that which was likely to happen from the close and frequent intercourse maintained between a mother city and its daughter colonies. From this Lydia, whose heart the Lord had opened to attend to the things spoken of Paul, the Church at Thyatira may have taken its beginnings; she who had gone forth for a while, to buy and sell and get gain, when she returned home may have brought home with her richer merchandise than any she had looked to obtain.

"*These things saith the Son of God, who hath his eyes like unto a flame of fire, and his feet are like fine brass.*"—The attributes which the Lord claims are again drawn from the description of the first chapter, ver. 14, 15, which see. The title "*Son of God*" (cf. xix. 13) is not indeed expressly and in so many words there; but it is involved in, and is the sum total of the impression left by the whole description. The actual form of this title is here drawn from the second Psalm, ver. 9, as is plain from more than one reference to that Psalm before this Epistle is ended; thus, compare ver. 26 with Ps. ii. 8; and ver. 27 with ii. 9. He who will presently give dominion to his servants, first claims it for Himself. The heathen have been given to Him for an inheritance, else He could not give them to his servants. If they are to rule them with a rod of iron, and break them in pieces like a potter's vessel, it is only as partakers in a power which He has Himself first received.

Ver. 19. "*I know thy works, and charity, and service, and faith, and thy patience, and thy works; and the last to be more than the first.*"—Omit "*and thy works*" on its second occurrence, which has no right to a place in the text, and which mars the symmetry of all. We shall then have two pairs, —first, "*thy charity and thy service*," for the article prefixed to all these words shows that the concluding σοῦ belongs to them all,—the "*charity*," or love, being the more inward thing, the "*service*" (διακονία) the outward ministrations, the helps of all kind shown first to the household of faith, and then to all others, in which this "*charity*" found its utterance (Acts xi. 29; 1 Cor. xvi. 15; 2 Cor. xii. 9; Heb. vi. 10). As the first pair have a very close inner connexion, so have also the next pair, "*thy faith and thy patience*." It needs but to refer in proof to Heb. xi. 27: "He endured, as seeing Him that is invisible;" and indeed Scripture everywhere declares that faith is the root and source of all patient continuance in well-doing.—"*And the last to be more than the first*." The faithful in Thyatira were growing and increasing in this service of love, this patience of faith; herein satisfying the desire of Him, who evermore desires for his people that they should abound more and more in all good things. How much better this τὰ ἔσχατα πλείονα τῶν πρώτων than that of which St. Peter elsewhere speaks as the state of some, τὰ ἔσχατα χείρονα τῶν πρώτων (2 Ep. ii. 20; cf. Matt. xii. 45), which, as regards the most excellent grace of all, the Lord has just declared to be the state of the Ephesian Church (ver. 4).

Ver. 20. "*Notwithstanding I have a few things against thee, because thou sufferest that woman Jezebel, which calleth herself a prophetess, to teach and to seduce my servants to commit fornication, and to eat things sacrificed unto idols.*"—Omit "*a few things*" (ὀλίγα), which has no business in the text, changing, as a consequence of this, "*because*" into "*that*"—but do not change "*that woman*" into "*thy wife*" (τὴν γυναῖκά σου), the authority for the insertion of σοῦ being insufficient to justify this. The whole condition of things at Thyatira was exactly the reverse of what it was at Ephesus. There much zeal for orthodoxy, and for the maintenance of sound doctrine, but little love, and as a consequence, no doubt, few ministrations of love. Here the activity of faith and love; but insufficient zeal for the maintenance of godly discipline and doctrine, a patience of error even where there was not a participation in it. Each of these Churches was weak in that wherein the other was strong.

But whom shall we understand by "*that woman Jezebel, which calleth herself a prophetess,*" whom the Lord proceeds presently to threaten with so terrible a doom? It will be expedient here to consider first the position which the literal and historic Jezebel occupies in the history of the Church of the Old

Testament. As Balaam, in the earlier history of the children of Israel, was the author of the great attempt to introduce heathenism with all its train of attendant impurities into the heart of the Church of God (Rev. ii. 14; Num. xxv.), so Jezebel in the later period of that same history. She was a daughter of Ethbaal, king of Sidon (1 Kings xvi. 13). The identity of this Ethbaal and *Εἰθώβαλος*, mentioned in a fragment of the *Tyrian Annals* of Menander, preserved by Josephus (*Con. Apion.* i. 18), is sufficiently made out, and is not, I believe, called in question by any. Of him then we there learn that he was priest of Astarte, and, by the murder of his predecessor Pheles, made his own way to the throne and kingdom. Jezebel, so swift to shed blood (1 Kings xviii. 4; xix. 2; xxi. 10), is a worthy offshoot of this evil stock. Nor less does she attest herself the daughter of the priest of Astarte. Hitherto the worship of the Calves had been the extent of the departure of the Ten Tribes from the Levitical institutions,—the true God worshipped still, the law of Moses in the main allowed and kept, however there might be a certain amount of sinful will-worship mingling with and spoiling all. But from the time of Ahab's marriage with the daughter of Ethbaal the apostasy of Israel assumes altogether a different character; the guilt of it is of quite another and an infinitely deadlier kind

(1 Kings xvi. 31; xxi. 25, 26). A fanatical promoter of the Baal worship (1 Kings xviii. 19), overbearing with her stronger will the weak will of her despicable husband, animated with the fiercest hatred against the prophets of Jehovah, the last witnesses for Him in Israel, now that the Levitical priesthood had been abolished there (1 Kings xxi. 31), she seeks utterly to exterminate these (1 Kings xviii. 13). She was probably herself, like her moral namesake here, a false prophetess; a priestess of that foul enthusiasm. Many arguments might be adduced to make this probable at the least. As much seems implied in Jehu's answer to Joram's question, "Is it peace?" "What peace, so long as the whoredoms of thy mother Jezebel, and *her witchcrafts* are so many" (2 Kings ix. 22)? While, again, when we keep in mind the essentially impure character of the Phœnician idolatries which she introduced,—Ashtaroth or Astarte was the Phœnician Aphrodite,—we have an explanation of the "whoredoms" which Jehu further lays to her charge, and which may thus have set an hideous contradiction between her and her name, if indeed that derivation which would make it etymologically to signify The Chaste (our *Agnes*) is the true one. Nor is this the only passage where these impurities are ascribed to her. There is at Jeremiah iv. 30 an allusion, often overlooked, but, so soon as attention is called to it, not

to be gainsaid, to 2 Kings ix. 30; and there the lovers or paramours of Jezebel appear.

Such was the elder Jezebel. And the later, assuredly not a sect of evil-workers personified, but some single wicked woman in the Church of Thyatira, inheriting from her this name of infamy in the Church of God, would seem to have followed hard in the steps of her Jewish prototype (for a like transfer of an evil name see Isai. i. 10). She gave herself out for a prophetess, and in one sense probably was so,—no mere *teacher* of perverse things, employing her intellectual faculties in the service of Satan, and not of God; but claiming inspiration, and probably possessing it, wielding spiritual powers, only they were such as reached her from beneath, not such as descended on her from above; for as at this time miraculous gifts of grace and power were at work in the Church, so were also their counterparts. And thus, by aid of these, she seduced the servants of Christ "*to commit fornication, and to eat things sacrificed to idols;*" see ver. 14. The attempt to restrain "*servants*" here to those who hold office in the Church is certainly a mistake. *Δοῦλος* may very well have this narrower meaning at i. 1; but that δοῦλοι includes the whole body of the faithful at vii. 3; xxii. 3, is evident. A comparison of this verse with ver. 14-16 leaves no doubt that the Jezebelites, and Balaamites, and Nicolaitans, with secondary differences no doubt, were yet substantially the same;—all libertine sects, disclaiming the obligations of the moral law; all starting with a denial that Jesus Christ was come in the flesh, and that in the flesh therefore men were to be holy; false spiritualists, whose high pretensions did not hinder them from ending in the foulest fleshly sins.

Ver. 21. "*And I gave her space to repent of her fornication, and she repented not.*"—The fact that punishment does not at once overtake sinners is constantly perverted by them as an evidence that it never will overtake them (Eccl. viii. 11; Isai. xxvi. 10; Ps. xxvi. 11); that God does not see, or, seeing, does not care to avenge. Christ opens out here another aspect under which this delay in the divine revenges may be regarded. The very time during which ungodly men are heaping up for themselves greater wrath against the day of wrath, was a time lent them for repentance (Rom. ii. 4; 2 Pet. iii. 9), if only they would have understood the object and the meaning of it.

Ver. 22. "*Behold, I will cast her into a bed, and them that commit adultery with her into great tribulation, except they repent of their deeds.*"—These last words imply that even now the day of grace was not expired for these transgressors, however near at hand the close of it might be. "*I will cast her into a bed;*"[1] there where she has sinned shall she also be punished (cf. 1 Kings xxi. 19); the bed of sin shall be the bed of languishing, of sickness, and of death. The allusion which Vitringa traces here to the bed on which Ahab cast himself down heavy and displeased (1 Kings xxi. 4) is ingenious, but exceedingly far-fetched.

Ver. 23. "*And I will kill her children with death.*"—If her lovers, those "*that commit adultery with her*" (ver. 22), can only mean the chief furtherers and abettors of those evil things (she may have seduced them to fleshly as well as spiritual wickedness), "*her children*" must be rather the less prominent, less forward members of the same wicked company, more the deceived, while the others were the deceivers (Isai. lvii. 3), who yet should be overtaken with those others in a common doom (Ezek. xxiii. 47). The words "*with death*" must plainly be accepted as emphatic;

[1] A curious testimony to the entire disappearance of Greek, and of the power of appealing to Greek copies of Scripture, probably to the total absence of Greek copies in Western Europe to appeal to, and the consequent exclusive dependence on the Vulgate, occurs here in the Commentary of Richard of St. Victor, one of the most learned men of perhaps the most learned monastic foundation in France. He observes that some copies here read 'lectum,' some 'luctum;' discusses at length the relative advantages and probabilities of the two readings, without a word implying the possibility of settling the question at once by a glance at the original.

some understand, with pestilence and plague (see Jer. xxi. 7), relying mainly on Rev. vi. 8; which, however, is insufficient to bear out this view, seeing that θάνατος in that passage itself cannot be proved to mean this; a reference to 2 Sam. xxiv. 13, 15, LXX. would be more to the point. Hengstenberg detects an allusion to the death of the adulteress (Lev. xx. 10; cf. John viii. 5); but this can scarcely be; for it is the "*children*" of the adulteress, not the adulteress herself, who are here threatened with death. Others find a reference to the two sweeping catastrophies which overtook the Baal priests and votaries at exactly that period of Jewish history to which the mention of Jezebel here points (1 Kings xviii. 40; 2 Kings x. 25). To me it seems no more than a threat that their doom should be a signal one, that they should not die the common death of all men, nor be visited after the visitation of all men (Num. xvi. 29), but leaving the precise manner of that doom undefined.

"*And all the Churches shall know that I am He which searcheth the reins and hearts.*"—The judgment on this brood of transgressors shall be so open and manifest, their sin shall so plainly find them out, that, not the wicked, for God's judgments are far above out of their sight, whether those judgments overtake themselves or others, but "*all the Churches,*" all who ponder these things and lay them to heart, shall confess that He who moves up and down in the midst of his Church, beholding the evil and the good, is a God of knowledge (see ii. 2), who is not mocked; "*which searcheth the reins and hearts*" (ταῖς ἐννοίαις ἐμβατεύων, as Olympiodorus explains it),—"*the reins*" being regarded as the seat of the passions, "*the heart*" of the affections; cf. Jer. xvii. 10; xx. 12. But this searching of the hearts and reins being, as it is, a prerogative of Deity (Mark ii. 8), God only knowing the hearts of men (ὁ καρδιογνώστης Θεός, Acts xv. 8; i. 24; 1 Chron. xxix. 17), it is plain that Christ, claiming this to Himself, is implicitly claiming to be God.—Ἐρευνᾶν is used in this same sense of searching, Rom. viii. 27, and always expresses a *careful* investigation, a following up of tracks or indications as far as they will lead, as the dog the footprints of the chase, the miner the veins of the metal (Gen. xxxi. 35; 1 Kings xx. 6; Prov. xx. 27; 1 Cor. ii. 10; 1 Pet. i. 11). Expressing, as the word does, this laborious and even painful investigation, leading step by step to its result, it, in the same way as every other *discursive* act, can only ἀνθρωποπαθῶς be ascribed to God; to whom by absolute and immediate intuition all hearts at all times lie open and manifest; who needs not to search out, and in this way to find, that which He always knows. For ἐρευνῶν the Septuagint Translators prefer ἐτάζων (Ps. vii. 10; 1 Chron. xxix. 17; Ps. cxxxviii. 22; Jer. xvii. 10), which does not occur in the New Testament.

"*And I will give unto every one of you according to your works.*"—This promise, or this threat, for it may be either, is one which we commonly keep at this time too much in the background; but it is one which we should press on ourselves and on others with the same emphasis wherewith Christ and his Word presses it upon us all (Ps. lxii. 13; Matt. xvi. 27; Rom. ii. 6; Job xxxiv. 11; Prov. xxiv. 12; Jer. xxii. 19). It is indeed one of the gravest mischiefs which Rome has bequeathed to us, that in a reaction and protest, itself absolutely necessary, against the false emphasis which she put on works, unduly thrusting them in to share with Christ's merits in our justification, we often fear to place upon them the true; being as they are, to speak with St. Bernard, the "via regni," however little the "causa regnandi;" though here too it must of course never be forgotten that it is only the good tree which brings forth good fruit; and that no tree is good until Christ has made it so.

Ver. 24. "*But unto you I say, and unto the rest in Thyatira, as many as have not this doctrine, and which have not known the depths of Satan, as they speak; I will put upon you none other burden.*"—Leave out the καί with which the second clause in this sentence begins, and read, "*But unto you I say, the rest in Thyatira*, &c." The Gnostics, starting probably from 1 Cor. ii. 10, were ever boasting their acquaintance with mysteries, the deep things of God; could speak much about the βυθός, "vere cæcutientes, qui profunda Bythi adinvenisse se dicunt" (Irenæus; cf. Tertullian, *Adv. Valentin.* § 1). A question is often here raised, whether these evil-workers spoke of "*depths of Satan;*" or only of "*depths*," while "*of Satan*" is a further characteristic of these "*depths*," added by the Lord Himself; who thus intimates with a keen irony what was the real character of those "*depths*" into which they professed themselves to have entered, and into which they sought to guide others. In this last way the words are generally understood, the Lord declaring what, in his all-seeing eye, was the true nature of the μεγαλοῤῥημοσύναι (such Ignatius, *Ep. ad Ephes.* 10, calls them), the "great swelling words of vanity" which these Gnostics vented; promising liberty to others, being themselves servants of corruption. I should be disposed, however, to think with Hengstenberg, that it was they themselves who talked of "*depths of Satan*,"—the position of ὡς λέγουσι seems to imply as much,—that in that fearful sophistry wherein they were such adepts, and whereby they sought to make a religion of every corrupt inclination of the natural mind, they talked much of "*depths of Satan*," which it was expedient for them to fathom. We know concerning them how they taught that it was a small thing for a man to despise pleasure and to show himself superior to it, while at the same time he fled from it. The true, the glorious victory was, to remain superior to it, even while tasting it to the full; to give the body to all the lusts of the flesh, and yet with all this to maintain the spirit in a region of its own, uninjured by them; and thus, as it were, to fight against pleasure with the arms of pleasure itself; to mock and defy Satan even in his own kingdom and domain. We have an anticipation of this sophistry of sin, with its flatteries at once of the pride and corruption of the human heart, in the well-known *mot* of Aristippus, the Cyrenian philosopher, who being upbraided on the score of his relations with a Corinthian courtesan, defended himself with the reply, difficult adequately to render in English, *Ἔχω Λαΐδα, οὐκ ἔχομαι ὑπ' αὐτῆς* (Clemens Alex. *Strom.* ii. 20). Here, however, were but the germs of that which in some of the Gnostics appears fully blown.

"For you," says the Lord, "who have not gone to this Satanic school, who have been content with the simple knowledge of the good, and not thought it needful to know the evil as well, not good and evil, but only good, *I will put upon you none other burden*." If it be asked, "*none other burden*" than what?—the answer no doubt is, none other than a continued abstinence from, and protest against, these abominations. It was the master-stroke of the antinomian Gnostics to exaggerate, to distort, to misapply, all which St. Paul had spoken about the freedom of the Christian man from the law. They were the ultra-Paulines, who caricatured his doctrine, till of God's truth they had made a devil's lie. St. Paul had said of the law that it was not the ground of the Christian man's justification, nor yet the source of his holiness; they made him to say that it was not the rule of his life; as though he had rejected it altogether as a burden no longer to be borne by the redeemed. The Lord takes up this word "*burden;*"—"I do lay on you a burden, but it is a burden which it is your blessedness to bear, and over and above which I will impose no other." Compare Matt. xi. 30, where, however, *φορτίον*, not *βάρος*, stands in the original, and Acts xv. 28, 29, where *βάρος* occurs in this very sense of abstinence from idol-meats and fornication; and where exactly in the same sense, and almost in the same words, the Apostles declare that they will lay on the faithful of the Gentiles "no greater burden than these necessary things."

Ver. 25. "*But that which ye have already hold fast till I come.*"—It is on this condition that He will impose on them no additional burden. What they have of sound doctrine, of holy living, this they must hold fast, must so grasp it that none shall wrest it from them, till the day when the Lord shall come, and bring this long and painful struggle for the maintenance of his truth to an end. Ever and ever in Scripture, not the day of death, but the day of the Lord Jesus, is put as the term of all conflict.

Ver. 26. "*And he that overcometh, and keepeth my works unto the end, to him will I give power over the nations.*"—By "*my works*" we must understand, "works which I have commanded, in which I find pleasure, which are the fruit of my Spirit;" cf. John vi. 27, where "works of God" are to be understood in the same sense as "godly works." Here again that which is praised, that which will be crowned, is the keeping of these his works to the end; for Christ, the great ἐπιστάτης in the games, of which the Father is the ἀγωνοθέτης, and, still to keep the language of Tertullian, the Holy Ghost the ξυστάρχης, eternal life the βραβεῖον, promises here this reward, not to him who enters the lists and endures for a time, but to him who, having begun well, continues striving lawfully to the last. "*To him will I give power over the nations*." The royalties of Christ shall by reflection and communication be the royalties also of his Church. They shall reign; but only because Christ reigns, and because He is pleased to share his dignity with them (iii. 21; Rom. v. 17; 2 Tim. ii. 12). When we ask ourselves in what sense, at what time, and in what form this "*power over the nations*" shall be the prerogative of the Church, we must find our answer in such passages as Rev. xx. 4; xxii. 5; 1 Cor. vi. 2; Ps. cxlix. 9, 6; and above all Matt. xix. 28.; cf. also Wisd. iii. 8.

Ver. 27. "*And he shall rule them with a rod of iron; as the vessels of a potter shall they be broken to shivers*."—As this is a dignity which is originally Christ's (Ps. ii. 9; Rev. xii. 5; xix. 15), and only by Him made over to his servants, it is needful first to inquire what it means in respect of Him; and we may then understand what it means in respect of them. The passage in the second Psalm is no doubt that on which the three in this Book repose. It is there, "Thou shalt *break* them with a rod of iron;" but this Book throughout is in agreement with the Septuagint, "Thou shalt *rule* [ποιμανεῖς] them with a rod of iron." The Hebrew words for "Thou shalt break" and "Thou shalt rule" only differ in their vowels; their consonants are identical; at the same time the parallelism of the latter half of the verse, "Thou shalt dash them in pieces like a potter's vessel," leaves no doubt that "Thou shalt break" was the intention of the Psalmist. Shall we therefore conclude not merely that the Septuagint Translators mistook, which happens too frequently to be a matter to us of any serious wonder, but that the Lord set his seal to their error? Not so; He indeed accepts the pregnant and significant variation which they, intentionally or unintentionally, drew out of the language before them; and which was justified by the root common to both words; and instead of the mere unmingled judgment which lay in the passage as it originally stood in that Psalm, He expresses by it now judgment mingled with mercy, judgment behind which purposes of grace are concealed, and only waiting their due time to appear. Such a *παιδευτικὴ ἐνέργεια*, as Theodoret terms it, must be recognized in the *ποιμαίνειν*; which our "*Thou shalt rule*," and the Latin "reges," only imperfectly give back; as, in regard of the Latin, Hilary (*in Ps.* ii.) urged long ago: "Reges eos in virgâ ferreâ; quanquam ipsum *reges* non tyrannicum neque injustum sit, sed ex æquitatis ac moderationis arbitrio regimen rationale demonstret, tamen molliorem adhuc regentis affectum proprietas, Græca significat. Quod enim nobiscum est, *reges eos*, cum illis est *ποιμανεῖς αὐτούς*, id est, *pastoraliter* reges, regendi scilicet eos curam affectu pastoris habiturus." For a still tenderer use of *ποιμαίνειν* see John xxi. 16; Acts xx. 28. I do not in the least mean to affirm that the words do not contain a threat for the nations; but it is a threat of love. Christ shall rule them with a sceptre of iron to make them capable of being ruled with a sceptre of gold; severity first, that grace may come after; they are broken in pieces, that they may know themselves to be but men; that, their fierceness and pride being brought down, they may accept the yoke of Christ (Ps. lxxxiii. 16). And indeed how often the great tribulations of a people have been the *προπαιδεία*, through which the Son of God has broken their pride, and made them capable of receiving his gospel, which, but for this, they would in their presumption and self-confidence have rejected to the end.

Our Translators have only rendered *ῥάβδος* by 'sceptre' on a single occasion in the New Testament (Heb. i. 8). It were to be wished they had done so here, and at xii. 5; xix. 15. The word in the second Psalm שֵׁבֶט has this meaning; cf. Ps. xliv. 8, where in like manner it occurs; and every thing else speaking of royalty here, this should do the same. It may be urged, indeed, that royal sceptres are not usually of iron, but of wood overgilded, or of silver, or of gold. This may be quite true, but, if so, only makes more striking the exception in the present instance. "*He shall rule them with a sceptre of iron*," which, harder and stronger than any other, shall dash them who oppose themselves to it in pieces like a potter's vessel; this image implying the ease with which all resistance shall be overcome, the utter destruction which shall overtake all them who attempt it (Jer. xix. 11; Isai. xxx. 14). Ewald: "Imago regis hostes suos facillimâ operâ conterentis et dispergentis."

"*Even as I received of my Father.*"—There was one who offered to inaugurate Him at once in the possession of all the kingdoms of the world and the glory of them; and the Lord had put back him and his offer with indignation (Luke iv. 5-8), not because these were not his just expectation and his due inheritance; but because He would receive them at no other hands than his Father's. And now we find that He *has* received them at these hands, and they are his; his to impart to his servants; and that which was a lying boast on the lips of the usurper, that he could give them to whom he would, is a truth on the lips of the rightful Lord. Even while upon earth He could say to his own (and the words constitute a very remarkable parallel to these), "I appoint unto you a kingdom, as my Father hath appointed unto Me" (Luke xxii. 29). Richard of St. Victor: "Magna promissio, magnum donum: hoc promittit, hoc tribuit, quod Ipse accepit."

Ver. 28. "*And I will give him the morning star.*"—Compare xxii. 16, where the Lord Himself is "the bright and morning star" (ὁ ἀστὴρ ὁ λαμπρὸς ὁ πρωϊνός). Whether He is meant by "the day-star" (φωσφόρος) of 1 Pet. ii. 19, may be a question. This star, as light-bringer, herald and harbinger of day, goes by many names; it is ἀστὴρ ἑωθινός (Ecclus. l. 6), ὁ ἑωσφόρος ὁ πρωῒ ἀνατέλλων (Isai. xiv. 12, "Lucifer, son of the morning," E. V.), the beauty and transcendant brightness of it being continually celebrated by poets, as by Homer (*Il.* xxii. 317); by Virgil (*Æn.* viii. 389); by Ovid (*Trist.* i. 3. 71: "cœlo nitidissimus alto"), and by Milton (*Par. Lost*, iv. 605:

> "Hesperus, that led
> The starry host, *rode brightest*").

So does the Lord claim all that is fairest and loveliest in creation as the faint shadow and image of his perfections. A comparison with that other passage in this Book referred to already (xxii. 16) conclusively proves that when Christ promises that He will give to his faithful ones the morning star, He promises that He will give to them Himself, that He will impart to them his own glory and a share in his own royal dominion (cf. iii. 21); for the star, as there has been already occasion to observe, is evermore the symbol of royalty (Matt. ii. 2), being therefore linked with the sceptre (Num. xxiv. 17). All the glory of the world shall end in being the glory of the Church, if only this abide faithful to its Lord.

Ver. 29. "*He that hath an ear, let him hear what the Spirit saith unto the Churches.*" Compare ii. 7.

V.

EPISTLE TO THE CHURCH OF SARDIS.

Rev. iii. 1–6.

Ver. 1. "*And unto the Angel of the Church in Sardis write.*"—Sardis, now Sart, was situated on the side of mount Tmolus, and on the river Pactolus. The ancient capital of Lydia, the kingdom of Crœsus, it maintained a certain portion of its old dignity and splendour in the time of the Persians, and had not wholly lost it in the Roman period. For the things in which the Sardians gloried the most, see Tacitus, *Annal.* iv. 55.

"*These things saith He that hath the seven Spirits of God, and the seven stars.*"—There has been already occasion to speak of "*the seven Spirits of God,*" and to claim for these that they in this complex can set forth no other than the one Holy Spirit, the third Person of the ever-blessed Trinity, in his sevenfold operation (i. 4). All that remains then is to consider the relation in which Christ, declaring that it is He "*that hath the seven Spirits of God*," claims to stand to these seven. How entirely He "*hath*" them, by how close a right they are his, may best be understood by the comparison of other words, presently occurring in this same Book; "I beheld a Lamb as it had been slain, having seven horns and seven eyes, which are the seven Spirits of God sent forth into all the earth" (v. 6; cf. Zech. iii. 9; iv. 10). It need hardly be observed how important a witness this verse, when the right interpretation of "*the seven Spirits*" has been seized, bears to the faith of the Western Church on that great point upon which it is at issue with the Eastern, in respect, namely, of the procession of the Holy Ghost. He is indeed the Spirit of the Father *and the Son*. The Son "*hath the seven Spirits*," or the Spirit; not because He has received; for though it is quite true that in the days of his flesh He did receive (Matt. iii. 16; John iii. 34; Heb. i. 9); yet now it is the Son of God, a giver therefore, and not a receiver, who is speaking; who "*hath*" the Spirit; "*hath*" to the end that He may impart it. If, too, the Spirit be admitted to be God, then the Son, who "*hath*" the Spirit, must be God likewise; as is well argued, though not with reference to this particular verse, by Augustine)*De Trin.* xv. 26): "Quomodo Deus non est, qui dat Spiritum Sanctum? Immo quantus Deus est, qui dat Deum?"

There is a special fitness in the assumption of this style by the Lord in his address to the Angel of the Church of Sardis. To him and to his people, sunken in spiritual deadness and torpor, the lamp of faith waning and almost extinguished in their hearts, the Lord presents Himself as one having the fulness of all spiritual gifts; able therefore to revive, able to recover, able to bring back from the very gates of spiritual death, those who would employ the little last remaining strength which they still retained, in calling, even when thus *in extremis*, upon Him.

"*And the seven stars.*"—This is the only approach to a repetition in the titles of the Lord throughout all the Epistles. He has already declared Himself "*He that holdeth the seven stars in his right hand*" (ii. 1), and now "*He that hath the seven stars.*" But "*the seven stars*" are brought there and here into entirely different combinations. There "*He that holdeth the seven stars*" is set forth as the same "*who walketh in the midst of the seven golden candlesticks;*" here "*He that hath the seven Spirits of God*" hath also "*the seven stars.*" But since "*the stars are the Angels of the seven Churches*" (i. 20), we must see in this combination a hint of the relation between Christ, as the giver of the Holy Spirit, and as the author of a ministry of living men in his Church; this ministry of theirs resting wholly on these gifts, even as the connexion between the two is often brought out in the New Testament. Of course the *locus classicus* on this matter is Ephes. iv. 7-12; but compare further John xx. 22, 23; Acts i. 8; xx. 28. His are the golden urns from which these "*stars*" must continually draw their light. They need not fear to be left destitute of his manifold gifts, for his is the Holy Spirit in all his sevenfold operations, with which evermore to furnish them to the full.

"*I know thy works, that thou hast a name that thou livest, and art dead.*"—A passage which at once suggests itself as parallel to this, is 1 Tim. v. 6, where St. Paul, of a woman living in pleasure, says, *ζῶσα τέθνηκε*; and compare, in the same sense, Matt. viii. 22; Luke xv. 24; Rom. vi. 13; Ephes. ii. 1, 5; Heb. vi. 1; ix. 14. Bengel suggests, though indeed earlier commentators had anticipated the suggestion, that the name of this Angel may have contained some assertion of life; which stood in miserable contradiction with the realities of death which the Lord beheld in him; a name therefore which in his case was not the utterance of a truth, but a lie; no *nomen et omen*, but the reverse; the name affirming and implying that he was alive, while in truth he was dead; *Ζώσιμος* would be such a name in Greek, Vitalis in Latin. Hengstenberg considers the suggestion not improbable; it appears to me exceedingly improbable and far-fetched. The use of "*name*" as equivalent to fame, reputation, character, is as common in Greek as in English. The fact that Sardis should have had this name and fame of life is very startling, and may well summon each and all to an earnest heart-searching. There would have been nothing nearly so startling, if Sardis had been counted by the Churches round about as a Church fallen into lethargy and death. But nothing of the kind. Laodicea, we know, deceived herself (iii. 17), but we do not find that she deceived others; counted herself rich, when she *was* most poor; but there is nothing to make us think that others counted her so as well; Sardis, on the other hand, had a name to live, was spoken of, we may well believe, as a model Church, can therefore have been by no means wanting in the outer manifestations of spiritual life; while yet all these shows of life did but conceal the realities of death; so He, before whose eyes of fire no falsehood can endure, too surely saw.

Ver. 2. "*Be watchful, and strengthen the things which remain, that are ready to die.*"—Translate rather, "*Become*" (*what thou art not now*) "*watchful* (*γίνου γρηγορῶν*)." Compare the many passages in which activity or vigilance of spirit is set forth under this same image, often by this same word (Matt. xxiv. 42, 43; xxv. 13; xxvi. 41; Mark xiii. 37; Acts xx. 31; 1 Cor. xiv. 13; 1

Thess. v. 6; 1 Pet. v. 9; Rev. xix. 15). Almost all better commentators are agreed that τὰ λοιπά here should not be rendered "*the things which remain*," "quæ huc usque tibi mansere virtutes" (Ewald); but rather, "*the persons which remain*," or "*the rest*,"=τοὺς λοιπούς, as many as are not yet dead, though now at the point of death. We gather from these words that, with few exceptions, the entire Sardian Church shared in this deadness of its chief pastor; while he, in seeking to revive their life, to chafe their dead limbs, would best revive and recover the warmth of his own (Ps. li. 13). Their present abject and fallen condition is excellently expressed by the use of the neuter; cf. 1 Cor. i. 26; Ezek. xxxiv. 4; Zech. xi. 9; nor indeed need the use of it surprise us, even without the sufficient explanation which this supplies. It is not here only that στηρίζειν is employed in this sense of establishing, confirming in the grace of God; thus compare Luke xxii. 32; Rom. i. 11; 2 Thess. iii. 3; 1 Pet. v. 10; βεβαιοῦν often occurs in the same sense (1 Cor. i. 8; 2 Cor. i. 21; Col. ii. 7); and θεμελιοῦν as well (Eph. iii. 17; Col. i. 23; 1 Pet. v. 10). This command to the Sardian Angel implies that the νεκρὸς εἶ of ver. 1 must not be taken absolutely. The dead can bury their dead; but this is all which they can do; they must be themselves alive, who are bidden to impart a savour of life to others.

The fire of grace may have burned very low in their hearts; but it cannot be quite extinguished; for how in that case could they kindle any flame in others?

"*For I have not found thy works perfect before God.*"—The word here employed is not that which we commonly render "*perfect;*" not τέλεια, but πεπληρωμένα; so that the Lord contemplates the works prepared and appointed in the providence of God for the faithful man to do as a definite sphere (Ephes. ii. 10), which it was his duty and his calling to have *fulfilled* or *filled to the full*,—the same image habitually underlying the uses of πληροῦν and πληροῦσθαι (Matt. iii. 15; Rom. xiii. 8). This sphere of appointed duties the Sardian Angel had not fulfilled; not, at least, "*before God;*" for on these last words the emphasis must be laid. Before himself and other men his works may very likely have been "*perfect;*" indeed, we are expressly told that he had "*a name to live*" (ver. 1); for we all very easily satisfy ourselves concerning our own works, neither is it very difficult to satisfy the world concerning them. But to have our works "*perfect before God,*" to fill up the measure of those that He has ordained, so to have them πεπληρωμένα, that is quite a different and a far harder thing. Very striking and very searching words on this matter are those of one whose own devotion to his work gave him a right to speak—Juan d'Avila, the apostle of Andalusia: "Tot tantæque sunt pastorum obligationes, ut qui vel tertiam earum partem reipsâ impleret, sanctus ab hominibus haberetur; cum tamen eo solo contentus, gehennam non esset evasurus;" and few, who have read, will forget some words of Cecil very nearly to the same effect,—that a minister of Christ is very often in highest honour with men for the performance of one half of his work, while God is regarding him with displeasure for the neglect of the other half.

It is a very instructive fact, that every where else, in the Epistles to all the Churches save only to this and to Laodicea, there is mention of some burden to be borne, of a conflict either with foes within the Church or without, or with both. Only in these two nothing of the kind occurs. The exceptions are very significant. There is no need to assume that the Church at Sardis had openly coalesced and joined hands with the heathen world; this would in those days have been impossible; nor yet that it had renounced the *appearance* of opposition to the world. But the two tacitly understood one another. This Church had nothing of the spirit of the Two Witnesses, of whom we read that they "*tormented* them that dwelt on the earth" (Rev. xi. 10), tormented them, that is, by their witness for a God of truth and holiness and love, whom the dwellers on the earth were determined not to know. There was nothing in it to provoke from the heathen, in the midst of whom it sojourned, any such words as those which the author of *The Wisdom of Solomon* puts into the mouth of the ungodly men (ii. 12-16). The world could endure it, because it too was a world. On the not less significant absence of all heretical opposition in these Churches, there will be something to say when we deal with the Epistle to Laodicea.

Ver. 3. "*Remember therefore how thou hast received and heard, and hold fast, and repent.*"—This "*how*" is by some interpreters referred to the *manner* of their former receiving, and by some to the *matter* which they formerly received and heard. Now if the character of the charges which the Lord is making against Sardis were that of holding, or even tolerating, any erroneous doctrine contrary to "the faith once delivered to the saints," I should certainly be on their side who referred this "*how*" to the matter, to the form of sound words which they had accepted at the first, and to which Christ would recall them now; I should see in these words a parallel to such passages as Col. ii. 6; 1 Tim. vi. 10; 2 Tim. i. 14. But the charge against Sardis is not a perverse holding of untruth, but a heartless holding of the truth; and therefore I cannot but think that the Lord is graciously reminding her of the heartiness, the zeal, the love with which she received this truth at the first. There was great joy in that city, no doubt, then; but now all was changed. Compare St. Paul to the Thessalonians, 1 Ep. i. 5-10, where, however, there is no such painful comparison to draw between their present and their past; also the same Apostle to the Galatians (iv. 13-15), a completer parallel to the words before us, St. Paul contrasting there their present disaffection and coldness of heart toward him and the Gospel of the grace of God which he brought, with the zeal and warmth and love wherewith they first received these glad tidings at his lips, the "*how*" of their present holding with the "*how*" of their past receiving. At the same time, this their joyful loving acceptance of the truth in times past is only one-half of the "*how*" of their receiving it. They are bidden, no doubt, in these words to remember as well "*how*" that truth itself came, that they *might* receive it; with what demonstration of the Spirit and of power from the lips of those ambassadors of Christ, whoever they may have been, who first brought it to Sardis; how holily, how unblamably these went in and out among them. And remembering all this, let them not guiltily let that go, which came so commended to them, which was so joyfully embraced by them, but rather hold it with a firm grasp. "Prize now"

—this is what Christ would say—" that which thou didst once prize so highly, which came to thee so plainly as a gift from God, accompanied with the Holy Ghost from heaven; and repent thee of all the coldness and heartlessness with which thou hast learned to regard it" (2 Pet. i. 9).

"*If therefore thou shalt not watch, I will come on thee as a thief, and thou shalt not know what hour I will come upon thee.*"—Augustine has pointedly said, "Latet ultimus dies, ut observetur omnis dies." But should this Angel refuse thus to observe and watch, the Lord takes up against him and repeats here his own words, twice spoken, with slight variations, in the days of his ministry on earth (Matt. xxiv. 42, 43; Luke xii. 39, 40); words which must have profoundly impressed themselves on those who heard them, and on the early Church in general, as is evidenced from the frequent references to them in other parts of the New Testament; as by St. Paul (1 Thess. v. 2, 4); by St. Peter (2 Ep. iii. 10); and by St. John (Rev. xvi. 15). It is the *stealthiness* of Christ's advent, and thus his coming upon the secure sinner when least He is looked for, which is the point of the comparison, not the violent taking away of the worldling's goods. In that case, he would be the ληστής rather than the κλέπτης, the robber, and not the thief which here he is (cf. Matt. xxiv. 36-51; xxv.

13). The grand Greek proverb, which affirmed that the feet of the avenging deities were shod with wool, awfully expressed the sense which the heathen had of this noiseless approach of the divine judgments, of their possible nearness at the moment when they were supposed the furthest off. So too in those sublime lines of Æschylus, the very turn of the phrase in the conclusion reminds one of these words of Christ:

δοκεῖς τὰ θεῶν σὺ ξυνετὰ νικῆσαί ποτε,
καὶ τὴν δίκην που μάκρ' ἀποκεῖσθαι βροτῶν;
ἡ δ' ἐγγύς ἐστιν, οὐχ ὁρωμένη δ' ὁρᾷ,
ὃν χρὴ κολάζειν τ', οἶδεν· ἀλλ' οὐκ οἶσθα σὺ,
ὁπόταν ἄφνω μολοῦσα διολέσῃ κακούς.

Ver. 4. "*Thou hast a few names even in Sardis which have not defiled their garments.*"—"*Names*" cannot here be slightingly used, any more than at Acts i. 15; cf. Rev. xi. 13; it must be simply equivalent to persons;—or there may be a tacit reference to ver. 1. The Angel of Sardis had a name that he lived, and was dead; but there were some there, however few, whose names were more than names; who had not merely the *form* of godliness (2 Tim. iii. 5, μόρφωσις there = ὄνομα here), but the *power*. It is very beautiful to observe the gracious manner in which the Lord recognizes and sets his seal of allowance to the good which any where He finds. Abraham said, "to slay the righteous with the wicked, that be far from Thee" (Gen. xviii. 25); but it is far from Him even to seem to include the righteous and the wicked in a common blame. He, the same who delivered Noah, a preacher of righteousness, from the destruction of the old world, who drew just Lot out of Sodom, who could single out from the whole wicked family of Jeroboam, and take from the evil to come, Ahijah, for some good thing toward the Lord his God which was found in him (1 Kings xiv. 13), beholds the few faithful in Sardis that had not defiled their garments, will not suffer them to suppose that they are overlooked by Him, or that his condemnation was intended to include them. The "*garments*" which these are thus declared not to have "*defiled*," are not to be identified with the "*white raiment*" of the next verse, nor with the "*white*" in the next clause of this. That "*white raiment*" there is the garment of glory,—this the garment of grace. That incapable of receiving a stain, being part of an inheritance which in all its parts is *ἀμίαντος* (1 Pet. i. 4); this something to which *σπῖλοι* (Ephes. v. 27; James iii. 6), *μιάσματα* (2 Pet. ii. 20), *μολυσμοί* (2 Cor. vii. 1), can only too easily adhere. That keeping itself, for nothing that defileth entereth the place where it is worn (Rev. xxi. 27); this needing to be kept, and above all keeping (Rev. xvi. 15), if the glory and brightness of it is not quite to disappear. This, itself a wedding garment (Matt. xxii. 11, 12), but not *necessarily* identical with "the fine linen, clean and white, the righteousness of saints" (Rev. xix. 8), is put on at our entrance by baptism into the kingdom of grace; that at our entrance by the resurrection into the kingdom of glory.

There were those at Sardis, a little remnant, who had thus kept their garments; or, according to the testimony of Christ, had "*not defiled*" them. Absolutely, and in the highest sense, no one has thus kept his garments, save only He who received more than a garment of grace at baptism; having been sanctified from his conception, and thus a "holy thing" (Luke i. 35) from the very first. But, in a secondary sense, and as compared with too many others, there are those who have not defiled these garments; the phrase is equivalent to St. James's "keeping oneself unspotted from the world" (i. 27). These are they who, if they do contract any defilement upon these, yet suffer it not to harden or become ingrained there; but go at once to the fountain open for all uncleanness, wash their garments and make them white again in the blood of the Lamb (Rev. vii. 14). *Μολύνειν* differs from *μιαίνειν*, as "inquinare" from "maculare," being not so much to stain as to besmear or besmirch with impurity (Cant. v. 3; Gen. xxxviii. 31). It is with reference to this word that Hengstenberg is convinced we are to find a covert allusion here to the name of this city, Sardis or Sardes, which is so near to *sordes;* Christ saying that, with the few exceptions which He has made, Sardes is become *sordes* ("*Sardes* ist *sordes* geworden"). But a *Latin* pun in the Apocalypse! A Hebrew, or even a Greek, play on words would be very conceivable in these Epistles; indeed, I am convinced that there is one in the name "Nicolaitans," given to the libertines of the apostolic period (see ii. 6). A deep sense of the significance of words and names will often find its utterance in such; but a Latin pun, and that without the slightest hint to set any looking for it, is about the unlikeliest thing in the world to encounter there. Not a few expositors, bringing this passage into connexion with Jude 23, find reference in both to those ceremonial uncleannesses spoken of Lev. xv. and elsewhere, which so very easily may be moral uncleannesses as well. I do not think this to lie in the words; but that *every* defilement (μολυσμός) of the flesh and spirit (2 Cor. vii. 1) is here intended.

"*And they shall walk with Me in white.*"—Here are many promises in one. The promise of life, for only the living walk, the dead are still; of liberty, for the free walk, and not the fast bound.

Much more too we may find in these words, "*they shall walk in white*," than if it had been merely said, "they shall be clothed in white." The grace and dignity of long garments only appears, at least only appears to the full, when the person wearing them is in motion; cf. Luke xx. 46: "the scribes desire to walk in long robes." And all this has its corresponding truth in the kingdom of heaven. God's saints and servants here in this world of grace, and no doubt also in that world of glory, are best seen and most to be admired when they are engaged in active services of love. And such they shall have. They shall walk (cf. Zech. iii. 7) with their Lord, shall be glorified together with Him (Rom. viii. 17; John xvii. 24); his servants shall serve Him (Rev. xxii. 3).

"*For they are worthy.*"—God's Word does not refuse to ascribe a worthiness to men (Matt. x. 10, 11; xxii. 8; Luke xx. 35; xxi. 36; 2 Thess. i. 5, 11); although this worthiness must ever be contemplated as relative, and not absolute; as grounding itself on God's free acceptance of an obedience which would fain be perfect, even while it actually is most imperfect, and on this his acceptance and allowance of it alone. There are those who "*are worthy*" according to the rules which free grace *has*, although there are none according to those which strict justice *might have*, laid down; and

God is "faithful" (1 John i. 9), in that having laid these rules down, He will observe and abide by them. Vitringa well: "Dignitas hic notat proportionem, et congruentiam, quæ erat inter statum gratiæ quo fuerant in his terris, et gloriæ quam Dominus ipsis decreverat, *æstimandam ex ipsâ lege gratiæ.*" There is another very fearful "They are worthy" in this Book (xvi. 6), where no such observation would need to be made, where no such mitigation of the word's force would be required; for see the antithesis between death as the *wages* (ὀψώνια) of sin, and eternal life as the *gift* (χάρισμα) of God, Rom. vi. 23.

Ver. 5. "*He that overcometh, the same shall be clothed in white raiment.*"—A repetition of the promise of the verse preceding. They who have kept their garments here, as a few in Sardis to whom the Lord bears testimony (ver. 4) had done, shall have brighter garments given to them there, "vestes vitæ," as in the book of Enoch they are called. Of white as the colour of heaven, and of white garments as shining ones, there has been already occasion to speak; see p. 170. Add the words of Grotius: "λευκὰ ἱμάτια, hoc loco et infra, iii. 18; iv. 4, sunt vestes *coruscantes*, et sic sume στολὰς λευκάς, infra, vi. 11; vii. 9, 13." It is not in Scripture merely that white is thus presented as the colour of heaven, and white garments the suitable investiture of the blessed inhabitants of heaven. The same, out of a deep inborn symbolism, repeats itself in heathen antiquity as well; thus see Plato, *Legg.* xii. 956; Cicero, *Legg.* ii. 18; Virgil, *Æn.* vi. 665; Ovid, *Fast.* iii. 363; iv. 419, 420; *Metam.* x. 432. As we cannot conceive of any room in heaven for raiment in the literal sense of the word, we must understand by this that vesture of light, that clothing with light as with a garment, which shall be theirs who shall then "*shine out* (*ἐκλάμψουσι,* Matt. xiii. 43) as the sun in the kingdom of their Father;" their raiment, and yet for all this not something external to them, but the outward utterance of all which now inwardly they are, who have left all sin behind them for ever. The glorified body, defecated of all its dregs and all its impurities, transformed and transfigured into the likeness of Christ's body (Phil. iii. 21), this, with its robe and atmosphere of light, is itself, I believe, the "*white raiment*" which Christ here promises to his redeemed.

I have alluded already, see p. 147, to the frequency, as it appears to me, of the scoffing side-glances at Scripture which occur in the writings of Lucian. It would be curious to know whether he intended a mock at this and at the glorious hope of the Christian, when, relating the tales current about Peregrinus, after his fiery passage in the spirit of Empedocles to a mock immortality, he makes one of this impostor's followers assure his hearers that shortly after the disappearance of Peregrinus in his funeral-pile he beheld him *walking in a white garment, shining*, and crowned with a garland of olive (ἐν λευκῇ ἐσθῆτι περιπατοῦντα, φαιδρόν, κοτίνῳ τε ἐστεμμένον, *De Mort. Pereg.* 40). One or two such passages we might attribute to accident; but they seem to me to occur too often for any such explanation. See a very good article by Planck, *Lucian und das Christenthum*, in the *Theoll. Stud. und Krit.* 1851, pp. 826-902.

"*And I will not blot out his name out of the book of life.*"—It is much more than a simple negative; οὐ μὴ ἐξαλείψω = "*nequaquam* delebo." We read of a "*book of life*," Exod. xxxii. 32; Ps. lxix. 29; Dan. xii. 1; Phil. iv. 3; Rev. xiii. 8; xx. 15; xxi. 27; of those "written among the living" (Isai. iv. 3); and resting on the same image, our Lord speaks of some whose names "are written in heaven" (Luke x. 20; cf. Heb. xii. 23). These are the τεταγμένοι εἰς ζωήν of Acts xiii. 48. At the same time the pledge and promise which is here given, implying, as on the face of it it does, that there are names, which, having been once written in that book, might yet be afterwards blotted out of it, has proved not a little perplexing to those followers of Augustine, who will not be content in this mystery of predestination with having *some* Scriptures on their side, and leaving the reconciliation of these and those others which are plainly against them, and apparently contradictory to these, for another and a higher state of knowledge; but who would fain make it appear that *all* Scripture is on their side (see Turretine's treatise, *De Libro Vitæ*, pp. 9-22). If this passage had stood by itself, it would not have been hard for them to answer, as indeed they do answer, that all who are written in the book of life overcome; therefore this promise holds good for them all, and none who are there written have their names blotted out from thence. But, unhappily, beside and behind this passage, there are others not capable of this solution, and principally Exod. xxxii. 32; Ps. lxix. 29; Rev. xxii. 19. To what hard shifts they are put in forcing these statements within the limits of their system may be judged from Augustine's comment on the second of these passages (*Enarr. in Ps.* lxix.): "Deleantur de libro viventium, et cum justis non scribantur, non sic accipere debemus quod quemquam Deus scribat in libro vitæ, et deleat illum; si homo dixit, Quod scripsi scripsi, Deus quemquam scribit et delet? . . Isti ergo quomodo inde delentur, ubi nunquam scripti sunt? Hoc dictum est *secundum spem ipsorum, quia ibi se scriptos putabunt.* Quid sit, deleantur de libro vitæ? Et ipsis constet non illos ibi esse."

"*But I will confess his name before my Father, and before his Angels.*"—Christ had spoken when on earth of confessing those who confessed Him, before his Father in heaven (Matt. x. 32, 33), and before the Angels (Luke xii. 8, 9). That "in heaven" is of course omitted now, for there is no longer any contrast between the Father *in heaven* and the Son *on earth;* but the two confessions, which were separated before, appear united now; and in general we may observe of this Epistle that in great part it is woven together of sayings which the Lord had already uttered once or oftener in the days during which He pitched his tent among men; He now setting his seal from heaven upon his words uttered on earth. On these costly mosaic-works of Scripture, which in our careless reading of it we so often overlook, there are some beautiful remarks in Delitzsch, *Commentar über den Psalter*, on Ps. cxxxv.; which is itself, as are also Ps. xcvii. xcviii. striking examples of the skill of a divine Artificer herein.

Nor will it be inopportune to observe further what signal internal evidence this same fact, analysed a little closer, will supply on another point; upon this, namely, that these Epistles are what they profess themselves to be, namely Epistles, directly, and in their form no less than their substance, from Christ the Lord. With no unworthy thought about their inspiration, we might very easily come to regard them as having past through the mind of St. John, and having been recast, in their form at least, in the passage. What they would have been, if they had undergone any such modifying process as this, St. John's own Epistles tell us. But no; it is the Lord Himself who speaks throughout; who not merely suggests the thoughts, but dictates the words. That St. John is here merely his mouthpiece, that the Master is speaking and not the servant, is, I say, remarkably witnessed for in the fact of the numerous points of contact and coincidence between these seven Epistles and the words of Christ as recorded in the Gospels, in the three synoptic Gospels above all. Had such only been found in St. John's own Gospel, this might have suggested quite a different explanation. But it is mainly the other Gospels which furnish these. Thus in this Sardian Epistle alone, where, it is true, the points of resemblance are more numerous than any where else, spiritual activity is set forth as a watching, ver. 3; with which compare Matt. xxiv. 42; xxv. 13; xxvi. 41; Mark xiii. 37. Christ likens his unlooked-for coming to that of a thief (ibid.); compare Matt. xxiv. 43; Luke xii. 39. He speaks here of blotting out a name from the book of life (ver. 5), there of names written in the book of life (Luke x. 20); here of confessing his servants before his Father (ibid.), with which the parallels from the Gospels have just been given. The remarkable reappearance in this and in all these Epistles of the words so often on our Lord's lips, according to the three first Gospels, but never noticed in the fourth, "*He that hath an ear to hear, let him hear*" (Matt. xi. 15; xiii. 9, 45; Mark iv. 9, 23; vii. 16, 33; Luke viii. 8; xiv. 35), has been dwelt on already, p. 120.

Ver. 6. "*He that hath an ear, let him hear what the Spirit saith unto the Churches.*"—Compare ii. 7.

VI.

EPISTLE TO THE CHURCH OF PHILADELPHIA.

Rev. iii. 7–13.

Ver. 7. "*And to the Angel of the Church in Philadelphia write.*"—Philadelphia, at the foot of mount Tmolus, on the banks of the little river Cogamus, which not far from the city falls into the Hermus (Pliny, *H. N.* v. 29, 30), was built by Attalus Philadelphus, king of Pergamum (he died B.C. 138), from whom it derives its name. No city of Asia Minor suffered more, or so much, from frequent earthquakes—πόλις σεισμῶν πλήρης Strabo calls it (xiii. 4), and describes it as almost depopulated in consequence of these. In the great earthquake in the reign of Tiberius Philadelphia was nearly destroyed (Tacitus, *Ann.* ii. 47).

"*These things saith He that is Holy.*"—Christ claims here to be ὁ Ἅγιος, The Holy One; cf. Acts ii. 27; xiii. 35; Heb. vii. 26. In all these passages, however, ὅσιος, not ἅγιος, stands in the original; nor are these words perfectly identical, though we have but the one word "holy" by which to render them both. The ὅσιος, if a man, is one who diligently observes all the sanctities of religion; anterior, many of them, to all law, the "jus *et fas*," with a stress on the latter word. If applied to God, as at Rev. xv. 4; xvi. 5, and here, He is One in whom these eternal sanctities reside; who is Himself the root and ground of them. The ἅγιος is the separate from evil, with the perfect hatred of the evil. But holiness in this absolute sense belongs only to God; not to Angels, for He chargeth his Angels with folly (Job iv. 18), and certainly not to men (Jam. iii. 2; Gen. vi. 5; viii. 21). He then that claims to be "*The Holy One*," —a name which Jehovah in the Old Testament continually claims for Himself,—implicitly claims to be God; takes to Himself a title which is God's alone, which it would be blasphemy for any other to appropriate, and, unless we allow the alternative that He is guilty of this, can only be accepted as Himself God.

"*He that is true.*"—We must not confound ἀληθινός (= "verus") with ἀληθής (= "verax"). God is ἀληθής (= ἀψευδής, Tit. i. 2), as He cannot lie, the truth-speaking and truth-loving God; with whom every word is Yea and Amen; but He is ἀληθινός, as fulfilling all that is involved in the name God, in contrast with those which are called gods, but which, having the name of gods, have nothing of the truth, wicked spirits, or dead idols. That is ἀληθινός which fulfils its own idea to the highest possible point; as Origen (*In Joan.* tom. ii. § 4) well puts it: ἀληθινός, πρὸς ἀντιδιαστολὴν σκιᾶς καὶ τύπου καὶ εἰκόνος. Nor is ἀληθινός only, as in this case of God, the true as contrasted with the absolutely false; but as contrasted with the subordinately true, with all imperfect and partial realisations of the idea; thus Christ is φῶς ἀληθινόν (John i. 9; 1 John ii. 8), ἄρτος ἀληθινός (John vi. 32), ἄμπελος ἀληθινή (John xv. 1); there is a σκηνὴ ἀληθινή in heaven (Heb. viii. 2). In each of these cases the antithesis is not between the true and the false, but between the perfect and the imperfect, the idea fully, and the idea only partially, realized; for John the Baptist also was a light (John v. 35), and Moses gave bread from heaven (Ps. cv. 40), and Israel was a vine of God's planting (Ps. lxxx. 8), and the tabernacle pitched in the wilderness, if only a figure of the true, was yet pitched at God's express command (Exod. xxv.).

"*He that hath the key of David.*"—Let us note here, but only that we may avoid it, a not uncommon error of interpretation, namely, the identifying, or confounding, of this "*key of David*" with "the key of knowledge," which in the days of his earthly ministry Christ accused the Scribes that they had taken away (Luke xi. 52). They who thus identify the two regard Him as here claiming to be the One who unlooses the seals of Scripture, opens the closed door into its inner chambers; who by his advent first made intelligible the dark and obscure prophecies of the Old Testament, and by his Spirit opens and enlightens the eyes of men to see and understand the deep things which are written in his Word. Into this erroneous interpretation Origen not unfrequently falls, bringing Rev. v. 7-9 into relation with these two passages as a third, having the same import; thus *In Joan.* tom. v. § 4; *Sel. in Psalm.* Ps. i.; Hilary no less (*Prol. in Libr. Psalm.* §§ 5, 6); and Jerome (*Ep.* 50, *de Stud. Script.*).

"*The key*" is of course here and elsewhere, as Andreas expresses it, *ἐξουσίας σύμβολον,* the symbol of power (cf. xxii. 1); and "*the key of David*" is "the key of the house of David," of that royal household whereof David was chief, and all his servants members. Cocceius: "Clavem Davidis vocat, quia ea regia clavis, et is tempore ministerii sui clausit et aperuit, typum Christi gerens; vide Ps. ci. 4-8." But David being a type of Christ, nay often his name being actually named for the name of Christ (Ezek. xxxiv. 23, 24), "the house of David" alluded to thus can mean nothing less than the heavenly house, the kingdom of heaven; and the Lord is, in fact, declaring, "I have the keys of the kingdom of heaven." Those keys which He committed to Peter and his fellow Apostles (Matt. xvi. 19), He announces to be in the highest sense his own. It depends on Him, the supreme κλῃδοῦχος in the house of God, who shall see the King's face, and who shall be excluded from it. Men are admitted into, or shut out from, that presence according to the good pleasure of his will; for it is He, and no other, "*that openeth, and no man shutteth, that shutteth, and no man openeth.*" Christ teaches us here that He has not so committed the keys of the kingdom of heaven, with the power of binding and loosing, to any other, his servants, here, but that He still retains the highest administration of them in his own hands. If at any time there is error in their binding and loosing, if they make sad the heart which He has not made sad, if they speak peace to the heart to which He has not spoken peace, then his judgment shall stand, and not theirs. For the promise that He would ratify and confirm in heaven the judgments of his Church on earth, could only be absolute and unconditional so long as the Church retained a discernment of spirits which was never at fault. When once this had departed from it, when therefore it was liable to mistake and error, from that moment the promise could be only conditional.

From the highest tribunal upon earth there lies an appeal to a tribunal of yet higher instance in heaven; to his, who opens and none can shut, who shuts and none can open; and when through ignorance, or worse than ignorance, any wrong has been done to any of his servants here, He will redress it there, disallowing and reversing in heaven the erring or unrighteous decrees of earth. It was in faith of this that Hus, when the greatest Council which Christendom had seen for a thousand years delivered his soul to Satan, did himself confidently commend it to the Lord Jesus Christ; and many a faithful confessor that, at Rome or Madrid, has walked to the stake, his yellow *san-benito* all painted over with devils in token of those with whom his portion was to be, has never doubted that his portion should be indeed with Him who retains in his own hands "*the key of David;*" who thus could open for him, though all who visibly represented here the Church had shut him out with extreme malediction at once from the Church militant on earth and the Church triumphant in heaven.

That the substrate of this language, and, so to say, the suggestion of this thought, is to be sought at Isai. xxii., there can be no reasonable doubt. The Prophet there describes the removal, indeed the shameful rejection, of Shebna, the chief οἰκονόμος of the king, who had occupied for a while the place of highest dignity and honour, but whom the Lord beheld as unworthy of this, and from which He puts him down with shame and dishonour, with the substitution in his room of his servant Eliakim, and his inauguration into the honours and dignities which the other had lost. It needs only to quote the words as they occur in the Septuagint: *δώσω αὐτῷ τὴν κλεῖδα οἴκου Δαυὶδ ἐπὶ τῷ ὤμῳ αὐτοῦ, καὶ ἀνοίξει καὶ οὐκ ἔσται ὁ ἀποκλείων, καὶ κλείσει καὶ οὐκ ἔσται ὁ ἀνοίγων.* The Prophet describes all this with an emphasis and fulness, which, however highly we may conceive of Eliakim, is surprising and inexplicable, until we look beyond that present, and see in that Scripture not merely the history of a revolution in the royal palace or house of David, —a putting down of one and setting up of another; but, over and above this, the type and real prophecy of something immeasurably greater, the indignant rejection of all those unworthy stewards who in God's spiritual house had long abused their position, and the exaltation of the true Steward of the mysteries of God, who should be faithful in all his house, in their room. Vitringa (*Comm. in Esai.* xxii.): "Quæ Eliakimo promittitur prærogativa dignitatis, fore ut claves gerens Domûs Davidis clauderet et aperiret solus, et omnis ab eo suspenderetur sarcina et decus Domûs Davidis (in quam hic cadit emphasis): tam magnifice et ample dictum est, ut plus dixisse videretur Propheta quam debebat, si id in aliquo subjecto nobiliore, cujus Eliakimus typum gerere poterat, olim illustrius non consequeretur exemplum. Certe sunt verbi prophetici recessus profundi."

Ver. 8. "*I know thy works: behold, I have set before thee an open door, and no man can shut it.*" —This "*open door*" is best explained by a reference to 1 Cor. xvi. 9; 2 Cor. ii. 12; Acts xiv. 27; Col. iv. 3. Vitringa: "Notat commodam Evangelii prædicandi occasionem." To this Philadelphian Church, weak probably in numbers, weak in worldly advantages, God had opened "a great door and effectual" for the declaring of his truth; and, though there were many adversaries, no man could shut it. For was not He who opened, the same who had the key of David? and when He opened none could shut, when He made room for his truth in the heart of one or of many, none could hinder it from having free course and being glorified; even as, if He shut and withheld a blessing, all other might and power would be wholly unavailing to make for it an entrance there.

"*For thou hast a little strength, and hast kept my word, and hast not denied my name.*"—They were probably but a little flock, poor in worldly goods, of small account in the eyes of men (cf. 1 Cor. i. 26-28), having "*little strength*"—not "*a little strength,*" which would rather be an acknowledgment of power than of weakness—the fitter therefore that God should be glorified in them and by them; even as He *had* been; for, put to the proof, they had kept his word, and had not denied his name. The aorists, ἐτήρησας, οὐκ ἠρνήσω, refer to some distinct occasions in the past, when, being thus put to the test, they had approved themselves faithful to Him.

Ver. 9. "*Behold, I will make them of the synagogue of Satan, which say they are Jews, and are not, but do lie; behold, I will make them to come and worship before thy feet, and to know that I have loved thee.*"—Here is the reward of their faithfulness, of the entrance which they had made by that open door which the Lord set before them. The promise to Philadelphia, in respect of Jewish adversaries, is larger and richer than that to Smyrna. The promise there did but amount to this, that these enemies should not prevail against them (ii. 9, 10); but here are better promises, namely, that they shall prevail against their enemies; and that with a victory the most blessed of all, in which conquerors and conquered should be blessed alike, and should rejoice together. In reward of their faithfulness, they should see some of these fierce gainsayers and opposers, some of this "*synagogue of Satan*" (see ii. 9), falling on their faces, and owning that God was with them of a truth. The "*worship*" before their feet, of course, does not mean more than this; compare Isai. xlix. 23; lx. 14, to which last verse is manifest allusion here. It is only *some* of them who shall worship thus; for there is no promise during the present dispensation that *all* Israel, but only that a remnant, shall be saved (Rom. ix. 27). In our Version we have failed to express this, that they are only *some* of the synagogue of Satan who should thus acknowledge the presence of God in the Church of his dear Son, should look at Him whom they had pierced, and own that this Jesus of Nazareth was indeed He of whom Moses and the Prophets did write, the promised Messiah, the King of Israel, who should turn iniquity from Jacob. In connexion with this promise, there is an interesting passage in the Epistle of Ignatius to this same Philadelphian Church (c. 6), implying the actual presence in the midst of it, of converts from Judaism, who now preached the faith which once they persecuted. We may say too that this same promise has been gloriously fulfilled to other Churches in our own days, or almost in our own days, as we call to mind the many of Germany's noblest theologians and philosophers, her Neanders and her Stahls; who, being of the stock of Abraham, have yet had the veil taken from their hearts, and owned of the Church of Christ that God was with it of a truth.

Ver. 10. "*Because thou hast kept the word of my patience, I also will keep thee from the hour of temptation, which shall come upon all the world, to try them that dwell upon the earth.*"—What does the Lord exactly mean here by "*the word of my patience*"? There are some who find reference to certain special words and sayings of Christ's, in which He has exhorted his servants to patience, or declared the need which they would have of it; such words as occur at Luke viii. 15; Matt. x. 22; xxiv. 13; cf. Rev. i. 19. Better, however, to take the whole Gospel as "*the word of Christ's patience*," everywhere teaching, as it does, the need of a patient waiting for Christ, till He, the waited-for so long, shall at length appear. Observe, "*Because thou hast kept*" (ἐτήρησας), therefore "*I also will keep*" (τηρήσω); the *benigna talio* of the kingdom of God; "because thou hast *kept* my word, therefore in return I will *keep* thee." The promise does not imply that the Philadelphian Church should be exempted from persecutions which should come on all other portions of the Church; that by any special privilege they should be excused from fiery trials through which others should have to pass. It is a better promise than this; and one which, of course, they share with all who are faithful as they are—to be kept *in* temptation, not to be exempted *from* temptation (τηρεῖν ἐκ not being here = τηρεῖν ἀπό, Jam. i. 27; Prov. vii. 5; cf. 2 Thess. iii. 3); a bush burning, and yet not consumed (cf. Isai. xliii. 2). They may take courage; the blasts of persecution will blow; but He will not winnow his barn-floor with so rough a wind that chaff and grain shall be borne away together. This "*hour of temptation*" is characterized as coming "*upon all the world, to try them that dwell upon the earth.*" These, according to the constant use of the Apocalypse, include all mankind, with the exception of the ἀπαρχή of the Church (vi. 10; xi. 10; xiii. 8, 14); who are already seated in heavenly places with Christ Jesus. The great catastrophies which come upon the earth are "*temptations*" to the world no less than to the Church. God is then putting "*them that dwell upon the earth*" to proof, whether now at least they will not repent, and, when his judgments are in the world, learn righteousness, however they may have in times past hardened themselves against Him. So too such times of great tribulation are trials or "*temptations,*" because they bring out the unbelief, hardness of heart, blasphemy against God, which were before latent in these children of this world; hidden from others, hidden from themselves, till that "*hour of tempta-*

tion" came and revealed them (Rev. ix. 20, 21; xvi. 9, 11, 21). Thus Moses speaks of the plagues as the "temptations of Egypt" (Deut. iv. 34; vii. 19; xxix. 3). They were such, inasmuch as they brought out the pride and obduracy that were in Pharaoh's heart and in his servants', as these would never have been otherwise revealed either to themselves or to others.

Ver. 11. "*Behold, I come quickly: hold that fast which thou hast, that no man take thy crown.*" —This announcement of the speedy coming of the Lord, the ever-recurring key-note of this Book (cf. xxii. 7, 12, 20), is sometimes used as a word of fear for those who are abusing the Master's absence, wasting his goods and ill-treating their fellow-servants; careless and secure as those for whom no day of reckoning should ever arrive (Matt. xxiv. 48-51; 1 Pet. iv. 5; cf. Jam. v. 9; Rev. ii. 5, 16); but sometimes as a word of infinite comfort for those with difficulty and painfulness holding their ground; He that should bring the long contest at once to an end; who should at once turn the scale, and for ever, in favour of righteousness and truth, is even at the door (Jam. v. 7, 9; Phil. iv. 5). Such a word of comfort is this announcement here: "Yet a little while, and thy patience shall have its full reward; only in the interval, and till I come, *hold that fast which thou hast.*" That which Philadelphia "*had*" we have just seen—zeal, patience, with little means accomplishing no little work: "Continue as thou hast begun; hold the beginning of thy confidence firm unto the end, *that no man take thy crown.*"

It may be needful to observe, as some have misunderstood these last words, that they do not signify, "Let no man step into that place of glory which was designed for thee;" for example, after the manner that Jacob stepped into Esau's place (Gen. xxv. 34; xxvii. 36); Judah into Reuben's (Gen. xlix. 4, 8); David into Saul's (1 Sam. xvi. 1, 13); Eliakim into Shebna's (Isai. xxii. 15-25); Matthias into Judas's (Acts i. 25, 26); Gentiles into the place of Jews (Rom. xi. 11); men into that of angels; the number of the elect, as Gregory the Great concludes from these words, remaining still the same, only some filling the places which others have left empty (*Moral.* xxxiv. 20), and thus taking their crown. These *received* indeed a crown, which others lost; they did not *take* it (the 'accipiat' of the Vulgate is wrong here; it should be rather 'auferat'); and it is quite inconceivable that any who should ever himself wear the crown, should be set forth as *taking* it from another. This taking, or seeking to take, the crowns from others' brows is the part, not of the good who would wear them on their own, but of the wicked who would have others discrowned like themselves. Instead of ascribing to the words any such meaning, we must regard them as simply equivalent to those of St. Paul: "Let no man beguile you of your reward" (καταβραβευέτω ὑμᾶς, Col. ii. 18); and as giving no least hint that what this Angel lost another would gain; the crown which he forfeited, another would wear. "*Thy crown*" is not the crown "*which thou hast*," but "*which thou mayest have*" (cf. 2 Tim. iv. 8: ἀπόκειταί μοι ὁ τῆς δικαιοσύνης στέφανος). "Let no man," Christ would say, "deprive thee of the glorious reward laid up for thee in heaven, of which many, my adversaries and thine, would fain rob thee; but which only one, even thyself, can ever cause thee to lose indeed."

Ver. 12. "*Him that overcometh will I make a pillar in the temple of my God, and he shall go no more out.*"—It need hardly be said, except that some have denied it, that this is a promise, as are all the others, of *future* blessedness, belonging not to the members of the Church militant here on earth, but of the Church triumphant in heaven. "*Pillar*" is not to be interpreted here exactly as it is at Gal. ii. 9. There the "pillars" (στῦλοι) are certain eminent Apostles, the main supports, under Christ, of the Church in its militant condition here upon earth; and, as such, towering above the rest of the faithful. But there is no such comparative preëminence indicated here; as is evident from the fact that the promise *to every one* of the faithful, to each that has overcome, is, that he shall be made "*a pillar in the temple of God;*" Christ so speaks, as Jerome (*In Gal.* ii. 9) says well, "docens *omnes* credentes qui adversarium vicerint, posse columnas Ecclesiæ fieri." To find any allusion here, as Vitringa and others have done, to the two monumental pillars, Jachin and Boaz, which Solomon set up, not in the Temple, but in the open vestibule before the Temple (1 Kings vii. 21; 2 Chron. iii. 15, 17), I must say, appears to me quite beside the mark; and if there were any question on this point, the words which follow, "*and he shall go no more out,*" would seem perfectly decisive upon this point. The pillars just named were *always without* the Temple; they would therefore have served very ill to set forth the blessedness of the redeemed, who should be *always within* it. Other pillars might do this, but certainly not these, which contradicted in their position the central intention of Christ's words here, which is to declare that he who overcomes shall dwell in the house of God for ever. "*He shall go out no more;*" for, as the elect angels are *fixed* in obedience, and have over-lived the possibility of falling, have attained what the Schoolmen call the *beata necessitas boni,* so shall it be one day with the faithful. Gerhard (*Locc. Theoll.* xxxii. 2): "Erit perpetuus heres æternorum bonorum, nec ullius ἐκπτώσεως ipsi imminebit periculum, qui columna est, symbolum immobilitatis in statu gloriæ cœlestis." Once admitted into the heavenly kingdom, they are admitted for ever; the door is shut (Matt. xxv. 10), not merely to exclude others, but safely to include these. In that heavenly household the son, every son who has once entered, abideth for ever (John viii. 35; cf. Isai. xxii. 23); so that, in the language of Augustine, "Who is there that would not yearn for that City, out of which no friend departs, and into which no enemy enters?"[1]

"*And I will write upon him the name of my God.*"—Christ will write this name of his God upon *him* that overcometh—not upon *it*, the pillar. It is true indeed that there were sometimes inscriptions on pillars,—which yet would be στῆλαι rather than στῦλοι,—but the image of the pillar is now dismissed, and only the conqueror remains. In confirmation of this, that it is the person, and not the pillar, whom the Lord contemplates now, we find further on the redeemed having the name of God, or the seal of God, on their foreheads (vii. 3; ix. 4; xiv. 1; xxii. 4), with probable allusion to

[1] "Quis non desideret illam Civitatem, unde amicus non exit, quo inimicus non intrat?"

the golden plate inscribed with the name of Jehovah, which the High Priest wore upon his (Exod. xxviii. 36-38). In the "kingdom of priests" this dignity shall not be any more the singular prerogative of one, but the common dignity of all. Exactly in the same way, in the hellish caricature of the heavenly kingdom, the votaries of the Beast are stigmatics, with *his* name upon their foreheads (xiii. 16, 17; xvii. 5; and cf. xx. 4).

"*And the name of the City of my God, which is New Jerusalem, which cometh down out of heaven from my God.*"—What the name of this City is we are told Ezek. xlviii. 35: "The Lord is there." Any other name would but faintly express the glory of it; "having the glory *of God*" (Rev. xxi. 11, 23). He that has the name of this City written upon him is hereby declared free of it. Even while on earth he had his true *πολίτευμα ἐν οὐρανοῖς* (Phil. iii. 20; see Ellicott thereon), the state, city, or country to which he belonged was a heavenly one; but still his citizenship was latent; he was one of God's hidden ones; but now he is openly avouched, and has a right to enter in by the gates to the City (xxii. 14). This heavenly City, the City which hath the foundations, and for which Abraham looked (Heb. xi. 10; cf. xiii. 14), is but referred to here; the full and magnificent description of it is reserved as the fitting close of the Book

(xxi. 10—xxii. 5). It goes by many and glorious names in Scripture. "That great city, the holy Jerusalem," St. John calls it (xxi. 10); claiming for it this title of "the holy," which the earthly Jerusalem once possessed (Matt. iv. 5), but which it had forfeited for ever. "Jerusalem which is above," St. Paul calls it (Gal. iv. 26). It is "the city of the living God, the heavenly Jerusalem" (Heb. xii. 22). It is the true **Καλλίπολις, ἡ ἄνω Καλλίπολις,** as Cyril of Alexandria has strikingly named it; being indeed that *Beautiful City*, of which Plato did but dream, when he devised this name (*Rep.* vii. 527 c). It is the **Οὐρανόπολις,** as Clement of Alexandria (*Pæd.* ii. 12) has called it, recovering and reclaiming for it this magnificent title; which Greek sycophants in profane flattery had devised for another city (*Athenæus*, i. 36), one, if we may trust the pictures of it drawn by those who saw it closest and knew it best, far better deserving a name drawn from beneath than from above.

The epithet "*new*," which is given here to the heavenly City, "*the new Jerusalem*," sets it in contrast with the old, worn-out, sinful city bearing the same name; for **καινός** expresses this antithesis of the new to the old *as the out-worn;* thus **καινὴ** κτίσις, καινὸς ἄνθρωπος, καινὸν ἱμάτιον; while **νέα** would but express that which had recently come into existence, as contrasted with that which had subsisted long; thus Νεάπολις, the city *recently* founded. There would therefore have been no fitness in this last epithet here, for this New Jerusalem, "whose builder and maker is God," is at once new, in that sin has never wasted it, and at the same time the oldest of all. Bengel has well observed, that St. John writes always in his Gospel Ἱεροσόλυμα, in the Apocalypse always Ἱερουσαλήμ; and gives, no doubt, the true explanation of this: "Non temere Johannes in Evangelio omnibus locis scribit Ἱεροσόλυμα de urbe veteri: in Apocalypsi semper Ἱερουσαλήμ de Urbe Cœlesti. Ἱερουσαλήμ est appellatio Hebraica, originaria et sanctior; Ἱεροσόλυμα deinceps obvia, Græca, magis politica."

Strange conclusions have been drawn from the words that follow: "*which cometh down out of heaven from my God.*" The dream of an actual material city to be let down bodily from heaven to earth, an "aurea atque gemmata in terris Jerusalem," as Jerome somewhat contemptuously calls it (*In Isai. Præf. ad Lib.* 18; and compare Origen, *De Princ.* ii. 11. 2), has been cherished in almost all times of the Church by some, who have been unable to translate the figurative language of Scripture into those far more glorious realities of the heavenly πολιτεία, whereof those figures were the vesture and the outward array. Thus the Montanists believed that the New Jerusalem would descend at Pepuza in Phrygia, the head-quarters of their sect; and already, according to Tertullian (*Adv. Marc.* iii. 24) there were vouchsafed from time to time signs and prophetic outlines in heaven of the city which should come down to earth. For forty days, morning and evening, the splendid vision and sky-pageant of this City had been suspended in the sky. But if only it be a City "in which righteousness dwelleth," it will little matter whether we go to it, or it come to us; and in this shape assuredly it will not come.[1]

[1] Glorious things have been spoken of this City of God, and not in the sacred Scriptures only, but also in the writings of uninspired men, in whose hearts, while they have mused on that Heavenly Jerusalem, the fire has kindled, and they have spoken with their tongues. Thus our own "Jerusalem, my happy home," is worthy of no mean place among spiritual songs. But the German and the Latin hymnologies are far richer, both indeed are extraordinarily rich, in these hymns celebrating the glories of the New Jerusalem. Thus in German how lovely is Meyfart's (1590-1642) "Jerusalem, du hochgebaute Stadt" (Bunsen, *Gesangbuch*, no. 495); but grander still, and not in Bunsen's collection, Kosegarten's (1758-1818) "Stadt Gottes, deren diamantnen Ring;" and in the Latin, Hildebert, not to speak of Prudentius (*Psychom.* 823–887), Bernard of Clugny in his *Laus Patriæ Cœlestis*, and many others, has set forth the beauty and the blessedness of that City of the living God, and his own longing to be numbered among the citizens of it in verses such as these:

"Me receptet Sion illa,
Sion, David urbs tranquilla,
Cujus faber auctor lucis,
Cujus portæ lignum crucis,

"*And I will write upon him my new name.*"—This "*new name*" is not "The Word of God" (xix. 13), nor yet "King of kings, and Lord of lords" (xix. 16). It is true that both of these appear in this Book as names of Christ; but at the same time neither of them could be called his "*new name;*"

Cujus muri lapis vivus,
Cujus custos Rex festivus.
In hâc urbe lux solennis,
Ver æternum, pax perennis:
In hâc odor implens cœlos,
In hâc semper festum melos;
Non est ibi corruptela,
Non defectus, non querela;
Non minuti, non deformes,
Omnes Christo sunt conformes.
Urbs cœlestis, urbs beata,
Super petram collocata,
Urbs in portu satis tuto,
De longinquo te saluto,
Te saluto, te suspiro,
Te affecto, te requiro:
Quantùm tui gratulantur,
Quàm festivè convivantur,
Quis affectus eos stringat,
Aut quæ gemma muros pingat,
Quis chalcedon, quis jacinthus,
Norunt illi qui sunt intus.
In plateis hujus urbis,
Sociatus piis turbis,
Cum Moÿse et Eliâ,
Pium cantem Alleluia."

the faithful having been familiar with them from the beginning; but the "*new name*" is that mysterious, and in the necessity of things uncommunicated, and for the present time incommunicable, name, which in that same sublimest of all visions is referred to: "He had a name written, that no man knew, but He Himself" (xix. 12); for none but God can search out the deep things of God (1 Cor. ii. 12; cf. Matt. xi. 27; Judg. xiii. 18). But the mystery of this new name, which no man by searching could find out, which in this present condition no man is so much as capable of receiving, shall be imparted to the saints and citizens of the New Jerusalem. They shall know, even as they are known (1 Cor. xiii. 12).

Ver. 13. "*He that hath an ear, let him hear what the Spirit saith unto the Churches.*"—Compare ii. 7. I cannot leave this Epistle, so full of precious promises to a Church, which, having little strength, had yet held fast the word of Christ's patience, without giving a remarkable passage about it from Gibbon (*Decline and Fall*, c. lxiv.), in which he writes like one who almost believed that the threatenings and promises of God did fulfil themselves in history: "In the loss of Ephesus the Christians deplored the fall of the first angel, the extinction of the first candlestick of the Revelations; the desolation is complete; and the temple of Diana or the church of Mary will equally elude the search of the curious traveller. The circus and three stately theatres of Laodicea are now peopled with wolves and foxes; Sardis is reduced to a miserable village; the God of Mahomet, without a rival or a son, is invoked in the mosques of Thyatira and Pergamus, and the populousness of Smyrna is supported by the foreign trade of the Franks and Armenians. Philadelphia alone has been saved by prophecy, or courage. At a distance from the sea, forgotten by the emperors, encompassed on all sides by the Turks, her valiant citizens defended their religion and freedom above fourscore years, and at length capitulated with the proudest of Ottomans. Among the Greek colonies and churches of Asia, Philadelphia is still erect—a column in a scene of ruins,—a pleasing example that the paths of honour and safety may sometimes be the same."

VII.

EPISTLE TO THE CHURCH OF LAODICEA.

Rev. iii. 14–22

Ver. 14. "*And unto the Angel of the Church of the Laodiceans write.*"—Laodicea, called often Laodicea on the Lycus, to distinguish it from other cities (there were no less than six in all) bearing the same name, was a city in Southern Phrygia (Phrygia Pacatiana), midway between Philadelphia and Colosse. Its nearness to the latter city is more than once referred to in St. Paul's Epistle to the Colossians (iv. 13, 15, 16). Its earliest name was Diospolis, then Rhoas (Plin. *H. N.* v. 29). Being rebuilt and adorned by Antiochus the Second, king of Syria, he called it Laodicea, after his wife Laodice, by whom he was afterwards poisoned. In Roman times it was a foremost city among those of the second rank in Asia Minor; "celeberrima urbs" Pliny calls it. Its commerce was considerable, being chiefly in the wools grown in the region round about, which were celebrated for their richness of colour and fineness of texture. The city suffered grievously in the Mithridatic war, but presently recovered again; once more in the wide-wasting earthquake in the time of Tiberius, but was repaired and restored by the efforts of its own citizens, without any help asked by them from the Roman senate (Tacitus, *Annal.* xiv. 27).

Some have supposed that the negligent Angel of the Laodicean Church was that Archippus, for whom St. Paul, writing to the Colossians, adds the message, "And say to Archippus, Take heed to the ministry which thou hast received in the Lord, that thou fulfil it" (Col. iv. 17). The urgency of this monition certainly seems to imply that St. Paul was not altogether satisfied with the manner in which Archippus was then fulfilling the "ministry," whatever that might be, which he had undertaken; and affording a not inconsiderable support to this conjecture is the fact that in the *Apostolical Constitutions* (viii. 46), which with much of later times also contain much of the very earliest, Archippus is actually named as first bishop of Laodicea. Let him have been the son of Philemon (Philem. 2), a principal convert in the Colossian Church, whose son therefore might very probably have been chosen to this dignity and honour, and it would be nothing strange to find him some thirty years later holding his office stlill; while it would be only too consonant with the downward progress of things, that he who began slackly, should in the lapse of years have grown more and more negligent, till now he needed and received this sharpest reproof from his Lord. Whether the rebukes and threatenings contained in this Epistle did their work or not, it is only for Him who reads the hearts of men to know. But it is certain that the Church of Laodicea was in somewhat later times, so far as man's eye could see, in a flourishing condition. In numbers it increased so much that its bishop obtained metropolitan dignity; and in 361 an important Church Council, that in which the Canon of Scripture was finally declared, was held at Laodicea, and derives its name from thence. All has perished now. He who removed the candlestick of Ephesus, has rejected Laodicea out of his mouth. The fragments of aqueducts and theatres spread over a vast extent of country tell of the former magnificence of this city; but of this once famous Church nothing survives. Recent travellers with difficulty discovered one or two Christians in the poor village of Iski-Hissar, which stands on the site which Laodicea occupied of old.

"*These things saith the Amen, the faithful and true Witness.*"—"*The Amen*" (it is only here that the word is used as a proper name) is He who can add a "Verily, verily," an "Amen, amen," to every word which He utters; as so frequently He does—the double "Amen" indeed only in the Gospel of St. John, i. 51; iii. 3, 5, 11, and often. He is "*the Witness, the faithful and the true*," in that He speaks what He knows, and testifies what He has seen. The thought is a favourite and ever-recurring one in the Gospel of St. John (iii. 11, 32, 33); but does not appear in any other. It may be interesting here to call to mind how the confessors of Lyons and Vienne, referring to these very words, put back from themselves the name of "witnesses" (μάρτυρες), when others would have given it to them, saying that Christ was the faithful and true Witness, that this name was his and not theirs (Eusebius, *H. E.* v. 2).

Of the two epithets, the first, πιστός, expresses his entire trustworthiness. The word is employed in two very different senses in the New Testament as elsewhere—now as trusting or believing (John xx. 27; Acts xiv. 1), now as trustworthy or to be believed (2 Tim. ii. 22; 1 Thess. v. 27; 1 John i. 9). Men may be πιστοί in both senses, the active and the passive, as exercising faith, and as being worthy to have faith exercised upon them; God can be only πιστός in the latter. The Arians found this epithet applied to Christ (Heb. iii. 2), and, as though the word was and could be only used in the former sense, in that of exercising faith upon some higher object, itself of course a creaturely act, they drew from the application of this epithet to the Son an argument against his divinity. I quote the clear and excellent answer of Athanasius, and, as it has been well translated, use the translation (*Library of the Fathers, Treatises against Arianism*, p. 289): "Further, if the expression, 'Who was faithful,' is a difficulty to them from the thought that 'faithful' is used of Him as of others, as if He exercises faith and so receives the reward of faith, they must proceed to find fault with Moses, for saying, 'God faithful and true,' and with St. Paul for writing, 'God is faithful, who will not suffer you to be tempted above that ye are able.' But when the sacred writers spoke thus, they were not thinking of God in a human way, but they acknowledged two senses of the word 'faithful' in Scripture, first believing, then trustworthy, of which the former belongs to man, the latter to God. Thus Abraham was faithful because he believed God's word; and God faithful, for, as David says in the Psalm, 'The Lord is faithful in all his words,' or is trustworthy, and cannot lie. Again, 'If any faithful woman have widows,' she is so called for her right faith; but, 'It is a faithful saying,' because what He hath spoken hath a claim on our faith, for it is true, and is not otherwise. Accordingly the words, 'Who is faithful to Him that made Him,' implies no parallel with others, nor means that by having faith He became well-pleasing, but that, being Son of God the True, He too is faithful, and ought to be believed in all He says and does."

It will be seen that the *truthfulness* of Christ as a Witness is asserted in the πιστός, not, as might at first sight be assumed, in the ἀληθινός that follows, or at least in it only as one quality among many. Christ is a μάρτυς ἀληθινός (not ἀληθής), in that He realized and fulfilled in the highest sense all that belonged to a witness. Three things are necessary thereto. He must have been αὐτόπτης; having seen with his own eyes that which he professes to attest. He must be competent to relate and reproduce this for others. He must be willing faithfully and truthfully to do this. These three things meeting in Christ, and not the presence of the last only, constitute Him a "*true witness*," or one in whom all the highest conditions of a witness met.

"*The beginning of the creation of God*."—There are two ways in which *grammatically* it would be possible to understand these words. They might say that Christ was passively this "*beginning of the creation of God*," as the first and most excellent creature of God's hands; thus Jacob addresses Reuben as ἀρχὴ τέκνων μου (Gen. xlix. 3; cf. Deut. xxi. 17). Or, on the other hand, they might declare of Christ that He was the active source, author, and, in this sense, "*beginning*" and beginner of all creation; as in the words of the Creed, "by whom all things were made." But while both meanings are possible so long as the words are merely considered by themselves, and without reference to any other statements concerning Christ, the analogy of faith imperatively demands the adoption of the latter. The Catholic Church has ever rejected the other as an Arian gloss; impossible to accept, because it would place this passage in contradiction with every passage in Scripture which claims divine attributes, and not creaturely, for the Son. To go no further than these seven Epistles, all the titles which Christ claims for Himself in them are either necessarily divine, or, at any rate, not inconsistent with his divinity; and this must be so no less. He is not, therefore, the "principium *principiatum*," but rather the "principium *principians*,"—not He whom God created the first, but He who was the fountain-source of all the creation of God, by whom God created all things (John i. 1-3; Col. i. 15, 18); even as elsewhere in this Book Christ appears as the Author of creation (v. 13). The Arians, as is well known, explained these words in the same way as they explained Col. i. 15, which is indeed the great parallel passage, as though ἀρχή was "the begun," and not "*the beginning;*" and they brought Job xl. 19 into comparison. But for the use of ἀρχή in the sense and with the force which we here demand for it, as "principium," not "initium" (though these Latin words do not adequately reproduce the distinction), compare the *Gospel of Nicodemus*, c. 25, in which Hades addresses Satan as ἡ τοῦ θανάτου ἀρχὴ καὶ ῥίζα τῆς ἁμαρτίας; and further, Dionysius the Areopagite (c. 15): ὁ Θεὸς ἐστὶν πάντων αἰτία καὶ ἀρχή; and again, Clement of Alexandria (*Strom.* iv. 25): ὁ Θεὸς δὲ ἄναρχος, ἀρχὴ τῶν ὅλων παντελής. These and innumerable other passages abundantly vindicate for ἀρχή that active sense which we must needs claim for it here.

Ver. 15. "*I know thy works, that thou art neither cold nor hot: I would thou wert cold or hot.*"—ζεστός, from ζέω, ferveo, cf. Acts xviii. 25; Rom. xii. 11; ζέοντες τῷ πνεύματι, love to God being a divine heat, a divine fire (Cant. viii. 6; Luke xxiv. 32). Ὄφελον, properly the second aorist of ὀφείλω, but now grown into an adverbial use (= "utinam"), has so far forgotten what at the first it was, as to be employed promiscuously in all numbers and all persons; cf. 1 Cor. v. 8; 2 Cor. xi. 1. It governs an indicative, not an optative, here (ἦς, not εἴης, is the right reading), inasmuch as the Lord is not desiring that something even now *might be*, but only that something *might have been.* In form a wish, it is in reality a regret.

Shall we take this, "*I would thou wert cold or hot,*" merely as the expression of a holy impatience at the half-and-half position of this Laodicean Angel; without pushing the matter further, or attempting to explain to ourselves *how* the Lord should put coldness as one of two alternatives to be desired; as though He had said, "I would thou wouldst take one side or other, be avowedly with me, or avowedly against me, ranged under my banner, or under that of my enemies, that so I might understand how to deal with thee"? Hardly so. This impatience, looked at more closely, would not deserve to be called holy. It is the impatience of sinful man, not of the Son of God; to whom indecision between good and evil must be preferable to decision for evil. The state of lukewarmness must be in itself worse than even that of coldness, before the Lord could thus deliberately desire the latter as a preferable alternative. But how? for there is certainly a difficulty here. Lukewarmness is very inferior to heat, but *seems* preferable to absolute coldness in the things of God. To have only half a heart for these things is bad, but wherein is it better to have no heart at all? How shall we then understand this exclamation of the Saviour, "*I would thou wert cold or hot*"? Best, I think, in this way, namely, by regarding the "*cold*" as one hitherto untouched by the powers of grace. There is always hope of such a one, that, when he does come under those powers, he may become a zealous and earnest Christian. He is not one on whom the grand experiment of the Gospel has been tried and has failed. But the "*lukewarm*" is one who has tasted of the good gift and of the powers of the world to come, who has been a subject of Divine grace, but in whom that grace has failed to kindle more than the feeblest spark. The publicans and harlots were "*cold*," the Apostles "*hot*." The Scribes and Pharisees, such among them as that Simon in whose house the Lord sat and spake the parable of the fifty and the five hundred pence (Luke vii. 36-47), they were "*lukewarm*." It was from among the "*cold*," and not the "*lukewarm*," that He drew recruits; from among them came forward the candidates for discipleship and apostleship and the crown of life, Matthew, and Zacchæus, and the Magdalene, and the other woman that had been a sinner (if indeed another), and all those others, publicans and harlots, that entered into the kingdom of heaven, while the Scribes and Pharisees continued without. That woman which was a sinner, for example, having been "*cold*," passed from that coldness to the fervency of a divine heat, at which there is little or no likelihood that the "*lukewarm*" Simon ever arrived (Luke vii. 47).

It is thus that Gregory the Great explains these

words (*Reg. Past.* iii. 34): "Qui enim adhuc in peccatis est, conversionis fiduciam non amittit. Qui vero post conversionem tepuit, et spem, quæ esse potuit de peccatore, subtraxit. Aut calidus ergo quisque esse, aut frigidus quæritur, ne tepidus evomatur, ut videlicet aut necdum conversus, adhuc de se spem conversionis præbeat, aut jam conversus in virtutibus inardescat." Compare Origen (*De Princip.* iii. 4): "Forte utilius videatur obtineri animam a carne, quam residere in suis propriis voluntatibus. Namque quoniam nec calida dicitur esse, nec frigida, sed in medio quodam tepore perdurans, tardam et satis difficilem conversionem poterit invenire. Si vero carni adhæreat, ex his ipsis interdum malis quæ ex carnis vitiis patitur, satiata aliquando et repleta, velut gravissimis oneribus luxuriæ ac libidinis fatigata, facilius et velocius converti a materialibus sordibus ad cœlestium desiderium et spiritualem gratiam potest." Jeremy Taylor, too, in the second of his sermons, *Of Lukewarmness and Zeal*, discusses this point, *why* the Lord preferred "*hot*" or "*cold*" to "*lukewarm*," at considerable length; and urges well that it is the "*lukewarm*," not as a *transitional*, but as a *final* state, which is thus the object of the Lord's abhorrence: "In feasts or sacrifices the ancients did use *apponere frigidam* or *calidam;* sometimes they drank hot drink, sometimes they poured cold upon their gravies or in their wines, but no services of tables or altars were ever with lukewarm. God hates it worse than stark cold; which expression is the more considerable, because in natural and superinduced progressions from extreme to extreme, we must necessarily pass through the midst; and therefore it is certain a lukewarm religion is better than none at all, as being the doing some parts of the work designed, and nearer to perfection than the utmost distance could be; and yet that God hates it more, must mean, that there is some appendant evil in this state which is not in the other, and that accidentally it is much worse: and so it is, if we rightly understand it; that is, if we consider it not as a being in, or passing through, the middle way, but as a state and a period of religion. If it be in motion, a lukewarm religion is pleasing to God; for God hates it not for its imperfection, and its natural measures of proceeding; but if it stands still and rests there, it is a state against the designs and against the perfection of God: and it hath in it these evils."

I must not leave these words without observing that there is another way of explaining this, "*I would thou wert cold or hot*," which has found favour with some in modern times. Urging that food, when *either* cold or hot, is pleasant to the taste, and only when tepid unwelcome, they make *both* the "*cold*" and the "*hot*" to express spiritual conditions absolutely acceptable in themselves, the only *tertium comparationis* being the nausea created by the tepid, and affirm that nothing further has a right here to be pressed. But assuredly there is much more in these words than this.

Ver. 16. "*So then because thou art lukewarm, and neither cold nor hot, I will spue thee out of my mouth.*"—The land of Canaan is said to have *spued out* its former inhabitants for their abominable doings; the children of Israel are warned that they commit not the same, lest in like manner it *spue* out them (Lev. xviii. 28; xx. 22); but this threatening is more terrible still: it is to be spued *out of the mouth of Christ*, to be rejected as with nausea, with moral loathing and disgust, by Him; to exchange the greatest possible nearness to Him for the remotest distance. At the same time, in the original the language is not quite so severe as in our Version; the threat does not present itself as one about to be put into *immediate* execution. The long-suffering of Christ has not been all exhausted; μέλλω σε ἐμέσαι, "I am about," or "I have it in my mind, to spue thee out of my mouth," as the Vulgate seeks to express it, "*incipiam* te evomere;" that is, "unless thou so takest to heart this threat that I shall never need to execute this threat" (Jon. iii. 10; 1 Kings xxi. 29). But if executed, it implies nothing less than absolute rejection, being equivalent to that "*I will remove thy candlestick out of his place*" (ii. 5), uttered against the Ephesian Angel. Not very different is the tropical use of *πτύειν, καταπτύειν,* and in Latin of "respuere," "conspuere," as = "repudiare," "abhorrere ab aliquâ re."

Ver. 17. "*Because thou sayest, I am rich, and increased with goods, and have need of nothing; and knowest not that thou art wretched, and miserable, and poor, and blind, and naked.*"—There is a question whether this verse coheres the most closely with what goes before, or what follows after,—that is, whether Christ threatens to reject him from his mouth, because he says, "*I am rich, and increased with goods, and have need of nothing;*" or whether, because he says he is all this, therefore Christ counsels him to buy of Him what will make him rich indeed (ver. 18). Our Translators regard the latter connexion as the right one; and, by the punctuation which they have adopted, join this verse with that which follows after it, not with that which went before it—I doubt whether correctly. I should have preferred to place a colon at the end of ver. 16, and a full-stop at that of ver. 17, instead of the reverse, which they have done. —These riches and goods in which the Laodicean Church and Angel gloried we must understand as *spiritual* riches, in which they fondly imagined they abounded. Some interpreters take it in another sense, that they boasted of their worldly prosperity, their flourishing outward condition, and found in this a sign and token of God's favour towards them. But assuredly this is a mistake; it is in the sphere of spiritual things that the Lord is moving; and this language in this application is justified by numerous passages in Scripture: as by Luke xii. 21; 1 Cor. i. 5; 2 Cor. viii. 9; above all, by two passages of holy irony, 1 Cor. iv. 8 and Hos. xii. 8; both standing in very closest connexion with this; I can indeed hardly doubt that there is intended a reference to the latter of these in the words of our Lord. The Laodicean Angel, and the Church which he was dragging into the same ruin with himself, were walking in a vain show and imagination of their own righteousness, their own advances in spiritual insight and knowledge. That this may go hand in hand with the most miserable lack of all real grace, all true and solid advances in goodness, we have a notable example in the Pharisee of our Lord's parable (Luke xviii. 11, 12; cf. Luke xvi. 15; 1 Cor. xiii. 1); and so it was here. Rightly Richard of St. Victor: "Dicis quod sum dives et locupletatus, sive videlicet per scientiæ cognitionem, sive per Scripturæ prædicationem, sive per secularis eloquentiæ nitorem, sive per sacramentorum administrationem, sive per pontificialis apicis dignitatem, sive per vulgi laudem inanem."

Such was their estimate of themselves; but now follows the terrible reality, namely, Christ's estimate of them: "*And knowest not that thou art wretched, and miserable, and poor, and blind, and naked.*" Here, as so often, our Version, to its loss, has taken no note of the article which goes before the two first adjectives, and raises them to the dignity of substantives, while the three which follow are added as qualifying adjectives. Read rather, "*And knowest not that thou art the wretched and the miserable one,*[1] *and poor, and blind, and naked.*" *Ταλαίπωρος*, "*wretched,*" occurs only here and Rom. vii. 24; it is commonly derived by the grammarians from *τλάω* and *πῶρος* in the sense of grief, but thought now to be a poetical recasting of *ταλαπείριος*, in which case we should find *πειρά*, a sharp piercing point, in the latter syllables. *'Ελεεινός*, "*miserable,*" only here and 1 Cor. xv. 19, the object of extremest pity (*ἐλέους ἄξιος*, Suidas), as in certain peril of eternal death, if he should remain what he was. The charge of blindness would seem to imply that the Laodicean Church

[1] Compare, as an exact parallel, and, singularly enough, much more than a mere verbal parallel, Isai. xlvii. 8 (LXX.): *νῦν δὲ ἄκουε ταῦτα, τρυφερά, ἡ καθημένη, ἡ πεποιθυῖα, ἡ λέγουσα ἐν καρδίᾳ αὐτῆς, 'Εγώ εἰμι; καὶ οὐκ ἔστιν ἑτέρα, κ. τ. λ.*

boasted of spiritual insight. Like some before them, being blind, they yet said, "We see" (John ix. 21). This blindness, of course, was not absolute and complete; else the eyesalve which the Lord presently bids them to obtain of Him would have profited little. They were **μυωπάζοντες**, as St. Peter (2 Ep. i. 9) speaks of some, he too joining **τυφλός** and **μυωπάζων**.

Ver. 18. "*I counsel thee to buy of Me gold tried in the fire, that thou mayest be rich; and white raiment, that thou mayest be clothed, and that the shame of thy nakedness do not appear.*"—There is a certain irony, but the irony of divine love, in these words. He who might have commanded, prefers rather to counsel; He who might have spoken as from heaven, conforms Himself, so far as the outward form of his words reaches, to the language of earth. To the merchants and factors of this wealthy mercantile city He addresses Himself in their own dialect. Laodicea was a city of extensive money transactions; Cicero, journeying to or from his province, proposes to take up money there (*Epp. ad Div.* ii. 17; iii. 5); Christ here invites to dealings with Him: He has gold so fine that none will reject it. The wools of Laodicea, of a raven blackness, were famous throughout the world; but He has raiment of dazzling white for them who will put it on. There were ointments for which certainly many of the Asiatic cities were famous; but He, as He will presently announce, has eyesalve more precious than them all. Would it not be wise to transact their chief business with Him? Thus Perkins (*Exposition upon Rev.* i. ii. iii., *Works*, vol. iii. p. 363): "Christ saith, I counsel thee to buy of Me; where He alludeth to the outward state of this city, for it was rich, and also given to much traffic, as histories record, and therefore He speaks to them in their own kind, as if He should say, Ye are a people exercised in much traffic, and delighted with nothing more than buying and selling. Well, I have wares that will serve your turn, as gold, garments, and oil; therefore come and buy of Me."

But first on those words, "*buy*," and "*of Me*." We must not fail to put an emphasis on that "*of Me*." "In Me," Christ would say, "are hidden all the treasures of wisdom and knowledge." Christ's Apostle had once before to remind the Colossians, neighbours of the Laodiceans, that this was so; and that there was no growth for the Church, or for any member of the Church, except through holding the Head (Col. ii. 3, 19); that all self-chosen ways of will-worship might have a show of wisdom, but puffed up, and did not build up (ii. 10-15); and out of the deep anxiety which he evidently felt for both these sister Churches alike (ii. 1), he had desired that the Epistle to the Colossians should be read also in the Church of the Laodiceans (iv. 16). But they had not learned their lesson. St. Paul's "great conflict" for them had been well nigh in vain; and now the Lord, repeating his servant's lesson, gathers up into a single point, concentrates in that single phrase, "buy *of Me*," the whole lesson of the Epistle to the Colossians.

The "*buying*" of Christ, who in so many more passages is described as making a free gift of all which He imparts to men, is drawn from Isai. lv. 1, with which we may compare Matt. xiii. 44, 46. The price which they should pay was this, the renunciation of all vain reliance on their own righteousness and wisdom; the price which in another Epistle St. Paul declared he had so gladly paid, that so he might himself win Christ (Phil. iii. 7, 8); the *ἀποτάσσεσθαι πᾶσι*, which the Lord long before had declared to be the necessary condition of his discipleship (Luke xiv. 33). This is the price, as it is contemplated rather in its negative aspect; in its positive it is the earnest striving after, and longing for, the gift, the reaching out after it, the opening of the mouth wide that He may fill it. Vitringa: "Quæ beneficia Dominus vult ut emant, h. e. secundum conditiones fœderis gratiæ pro iis expendant pretium abnegationis sui ipsius et mundanarum cupiditatum; quod hic non habet rationem meriti, sed tamen pretii, quia in regeneratione homo aliis quibusdam, rebus sibi hactenus caris renunciat, ut pretioso dono justitiæ Christi potiatur."

And what does the Lord counsel him that he shall "*buy;*" which, when he has made them his own, he shall be no longer "*poor and blind and naked*"? Three things; and, first, as he is "*poor*"—"*gold tried in the fire, that thou mayest be rich.*" A comparison with 1 Pet. i. 7 (cf. Zech. xiii. 9; Matt. iii. 3; Prov. xvii. 3; Jam. i. 3) teaches us that by this is intended faith; for faith being a gift of God, must therefore be bought of Christ (Luke xvii. 5; cf. Ps. lxxii. 15, according to the right translation); and such faith as would stand the test, would endure in the furnace of affliction, in the πύρωσις (1 Pet. iv. 12); Vitringa: "Vera et solida fides, quæ sustinere possit afflictiones." Then shall he be rich indeed; this is the true πλουτίζειν (1 Cor. i. 5), better than that spoken of in the book of Job (xxii. 23, 24); though that, as God's gift, might be good; then should he be indeed one εἰς Θεὸν πλουτῶν (Luke xii. 21), rich toward God, not walking, as now, in a vain show of wealth which he had not. Πεπυρωμένον ἐκ πυρός = δοκιμαζόμενον διὰ πυρός, 1 Pet. i. 7; for, in the words of the Latin poet,

> "Omnia purgat ignis edax, vitiumque metalli
> Excoquit."

But, secondly, as he is "*naked*," he shall "*buy*" of Christ "*white raiment, that thou mayest be clothed, and that the shame of thy nakedness do not appear*."—Instead of the αἰσχύνη here, we have in the parallel passage, xvi. 15, ἀσχημοσύνη, translated also "shame," but better, "unseemliness," or "uncomeliness;" cf. τὰ ἀσχήμονα, 1 Cor. xii. 23. "*Do not appear*" is too weak a rendering of μὴ φανερωθῇ. Translate rather, "*be not made manifest;*" φανεροῦσθαι being constantly used for the manifestations or revelations which God makes of the hidden things of men (John iii. 21; 1 Cor. iv. 5; 2 Cor. v. 11; Eph. v. 13); either now, or at that last day when every guest that has not on a wedding garment is at the same instant discovered and cast out (Matt. xxii. 11-13; compare Isai. xlvii. 3: ἀνακαλυφθήσεται ἡ αἰσχύνη σου). As stripping, and laying bare the nakedness, is a frequent method of putting to open shame (cf. 2 Sam. x. 4; Isai. xx. 4; xlvii. 2, 3; Ezek. xvi. 37; Hos. ii. 3, 9; iii. 5; Nah. iii. 5; Rev. xvi. 15), so the clothing with comely apparel those unclothed or ill-clothed before, of imparting honour; cf. Gen. xli. 42; Esth. vi. 7-11; Luke xv. 22; Zech. iii. 3-5; and above all, Gen. iii. 7, 21, where it is shown that God, and not himself, is the true coverer of the nakedness of man; for while he can discover his own shame, it is God only who can cover it. This, the shame of the nakedness of him who, professing Christ, has not put on Christ (Col. iii. 10-14), may be, and often is, revealed in the present time; it *must* be revealed in the last day (Matt. xxii. 11-13; Dan. xii. 2; 2 Cor. v. 10). Therefore is it that the Psalmist exclaims, "Blessed is the man whose sin *is covered*" (Ps. xxxii. 1); and those interpreters seem to me to give too narrow a range of meaning to this "*white raiment,*" who limit it to the graces of the Christian life, and the putting on, in this sense, of the Lord Jesus Christ. We should understand by it not merely the righteousness of Christ imparted, but also that righteousness imputed; for both are needful, the one as needful as the other, if the shame of our nakedness is not to appear. So Vitringa: "Vestimenta alba, h. e. justitiam Christi, verâ fide acceptam, quæ nos obtegat quâ parte nudi, id est, expositi sumus ardenti iræ Dei; tum quoque habitus Christianarum virtutum, quæ faciunt ut quis cum fiduciâ absque pudore coram Deo et sanctis ausit comparere, inter quas eminent caritas, simplicitas, humilitas et zelus."

"*And anoint thine eyes with eyesalve, that thou mayest see.*"—The eye for which this salve is needed is, of course, the spiritual eye, the eye of the conscience, by which spiritual things are discerned and appreciated; which eye may be sound or simple (ἁπλοῦς, Matt. v. 29), or which may be evil (πονη ρός, Matt. vi. 23 ; cf. 1 John ii. 11) ; and according as it is this or that, the man will see himself as he truly is, or see nothing as he ought to see it. The beginning of all true amendment is to see ourselves as indeed we are, in our misery, our guilt, our shame ; and to enable us to do this is the first consequence of the anointing with that eyesalve which the Lord here invites this Angel to purchase of Him. The Spirit convinceth of sin, and by this "*eyesalve*" we must understand the illuminating grace of the Holy Ghost, which at once shows to us ourselves and God. And if it be true of the medicinal eyesalves of antiquity that they commonly caused the eye to smart on their first application (Tob. xi. 8, 12), "*mordacia* collyria," "*acre* collyrium," as Augustine therefore calls them (*In Joh. Tract.* xviii. § 11 ; *Conf.* vii. 8), this may fitly set forth to us the wholesome pain and medicinal smart which belong to the spiritual eyesalve as well ; making for us discoveries so painful as it does, causing us to see in ourselves a nakedness and poverty which had been wholly concealed from us before ; while yet only through the seeing and through the confessing of this can that poverty be ever exchanged for riches, or that nakedness for "durable clothing."

It has been already remarked (p. 211), and assuredly is very well worthy of notice, that the two

Churches which are spiritually in the most sunken condition of all, that, namely, of Sardis and this of Laodicea, are also the two in which alone there is no mention made either of adversaries from without, or of hinderers to the truth from within. Of the absence of heathen adversaries there has been occasion to speak already; but more noticeable still is the fact that there neither appear here nor there Nicolaitans, or Balaamites, or Jezebelites, or those who say they are Jews and are not; seeking to seduce Christ's servants, and making it needful for them earnestly to contend for the truth, if they would not be robbed of it altogether. In the coldness and deadness of these Churches, which had no truth to secure or defend from gainsayers, we may see a pregnant hint of all which the Church owes to the heresies and heretics that, one after another, have assailed her. Owing them no thanks for what she has gained by them, her gains themselves have been immense, and there are remarkable acknowledgments to this effect made by more than one of the early Fathers. Contending against these she has learned not merely to define more accurately, but to grasp more firmly, and to prize more dearly, that truth of which they would fain have deprived her. What would the Church of the second century have been, if it had never learned its strength, and the treasures of wisdom and knowledge which it had in Christ Jesus, in the course of that tremendous conflict with the Gnostics which it then sustained? Would the Church itself have ever been the *true* Gnostic, except for these *false* ones? Again, what an education for it were the fast-succeeding conflicts of the two next centuries; and not in intellectual education only, but "as iron sharpeneth iron," so the zeal of the adversaries of the truth served often to excite the zeal and love, which might else have abated, of its friends. Assuredly it was not good for the Sardian and Laodicean Churches to be without this necessity of earnestly contending for the truth. Perhaps they gloried in their freedom from conflicts which were agitating and troubling the other Churches around them. But we may be bold to say that in a world of imperfections like ours, it argued no healthy spiritual life that there should have been none there to call the truth into question and debate. Misgrowths are at all events growths; and if there is a spiritual condition which is *above* errors, so also there is one which is *beneath* them, when there is not interest enough in theology, not care enough to know any thing certain about God, or about man's relation to God, even to generate a heresy. As we read the history of the Church, we may perhaps find some consolation in thoughts like these. Assuredly in reading many a page in that history, we need the strongest consolations which we can any where find. But to return from this digression.

Ver. 19. "*As many as I love I rebuke and chasten; be zealous therefore, and repent.*"—He, the great Master-builder, polishes with many strokes of the chisel and the hammer the stones which shall find a place at last in the walls of the heavenly Jerusalem (cf. Prov. iii. 12; Job v. 17; Heb. xii. 6; 2 Chron. xxxiii. 11-13; Ps. xciv. 12). And this is a rule which endures no exception. In that "*as many*" (ὅσους) here lies the same emphasis as in the "*every* son" of Heb. xii. 6. *All* whom He loves are included in the same discipline of correction, are made sooner or later to be able to say, "Thy loving correction shall make me great" (Ps. xviii. 35). Of *all* it is true that, if not scourged, they are not sons (Heb. xii. 8); if not rebuked and chastened, they are not loved. Not a few, if their prosperity lasts a little longer than that of others, fancy that they are to be exceptions to this rule; but it is never so. They can only be excepted from the discipline through being excepted from the sonship; as Augustine excellently well (*Serm.* xlvi. § 11): "Flagellat, inquit, omnem filium quem recipit. Et tu forte exceptus eris? Si exceptus a passione flagellorum, exceptus a numero filiorum." Many other beautiful passages to the same effect may be found in his writings; thus

Enarr. in Ps. xxxi. 11; *in Ps.* xciii. 14; *in Ps.* cxiv. 5.

'Ἐλέγχειν and παιδεύειν are often found together, as here; thus Ecclus. xviii. 13; Ps. cxl. 5; so too παιδεία and ἔλεγχος, Prov. vi. 23, and compare Heb. xii. 5; but they are very capable of being distinguished. 'Ἐλέγχειν is more than ἐπιτιμᾶν, with which it is often joined; see my *Synonyms of the New Testament*, § 4. It is so to rebuke that the person rebuked is brought to the acknowledgment of his fault, is convinced, as David was when rebuked by Nathan (2 Sam. xii. 13); for, in the words of Aristotle (*Rhet. ad Alex.* 13), ἔλεγχος ἐστι μὲν ὃ μὴ δυνατὸν ἄλλως ἔχειν, ἀλλ' οὕτως ὡς ἡμεῖς λέγομεν; and this rebuking, or convincing of sin, is eminently the work and office of the Holy Ghost (John xvi. 8; cf. iii. 20; Ephes. v. 13). See upon this subject an admirable note by Archdeacon Hare in his *Mission of the Comforter*, vol. ii. p. 528. Παιδεύειν, being in classical Greek to instruct, to educate, is in sacred Greek to instruct or educate *by means of correction*, through the severe discipline of love (παιδεύειν and μαστιγοῦν are joined together, Heb. xii. 6), "per molestias erudire," as Augustine (*Enarr. in Ps.* cxviii. 66), tracing the difference between its sacred and profane uses, explains it. As David had found his ἔλεγχος when he exclaimed, "I have sinned against the Lord"

(2 Sam. xii. 13), so his παιδεία was announced to him in the words which followed: "The child also that is born unto thee shall surely die" (ver. 14)—which passage is alone sufficient to refute those who affirm that we have in the ἐλέγχω καὶ παιδεύω a ὕστερον πρότερον. Not so. It will indeed continually happen that the same dealing of God with men is at once ἔλεγχος and παιδεία, but only παιδεία through having been first ἔλεγχος. This therefore, namely the ἔλεγχος, rightly precedes. Brightman: "Observandum est illum *arguere* et *castigare*; id est, convincere et plectere. Simul enim sunt hæc duo conjungenda. Inutilis est animadversio, ubi verba silent, verbera sæviunt. Unde recte vocatur castigatio, disciplina quâ delinquens una dolet et discit."—For ζήλωσον of the received text, read rather ζήλευε, from ζηλεύω, another form of ζηλόω. This word, through ζῆλος connected with ζέω and thus with ζεστός (ver. 15), is chosen as the word of exhortation, with special reference to the *lukewarmness* which the Lord so indignantly saw in the Laodicean Church. It was *warmth*, *heat*, *fervency*, which He required of it. St. Paul uses ζηλοῦν in a good sense, Gal. iv. 18, and also, which are the best parallels to its employment here, 1 Cor. xii. 31; xiv. 1.

Ver. 20. "*Behold, I stand at the door and knock.*"—The Hellenistic κρούω is here, as always in the New Testament, the word used to describe this knocking at the door (Luke xii. 36; xiii. 25; Acts xii. 13, 16). The Greek purists preferred *κόπτω*; yet see Lobeck, *Phrynichus*, p. 177. We have in these gracious words the long-suffering of Christ as He waits for the conversion of sinners (1 Pet. iii. 20); and not alone the long-suffering which waits, but the love which seeks to bring that conversion about, which knocks. He at whose door we ought to stand, for He is the Door (John x. 7), who, as such, has bidden *us* to knock (Matt. vii. 7; Luke xi. 9), is content that the whole relation between Him and us should be reversed, and instead of our standing at his door, condescends Himself to stand at ours,—*θυραυλεῖν*, as the Greeks termed this waiting and watching at the door of the beloved. Very beautiful on the matter of this infinite condescension on his part are the words of Nicolaus Cabasilas, a Greek divine of the fourteenth century: *ὁ περὶ τοὺς ἀνθρώπους ἔρως τὸν Θεὸν ἐκένωσεν. οὐ γὰρ κατὰ χώραν μένων καλεῖ πρὸς ἑαυτὸν, ὃν ἐφίλησε δοῦλον, ἀλλ' αὐτὸς ζητεῖ κατελθών, καὶ πρὸς τὴν καταγωγὴν ἀφικνεῖται τοῦ πένητος ὁ πλουτῶν, καὶ προσελθὼν δι' ἑαυτοῦ μηνύει τὸν πόθον, καὶ ζητεῖ τὸ ἴσον, καὶ ἀπαξιοῦντος οὐκ ἀφίσταται, καὶ πρὸς τὴν ὕβριν οὐ δυσχεραίνει, καὶ διωκόμενος προσεδρεύει ταῖς θύραις, καὶ ἵνα τὸν ἐρῶντα δείξῃ, πάντα ποιεῖ, καὶ ὀδυνώμενος φέρει καὶ ἀποθνήσκει.*

"*If any man hear my voice, and open the door, I will come in to him, and will sup with him, and he with Me.*"—Christ does not knock only; He also speaks; makes his "*voice*" to be heard—a more precious benefit still! It is true indeed that we cannot in our interpretation draw any strict line of distinction between Christ's knocking and Christ's speaking. They both represent his dealings of infinite love with souls, for the winning them to receive Him; yet at the same time, considering that in this natural world a knock may be any one's and on any errand, while the voice accompanying it would at once designate who it was that was knocking, and with what intention (Acts xii. 13, 14), we have a right, so far as we may venture to distinguish between the two, to see in the voice the more inward appeal, the closer dealing of Christ with the soul, speaking directly by his Spirit to the spirit of the man; in the knocking those more outward gracious dealings, of sorrow and joy, of sickness and health, and the like, which He sends, and sending uses for the bringing of his elect, in one way or another, by smooth paths or by rough, to Himself. The "*voice*" very often will interpret and make intelligible the purpose of the "*knock.*"

But that "*knock*" and this "*voice*" may both remain unheard and unheeded. It is in the power of every man to close his ear to them; therefore the hypothetical form which this gracious promise takes: "*if any man hear my voice, and open the door.*" There is no *gratia irresistibilis* here. It is the man himself who must open the door. Christ indeed knocks, claims admittance as to his own; so lifts up his voice that it may be heard, in one sense *must* be heard, by him; but He does not break open the door, or force an entrance by violence. There is a sense in which man is lord of the house of his own heart; it is for him to open, and unless he does so, Christ cannot enter. And, as a necessary complement of this power to open, there belongs also to man the mournful prerogative and privilege of refusing to open: he may keep the door shut, even to the end. He may thus continue to the last blindly at strife with his own blessedness; a miserable conqueror, who conquers to his own everlasting loss and defeat.

At the same time these words of Christ, decisive testimony as they yield against that scheme of irresistible grace which would turn men into mere machines, and take away all moral value from the victories which Christ obtains over the sullenness, the pride, the obstinacy, the rebellion of men, must not be pushed, as some have pushed them, in the other direction, into Pelagian error and excess; as though men could open the door of their heart when they would; as though repentance was not itself a gift of the exalted Saviour (Acts v. 31). They can only open when Christ knocks; and they would have no desire at all to open unless He knocked, and unless, together with the external knocking of the Word, or of sorrow, or of pain, or whatever other shape it might assume, there went also the inward voice of the Spirit. All which one would affirm is that this is a *drawing*, not a *dragging*—a knocking at the door, not a breaking open of the door. Hilary has here some words very much to the point (*In Ps.* cxviii. 89): "Vult ergo semper introire; sed a nobis ne introeat excluditur. Ipse quidem semper ut illuminet promptus est; sed lumen sibi domus ipsa obseratis aditibus excludit. Quæ si cœperit patere, illico introibit, modo solis, qui clausis fenestræ valvis introire, prohibetur, patentibus vero totus immittitur. Est enim Verbum Dei Sol justitiæ, adsistens unicuique ut introeat, nec moratur lucem suam repertis aditibus infundere."

Some, wishing to decry the *Song of Solomon*, to take it from its place in the Canon, and to set it down as a mere human love-poem, an idyl of an earthly love, have affirmed that there is no single allusion to it in the New Testament. This statement is altogether without warrant. In the words we have been just considering there is an undoubted allusion to Cant. v. 2-6; where indeed the very language which Christ uses here, the κρούειν ἐπὶ τὴν θύραν, the summons ἀνοίγειν recurs. Nor is the relation between the one passage and the other merely superficial and verbal. On the contrary, it lies very deep. The spiritual condition of the Bride there is in fact precisely similar to that of the Laodicean Angel here. Between sleeping and waking she has been so slow to open the door, that when at length she does so, the Bridegroom has withdrawn, and she has need to seek for and to follow Him (ver. 5, 6). This exactly corresponds to the lukewarmness of the Angel here. See the two passages brought into closest connexion in this sense by Jerome, *Ep.* xviii. *ad Eustochium.* Another proof of the connexion between them is this,—that although there has been no mention of any thing but a knocking here, Christ goes on to say, "*If any man hear my voice.*" What can this be but an allusion to the words in the *Canticle* which have just gone before, "It is the *voice* of my beloved that knocketh, saying, *Open* to me, my sister"? In the face of this, and much more of the same kind which might be adduced, Ewald asserts, "Cantico nunquam utuntur Scriptores Novi Testamenti;" and rather than look there for this "*I stand at the door and knock,*" he prefers to find an allusion here to Peter's standing and knocking at the door of Mary's house after he was released from prison by the Angel (Acts xii.

13, 14)! We shall not go far before we find further evidence of the intimate relation between these words of Christ and those of the Bridegroom in that Book. We trace it in the words which immediately follow: "*and will sup with him, and he with Me.*" There may possibly be in these a more immediate reference to Luke xii. 36; but that to the Song of Solomon, because it lies deeper, must not therefore be overlooked. There too the mutual feasting of Christ with the soul which opens to Him, and of the soul with Him, is all set forth. There too the bride prepares a feast for her Beloved: "Let my Beloved come into his garden, and eat his pleasant fruits" (iv. 16); but He had first prepared one for her: "I sat down under his shadow with great delight, and his fruit was sweet to my taste" (ii. 3). Few, I suppose, would be disposed to deny a mystical significance to that meal after the Resurrection on the shores of the Sea of Tiberias, recorded with so much emphasis by the beloved disciple (John xxi. 9-13); which wonderfully fulfils the same conditions, being made up of what the disciples bring and what Christ brings. This mutual feasting of Christ with his people, and of his people with Him, finds in this present life its culminating fulfilment in the Holy Eucharist; which yet is but an initial fulfilment; it will only find its exhaustive accomplishment in the marriage supper of the Lamb (Rev. xix. 7-9; Mark xiv. 25).

Ver. 21. "*To him that overcometh will I grant to sit with Me in my throne.*"—A magnificent variation of Christ's words spoken in the days of his flesh: "The glory which Thou gavest Me, I have given them. . . . Father, I will that they also whom Thou hast given Me, be with Me where I am" (John xvii. 22, 24); as also of the words of St. Paul, "If we suffer with Him, we shall also reign with Him" (2 Tim. ii. 12). Wonderful indeed is this promise, which, as the last and the crowning, is also the highest and most glorious of all. Step by step they have advanced, till a height is reached than which no higher can be conceived. It seemed much to promise the Apostles themselves that they should sit on thrones, judging the twelve tribes of Israel (Matt. xix. 28); but here is promised to every believer something more than was there promised to the elect Twelve. And more wonderful still, if we consider to whom this promise is here addressed. He whom Christ threatened just now to reject with loathing out of his mouth, is offered a place with Him on his throne. But indeed so it is; the highest place is within reach of the lowest; the faintest spark of grace may be fanned into the mightiest flame of divine love. It will be observed that the image here is not that of sitting upon seats on the right hand or on the left of Christ's throne (1 Kings ii. 19), but of sharing that throne itself. To understand this, we must keep in mind the fact, that the Eastern throne is much ampler and broader than ours; so that there would be room upon it for other persons, besides him who occupied as of right the central position there (Matt. xx. 21).

"*Even as I also overcame, and am set down with my Father in his throne.*"—The Son is σύνθρονος with the Father (Wisd. ix. 4), as the early Church writers loved to express it, with a word employed already in the heathen mythology, perhaps borrowed from it (see Suicer, s. v.); his faithful people shall be πάρεδροι with Him. These words, "*I overcame,*" remind us of other words spoken by the Lord while as yet He had not so visibly overcome as now: "Be of good cheer, I have overcome the world" (John xvi. 33); and the manner in which the overcoming the world and the sitting down with his Father in his throne are brought together here, puts this passage in closest connexion with Phil. ii. 9: "*Wherefore* God also hath highly exalted Him, and given Him a name which is above every name;" cf. Heb. i. 3.—On this "*my throne,*" and "*my Father's throne,*" Joseph Mede says well (*Works*, p. 905): "Here are two thrones mentioned. *My throne*, saith Christ; this is the condition of glorified saints who sit with Christ in his throne; but *my Father's* (*i.e.* God's) *throne* is the power of Divine majesty; herein none may sit but God, and the God-man Jesus Christ. To be installed in God's throne, to sit at God's right hand, is to have a god-like royalty, such as his Father hath, a royalty altogether incommunicable, whereof no creature is capable."

Ver. 22. "*He that hath an ear, let him hear what the Spirit saith unto the Churches.*"—Compare ii. 7.

A few words in conclusion upon the order in which the promises of the seven Epistles follow one another. It is impossible not to acknowledge such an order here,—an order parallel to that of the unfolding of the kingdom of God from its first beginnings on earth to its glorious consummation in heaven. Thus the promise of Christ to the faithful at Ephesus is, that He will give them to eat of the tree of life which is in the Paradise of God (ii. 7); thus taking us back to Genesis i. and ii. But sin presently entered into Paradise, and death, the seal and witness of sin (Gen. iii. 19); but for the faithful at Smyrna,—and the promise that is good for them is good for the faithful every where,—this curse of death is lightened. It shall be but the gate of immortality, for "*he that overcometh shall not be hurt of the second death*" (ii. 11). The next promise, that to the faithful at Pergamum, brings us to the Mosaic period, to the Church in the wilderness:

"*To him that overcometh will I give to eat of the hidden manna*" (ii. 17); and if the interpretation of the "*white stone*" which has been ventured here is the right one, that promise will also fall in perfectly with the wilderness period and the institution of the high-priesthood, which at that period found place. In the fourth, that namely to Thyatira, we have reached the full and final consummation, in type and prophetic outline, of the kingdom, the period of David and Solomon,—the triumph over the nations, the Church sharing in the royalties of her king (ii. 26, 27). Every reader will recognize this as a characteristic feature of those reigns (2 Sam. x. 19; xii. 29, 30; 1 Chron. xvii. 1-13).

Here there is a pause; and with this consummation reached, than which in type and prophecy there can be nothing higher, a new series begins; the heptad falling, as is so constantly the case, into two groups; either of three and four, as in the Lord's Prayer, or of four and three, as here. And now the scenery, if I may use the word, changes; it is not any longer of earth, but of heaven. The kingdom, not of David, but of David's Son, has come; all his foes are under his feet; his Church is not any longer contemplated as militant, but triumphant; and in the succession of the three last promises we learn that even for the Church triumphant there are steps and advances from glory to glory. Thus, in the promise addressed to the Angel of Sardis, we have the blessings of the judgment-day, the name found written in the book of life, Christ's confession of his own before his Father, the vesture of light and immortality, in other words, the glorified body which it shall be then given to the saints to wear (iii. 5). This, however, is a personal, a solitary benefit, belonging to each of them alone; not so the next. In the promise made to the faithful at Philadelphia, it is declared that as many as overcome shall have right to enter by the gates into the heavenly City, where City and Temple are one, shall be themselves avouched members of that heavenly *πολιτεία*, and shall have their place in it for evermore (iii. 12). And then, it having thus been declared what they have in themselves, namely, the glorified body, and what they have in and with the company of the redeemed, the citizenship of the heavenly Jerusalem, it is, last of all, in the concluding words to the Angel of Laodicea, declared what they possess with God and with Christ; that it shall be granted to them to sit down with Christ on his throne, as He has sat down with his Father in his Father's throne (iii. 21). There can be nothing behind and beyond this; and with this therefore is the close. It is here, to compare divine things with human, as in the *Paradiso* of Dante. There, too, there are different circles of light around the throne, each, as it is nearer to the throne, of an intenser brightness than that beyond it and more remote, till at last, when all the others have been past, the throne itself is reached, and the very Presence of Him who sits upon the throne, and from whom all this light and this glory flows.

EXCURSUS.

ON THE HISTORICO-PROPHETICAL INTERPRETATION OF THE EPISTLES TO THE SEVEN CHURCHES OF ASIA.

It is, doubtless, familiar to as many as have at all gone into the history of the exposition of these seven Epistles, that a large body of interpreters, several of these distinguished for their piety and their learning, have not been content to take them merely for what they seem to announce themselves to be, seven Epistles of instruction, warning, consolation, addrest by the great Bishop of the Church to seven Churches of Asia; but have loudly proclaimed that they look much farther than this, that they contain far deeper mysteries than these. In the Scripture are such depths of meaning, so much remains to be discovered in them, in addition to all which has yet been discovered, that any one, whose incapacity is not patent, has a right to claim from us a patient and attentive ear, when he offers to lead us into these depths, to show us that, where *we* thought there were but golden harvests, the food of all waving upon the surface, there are also veins of richest metal below, the wealth of those who will be at the pains to dig for these hid treasures. And yet, at the same time, before we accept any such discoveries of treasures hid in the field of Scripture, it will be good always to remember, that there is a temptation to make Scripture mean more than in the intention of the Holy Ghost it does mean, as well as a temptation to make it mean less; and that we are bound by equally solemn obligations not to put upon it something of ours, as not to subtract from it any thing of its own (Rev. xxii. 18, 19); the interpretation in excess proving often nearly, or quite, as mischievous as that in defect. One has well said, "Mali moris est sensum in S. Scripturam *inferre*, non *efferre*;" and yet it is a practice which is by no means unusual. To inquire into the motives which induce to it would lead me too far from my immediate subject; and some of them will, I think, appear before this essay is concluded.

But what, it may be asked, is this wider horizon, which, if we would meet the Divine intention, it is declared to us we should ascribe to these Epistles, and what the deeper mysteries which they contain? Before I attempt to answer this, let me first, by way of clearing the ground, set down what *all* are agreed on, matter on which there is no dispute; and then secondly, that which, if not all, yet the greater number of competent persons would admit; that so, this done, and these points of universal or general agreement separated off, we may better present to ourselves what are the precise points on which the controversy turns.

All, then, are agreed, and would freely allow, that these seven Epistles, however primarily addrest to these seven Churches of Asia, were also written for the edification of the Universal Church; in the same way, that is, as St. Paul's Epistle to the Romans, or to Timothy, or St. James' to the Dispersion, were written with this intention. The warnings, the incentives, the promises, the consolations, and, generally, the whole instruction in righteousness in these contained, are for every one in all times, so far as they may meet the several cases and conditions of men; what Christ says to those here addrest He says to all in similar conditions. So far there can be no question. "All Scripture," and therefore this Scripture, "was written for our learning."

But further, it may not meet with such universal acceptance, yet will, I suppose, be admitted by many thoughtful students of God's Word, probably by most who have entered into the mystery of the heptad in Scripture, that these seven Churches of Asia are not an accidental aggregation, which might just as conveniently have been eight, or six, or any other number; that, on the contrary, there is a fitness in this number, and that these seven do in some sort represent the Universal Church; that we have a right to contemplate the seven as offering to us the great and leading aspects, moral and spiritual, which Churches gathered in the name of Christ out of the world will assume. No one, of course, affirming this, would mean that they could be contemplated as exhaustive of these aspects; for the infinite depth and richness of that new life which Christ brought into the world testifies itself in nothing more than in this, the rich variety of forms which this new life of his, embodying itself in the lives of men, will assume, the very malformations themselves witnessing in this way for the fulness of this life. But though not exhaustive (for what could be that?), they give us on a smaller scale, ὡς ἐν τύπῳ, the grander and more recurring features of that life; are not fragmentary, fortuitously strung together; but have a completeness, a many-sidedness, being probably selected for this very cause; here, perhaps, being the reason why Philadelphia is included and Miletus past by; Thyatira, outwardly so insignificant, chosen, when one might have expected Magnesia or Tralles. Then what notable contrasts have we here,—a Church face to face with danger and death (Smyrna), and a Church at ease, settling down upon its lees (Sardis); a Church with abundant means and loud profession, yet doing little or nothing for the furtherance of the truth (Laodicea), and a Church with little strength and little power, yet accomplishing a mighty work for Christ (Philadelphia); a Church intolerant of doctrinal error, yet too much lacking that love towards its Lord for which nothing else is a substitute (Ephesus), and over against this a Church not careful nor zealous, as it ought to be, for doctrinal purity, but diligent in the work and ministry of love (Thyatira); or, to review these same Churches from another point of view, a Church in conflict with heathen libertinism, the sinful freedom of the flesh (Ephesus), and a Church or Churches in conflict with Jewish superstition, the sinful bondage of the spirit (Pergamum, Philadelphia); or, for the indolence of man a more perilous case than either, Churches with no active forms of opposition to the truth in the midst of them, to brace their energies and to cause them, in the act of defending the imperilled truth, to know it better and to love it more (Sardis, Laodicea). That these Churches are more or less *representative* Churches, and were selected because they are so; that they form a complex within and among themselves, mutually fulfilling and completing one another; that the great Head of the Church contemplates them for the time being as symbolic of his Universal Church, implying as much in that mystic seven, and giving many other indications of the same,—this also will be accepted, if not by all, yet by many.

But the Periodists, as they have been called, the upholders of what may be fitly termed the historico-prophetical scheme of interpretation, are by no means satisfied with these admissions. They demand that we should recognize in these Epistles very much more than this; they affirm that we have in them, besides counsels to the Churches named in each, a prophetic outline of seven successive periods of the Church's history; dividing, as they do, into these seven portions the whole time intervening between Christ's ascension and his return in glory. As in making a statement for others, especially for those from whom one is about to dissent, it is always fairest, or, at any rate, is most satisfactory, to cite their own words, I will here quote two passages, one from Joseph Mede, another from Vitringa, in which they severally set forth that historico-prophetical scheme; which they both favoured and upheld; and certainly the statement of the case could scarcely be in more prudent or in abler hands. The modesty with which the first propounds it, is in striking contrast with the arrogant confidence of some others, who were well nigh disposed to make here a new article of faith, and the acceptance or rejection of this interpretation a test of orthodoxy. These are his words; they occur in one of his sermons (*Works*, 1672, p. 296): "It belongs not much to our purpose to inquire whether those seven Epistles concern historically and literally only the Churches here named, or whether they were intended for types or ages of the Church afterwards to come. It shall be sufficient to say, that if we consider their number, being seven (which is a number of revolution of times, and therefore in this Book the seals, trumpets, and vials also are seven); or if we consider the choice of the Holy Ghost, in that he taketh neither all, no, nor the most famous Churches then in the world, as Antioch, Alexandria, Rome, and many other, and such, no doubt, as had need of instruction as well as those here named; if these things be well considered, it will seem that these seven Churches, besides their literal respect, were intended (and it may be chiefly) to be as patterns and types of the several ages of the Catholic Church from the beginning thereof unto the end of the world; that so these seven Churches should prophetically sample unto us a sevenfold temper and constitution of the whole Church according to the several ages thereof, answering the pattern of the Churches named here;" compare p. 905. Vitringa (*Anacrisis Apocalypsios*, p. 32): "Omnino igitur existimo Spiritum S. sub typo et emblemate septem Ecclesiarum Asiæ nobis mystice et prophetice voluisse depingere septem variantes status Ecclesiæ Christianæ, quibus successive conspiceretur usque ad adventum Domini et omnium rerum finem, phrasibus desumptis a nominibus, conditione et attributis ipsarum illarum Ecclesiarum Asiæ nobiliorum, quæ ad hunc usum et scopum sapienter adhibuit; sic tamen ut ipsæ illæ Ecclesiæ Asianæ simul in hoc speculo se ipsas videre, suasque tam virtutes quam vitia ex illis epistolis cognoscere, et quæ in iis sunt admonitiones et exhortationes ad se ipsas quoque referre et applicare possent; quippe quod summa suadet jubetque ratio. Quod enim alterius rei typum et figuram sustinebit symbolicam, ita affectum esse oportet ut attributa subjecti analogi in ipsâ illâ re figurante omnium primo demonstrari possint."

I have cited these two writers of a later age; but the scheme itself, in one shape or another, may be traced to a much earlier date; though, indeed, it is very far from being as old as its favourers would have us to believe, claiming, as not seldom they do, several of the early Fathers, as early at least as Augustine and Chrysostom, for the first authors and upholders of it. They are, however, quite without warrant in this. No passage has been quoted, and I am convinced none could be quoted, bearing out their assertion here. In the eager debate carried on upon this subject for a considerable part of a century, the opponents of this interpretation repeatedly challenged the advocates to bring forward a single quotation from one Father, Greek or Latin, in its support; but none such was ever produced; so that Witsius has perfect right when he affirms, "Nullibi id dicunt [antiqui] quod viri isti eruditi volunt, quibuscum hæc nobis instituta disputatio est; nimirum proprie, literaliter atque ex intentione Spiritûs Sancti verbis harum Epistolarum delineari, non quod Johannis tempore in Asiæ Ecclesiis agebatur, sed quod in universali Ecclesiâ septem temporum periodis ordine succedentibus futurum erat. Id non liquet antiquorum ulli vel in mentem venisse." This quotation is from his essay, *De Septem Eccles. Apocalyp. sensu historico an prophetico* (*Opp.* t. i. pp. 640-741), remarkable for the fairness and moderation with which all that can be said on one side and the other is considered. It is quite true that Augustine, with others before and after him, recognized that symbolic representative character of these Epistles, of which I just now spoke; saw a mystery in the seven;[1] but to recognize them as

[1] Andreas, the earliest commentator on the Apocalypse whose work has reached us, gives this as the reason why the Lord, through St. John, addressed Himself exactly to seven Churches; διὰ τοῦ ἑβδοματικοῦ ἀριθμοῦ τὸ μυστικὸν τῶν ἁπανταχῇ ἐκκλησιῶν σημαίνων. Au-

historico-prophetical is quite a different matter, and of any allowance of this there is no vestige among them; or that it had so much as come into their minds.

The Spiritualists, or extreme Franciscans, are the first among whom this scheme of interpretation assumed any prominence. It is well known to those who are at all familiar with this wonderful body of men, what an important part the distribution of the Church's history into seven ages played in their theology, and what weapons they found in this armoury for the assault of the dominant Church and hierarchy of Rome. Looking every where in Scripture for traces of these seven periods, it is not strange that they should have found such in these seven Epistles. At their first rise, one but recently dead, high in reputation for sanctity throughout

gustine (*De Civ. Dei*, xvii. 4), explaining the Canticle of Hannah, in which it is said, "The barren hath born seven" (1 Sam. ii. 5), goes on to say, "Hic totum quod prophetabatur eluxit agnoscentibus numerum septenarium quo est universa Ecclesiæ significata perfectio. Propter quod et Johannes Apostolus ad septem scribit Ecclesias, eo modo se ostendens ad unius plenitudinem scribere;" or, as the last clause of a similar statement reads elsewhere (*Exp. in Gal.* ii. 7): "quæ [Ecclesiæ] utique universalis Ecclesiæ personam gerunt;" cf. *Ep.* xlix. § 2. And Gregory the Great almost word for word (*Moral.* xvii. 27): "Unde et septem Ecclesiis scribit Johannes Apostolus, ut unam Catholicam, septiformis gratiæ plenam Spiritu designaret;" cf. *Præf.* c. 8.

the Church, himself regarded as little short of an apocalyptic seer, I mean the Abbot Joachim of Floris (he died in 1202), had already shown the way in this interpretation;[1] and the Spiritualists did not fail to adjust the seven ages of the Church and the seven Epistles prophetic of them, so as these should prophesy all good of themselves, and all evil of Rome.

It is evident that when the scheme was adopted two or three centuries later by theologians of the Reformed Church, it would require readjustment and redistribution throughout, at once chronological and dogmatic. This, however, was easily effected. The whole thing was a subjective fancy of men's minds, not an objective truth of God's Word, and would therefore oppose no serious resistance. It was easy to give it what new shape was required by the new conditions under which it should now appear. After the Reformation, the first in whom I meet this interpretation of the seven Churches, as predictive of the seven ages of the Church and foreshadowing their condition, is an English divine, Thomas Brightman (b. 1557, d. 1607). He belonged to the Puritan school of divines, as they existed within the bosom of the Anglican Church,

[1] For an account of Joachim of Floris' seven ages, see Hahn, *Gesch. d. Ketzer im Mittelalter*, vol. iii. p. 112; and Engelhardt, *Kirch. Gesch. Abhandl.* p. 107.

and though in opposition to its spirit, not as yet separated from it; but his work, *Apocalypsis Apocalypseos*, 1612, avouches him a man of no ordinary gifts, and of warm and earnest piety; and Marckius has perfect right when he says of this work, "eruditionem et pietatem non vulgarem spirat." But although he, and Joseph Mede, as we have seen (he died in 1638), and Henry More,[1] lent to this suggestion the authority of their names, it never seems to have struck any vigorous root in England, nor to have stirred up much controversy for or against it. It was in the Reformed Churches of Holland and Germany, but predominantly in the former, that this periodic interpretation first assumed any prominence or importance. There indeed, during the middle and latter part of the seventeenth century and beginning of the eighteenth, it was debated with animation, and often with something more than animation. The very able *Præfatio de Septem N. T. Periodis*, which Marckius has prefixed to his Commentary on the Apocalypse, 1699, shows how very angry the disputants could be on one side and the other.

The theologian who by his adoption of the historico-prophetical interpretation gave an impor-

[1] *Prophetical Exposition of the Seven Epistles sent to the Seven Churches in Asia from Him that is, and was, and is to come,—Theological Works*, London, 1708, pp. 719-764; first published in 1669.

tance to it, and procured for it an acceptance, which in any other way it would scarcely have obtained, was Cocceius (1603-1669). It is indeed with him only the part of a larger whole—one among many testimonies for a divinely-intended division into seven periods of the whole history of the Church. This division found favour with many; but in no one does it recur with so great a frequency, exercise so powerful an influence on his interpretation of Scripture, constitute so vital a portion of his theology, as in him. The fame of Cocceius, if it ever reached England, has now quite passed away; but his influence for good on the Protestant communities of Holland and also of Germany, as the promoter of a Biblical in place of a scholastical theology, leading as he did those Churches from the arid wastes of a new scholasticism to the living fountains of the Word of God, was immense, and survives to the present day. But this distribution into seven periods of the Church's history, seven before Christ's coming, and seven after, is a sort of "fixed idea" with him. It is indeed his desire to make Scripture the rule in every thing, and to find all that concerns the spiritual life and development of man cast in a scriptural framework, this desire in season and out of season, which has led him astray. And thus it is that he finds, or where he does not find he makes, a prophecy of these periods every where; in the seven days of creation, in the seven beatitudes, in the seven petitions of the Lord's Prayer, in the seven parables of Matthew xiii.; not seldom forcing into artificial arrangements by seven, Scriptures which yield themselves not naturally and of their own accord, but only under violent pressure and constraint, to any articulation of the kind, as Hannah's Prayer, the Song of Moses, of Deborah, the Song of Songs, not a few of the Psalms, and, I dare say, much else in Scripture besides.[1]

With all his excesses, however, I do not think Cocceius ever refused to these Epistles a true historical foundation. The historico-prophetic meaning was no doubt far the most precious in his eyes; and it had good right to be, if only it had

[1] Let me rescue from vast unread folios of his, as not very alien to the matter we have in hand, one noble passage, and he abounds in such, on the analogy of faith, and the help which the different portions of Scripture mutually afford to the right understanding of one another. It is from the *Præfatio ad Comm. in Proph. Min.*, *Opp.* tom. v., without pagination: "Habet enim divina institutio Scripturæ instar augusti palatii, in quo ordine consideant innumeri seniores, qui viritim admissum novum discipulum erudiant, a collegis suis dicta confirment, roborent, explicent, illustrent, nunc fusius dicta contrahant, nunc contractiora diffundant et diducant, generalius dicta distinguant, distincta generatim innuant, regulas exemplis fulciant, exempla in regulis judicent, ita ut omnium de eâdem re agentium dictorum is sensus accipi debeat, qui est ullius, et qui nulli refragetur, et plena institutio ea demum censeri quæ omnium virorum Dei sit vox, συμφωνία et ὁμόνοια."

been designed by the Spirit; but he did not deny that there had been actual Churches at Ephesus, Smyrna, and the rest, which were primarily addrest, and to whose condition, at the time they were written, these Epistles fitted. Others, however, have proceeded to far greater lengths. They have refused to see any reference whatever to Churches actually, at the time when this vision was seen, subsisting in these cities of Asia, and to their spiritual condition. These they regard merely as the machinery for the conveyance of the prophecy; the seven Epistles not in the least expressing, except, it might be, here and there by accidental and undesigned coincidence, the actual condition of these seven Churches. Despite of any thing which these Epistles seem to affirm to the contrary, the Church of Ephesus, according to their view, may at this time have been tolerant of false teachers, and Thyatira intolerant; Philadelphia may have been slack in deeds of faith and love, and Laodicea fervent in spirit, and Sardis with not a few only, but many names, that had not defiled their garments. No Antipas had actually resisted to blood at Pergamum; there was no tribulation of ten days imminent upon Smyrna.[1]

[1] Floerke, in an able work on the Millennium, *Lehre vom tausendjährigen Reiche*, Marburg, 1859, is the latest denier *in toto* of an historical element in these Epistles; see p. 59 sqq.

This extravagance may be dismissed in a few words. Origen is justly condemned, that, advancing a step beyond other allegorists, who *slighted* the facts of the Old Testament history for the sake of mystical meanings which they believed to lie behind them, he denied, concerning many events recorded there as historical, that they actually happened at all; rearing the superstructure of his mystical meaning, not on the establishment of the literal sense, but on its ruins. Every reverent student of the Word of God must feel that so he often lets go a substance in snatching at a shadow, that shadow itself really eluding his grasp after all. He who in this sense assails the strong historic substructures of Scripture, may not know all which he is doing; but he is indeed doing his best to turn the glorious superstructure built on these, which, though resting on earth, pierces heaven, into a mere sky-pageant painted on the air, a cloud-palace waiting to be shifted and changed by every breath of the caprice of man, and at length fading and melting into the common air. It was not without reason that Augustine, himself not wholly to be acquitted of excesses in this direction, did yet urge so strongly the necessity of maintaining, before and above all, the historic letter of the Scripture, whatever else to this might be superadded (*Serm.* ii. 6): "Ante omnia, fratres, hoc in nomine Domini et admonemus quantum possumus et præcipimus, ut quando auditis exponi sacramentum Scripturæ narrantis quæ gesta sunt, prius illud quod lectum est credatur sic gestum quomodo lectum est, ne subtracto fundamento rei gestæ, quasi in aëre quæratis ædificare." Similar warnings in his writings continually recur. Who indeed could continue sure that any thing presented in Scripture as history, with all apparent marks of history about it, was yet history at all, and not something wholly different, parable, or allegory, or prophecy, if these Epistles, which St. John is bidden to send to the seven Churches of Asia, which profess to enter minutely into their spiritual condition, were yet never sent to them at all, had no relation whatever to them, more, that is, than to any other portion of the universal Church?

But leaving these, and addressing ourselves only to the more moderate upholders of the periodic scheme of interpretation, to those, namely, who admit a literal sense, while they superinduce upon it a prophetical, we ask, what slightest hint or intimation does the Spirit of God give that we have here to do with the great successive acts and epochs of the kingdom of God in the course of its gradual evolution here upon earth? Where are the fingerposts pointing this way? What is there, for instance, of chronological succession? Does not every thing, on the contrary, mark *simultaneity*, and not *succession?* The seven candlesticks are seen at the same instant; the seven Churches named in the same breath. How different is it where succession *in time* is intended; see, for instance, Dan. ii. 32, 33, 39, 40; vii. 6, 7, 9. On this matter Marckius says very well (*Præf.* § 52): "Attamen ut Ecclesias has agnoscamus pro typicis, sive significantibus ex Dei intentione alias Ecclesias aliorum locorum et temporum, oportet nos a Deo doceri. Typos enim, non magis quam allegorias, pro lubitu nostro in Scripturam inferre licet, cum non sit ἰδίας ἐπιλύσεως, propriæ interpretationis, 2 Pet. i. 20. Non sufficit ad typum constituendum nuda convenientia, quæ inter res, personas, et eventus plurimos a nobis observari potest, sed oportet nobis amplius constet de divino consilio quo rem similem servire voluerit alteri præsignificandæ, cogitationibusque nostris illuc ducendis."

But all such objections, with all those others which it would only be too easy to make, might indeed be set aside or overborne, if any marvellous coincidence between these Epistles and the after-course of the Church's development could be made out; if history set its seal to these, and attested that they were prophecy indeed; for when a key fits perfectly well the wards of a very complicated lock, and opens it without an effort, it is difficult not to believe that they were made for one another. But there is nothing here of the kind. There is no agreement among themselves on the part of the interpreters of the historico-prophetical school. Each one has his own solution of the enigma, his own distribution of the several epochs ; or, if this is too much to affirm, there is at any rate nothing approaching to a general *consensus* among them. Take, for instance, the distribution of Vitringa. For him Ephesus represents the condition of the Church from the day of Pentecost to the outbreak of the Decian persecution ; Smyrna, from the Decian persecution to that of Diocletian, both inclusive ; Pergamum, from the time of Constantine until the close of the seventh century ; Thyatira, the Church in its mission to the nations during the first half of the middle ages ; Sardis, from the close of the twelfth century to the Reformation ; Philadelphia, the first century of the Reformation ; Laodicea, the Reformed Church at the time when he was writing ; compare Lange, *Das Apostolische Zeitalter*, vol. ii. p. 472, for a nearly similar distribution.

There are two or three fortunate coincidences here between the assumed prophecy and the fact ; without such indeed the whole notion must have been abandoned long ago as hopeless ; such could scarcely have been avoided. Smyrna, for instance, represents excellently well the *ecclesia pressa* in its two last and most terrible struggles with heathen Rome; so too for such Protestant expositors as see the Papacy in the scarlet woman of Babylon, the Jezebel of Thyatira appears exactly at the right time, coincides with the Papacy at its height, yet at the same time with judgment at the door in the great revolt which was even then preparing. But I would ask any one fairly grounded in the subject whether there is any true articulation of Church history in the distribution above made? any general felicity of correspondence between what are averred to be the prophetic outlines with the historic realities adduced as fulfilling them? Take, for instance, Philadelphia, as representing the Reformation period. The praise bestowed on the Philadelphian Angel may be said to culminate in these words, "*Behold, I have set before thee an open door, and no man can shut it*" (iii. 8). Can any thing, on the contrary, be sadder than the way in which, when "*an open door*" was set before the Reformers, they suffered it to so great an extent to be closed on them again? There was a time, some five and twenty or thirty years after Luther had begun to preach, when Austria and Bavaria and Styria and Poland, and, in good part, France, had all been won for the Reformation. Thirty years more had not elapsed when they all were lost again; and it was confined within the far narrower limits which it occupies at the present day (see Ranke, *History of the Popes in the Sixteenth and Seventeenth Centuries*)—this door, once open, having been closed mainly through the guilt of those contests, any thing but *Philadelphian* (for the names too are pressed into service) among the Reformers themselves.

Then, again, other interpreters, as I have already observed, distribute the epochs according to schemes altogether diverse from this. Thus it is far more common among the Protestant theologians of the seventeenth century to apportion, not five Churches, but only the first four, to the pre-Reformation period; to claim, as Brightman does, Philadelphia, with all its graces, for themselves, and, as must necessarily follow, to contemplate Sardis as representing the Church of the actual Reformation. Certainly the Reformation had blots and blemishes enough; but its faults were those of zeal and passion; had nothing in common with that hypocritical form of godliness, that death under shows of life, imputed to Sardis; and one might have expected that any dutiful child of the Reformation, who at all felt the immense debt of gratitude which he and the whole Church owed to it, notwithstanding all its shortcomings, would have hesitated long as to the accuracy of a scheme which should brand it with this dishonour. See on this, Marckius, *Præf.*

§ 55; and on the other hand as saying, and saying well, whatever there is to be said in support of the historico-prophetical school in this particular aspect, see Henry More, at pp. 756 sqq., in his treatise already referred to.

Much more might be urged on the arbitrary artificial character of all the attempted adaptations of Church history to these Epistles; but this Essay has already run to a greater length than I intended; and indeed it is not needful to say more. Where there were no preestablished harmonies in the Divine intention between the one and the other, as I am persuaded here there were none, it could not have been otherwise. The multitude of dissertations, essays, books, which have been written, and still are being written, in support of this scheme of interpretation, must remain a singular monument of wasted ingenuity and misapplied toil; of the disappointment which must result from a futile looking into Scripture for that which is not to be found there,—from a resolution to draw out from it that which he who draws out must first himself have put in. Men will never thus make Scripture richer. They will have made it much poorer for themselves, if they nourish themselves out of it with the fancies of men, in place of the truths of God.

THE END.

www.ingramcontent.com/pod-product-compliance
Lightning Source LLC
LaVergne TN
LVHW020232110826
845151LV00003B/900
9781425530846